STD

ACPL ITEM ☑ S0-CBG-970
DISCARDED

5-10-76

WHAT DO YOU
DO FOR A LIVING?

WHAT DO YOU DO FOR A LIVING?

Compiled By
PETER F. SPRAGUE

DOW JONES BOOKS
PRINCETON, N.J.

Introduction

"What do you do for a living?"

That question pops up so frequently and so naturally that when it isn't asked it is missed. A child at his parents' knees, people chatting at a party, new neighbors introducing themselves—all these are among the many occasions for inquiring about another's livelihood.

It isn't just a polite, small-talk question. People are fascinated by others' work. What is it like to be a gold miner in Canada, a poet or an astronomer? What does a social worker do, or a park ranger or a jet pilot for an airline? How does it feel to officiate a pro hockey game or find a dinosaur bone or make a very big sale?

These are the things that people like to learn about each others' work, and these are the questions that are answered in this collection of 43 profiles of people making their living. These stories originally appeared in the pages of The Wall Street Journal, where they drew far heavier response from the newspaper's four million readers than any stock-market or economic analysis. Most of the letters didn't complain about anything, as letters to editors often do, but rather expressed pleasure with the stories—and requested more.

In assembling the best of these articles from the past three years into book form, it seemed that this panorama of portraits of people at work held particular appeal for two groups of people who often don't enjoy reading the same things.

For the young, who are in the process of deciding how to spend their lives, these stories provide up-to-date, interesting and objective information about a wide variety of careers. For those who are older and already embarked on their careers, the book offers an opportunity to compare others' workaday lives with their own, to glimpse what it may have been like to walk down a different path in life.

Not all of these paths are desirable, and even those that at first glance seem glamorous or exciting have their periods of boredom, frustration and even physical agony. The profiles in this book candidly dig into the negative as well as the positive aspects of each job, providing well-rounded insights that usually aren't so easy to come by.

You will read about the hockey official who was promoted to referee and became so nervous about the responsibilities that he broke out into a terrible case of psoriasis. You will meet the prolific and financially success-ful novelist who is tormented because critics ignore him and his works.

On the other hand, you'll share the sense of challenge of a man starting his own business in tough times. You'll be taken behind the scenes of big courtroom trials and shown the cunning tricks of the attorneys. You'll sense the quiet pride of craftsmen as they stand back from their benches and smile their acceptance of their handiwork.

The profiles have been organized into groupings according to the dominant characteristic of work. These are more descriptive than the usual categories of white-collar blue-collar and so on, though they might seem to be arbitrary in some cases. For instance, the talented Indian potter is in the section entitled Working With Their Hands, not the one called Expressing Their Talents; but that's because the potter herself makes a point of the important role her hands play in her work.

One section deserves special mention: Not Working. It consists of profiles of people who do nothing for a living for one reason or another. These stories were included for con-trast, of course, but there is something ironically appro-priate about placing them at the end of a book about people at work. These stories remind us that even though we may be never fully satisfied with our work, and no matter how difficult it is to get up on Monday mornings, our jobs are central to our enjoyment of life. Wages and salaries aside, most of us couldn't live long or well without our work.

Contents

Contents

Part One

WORKING WITH THEIR HANDS

Many people's work involves physical movement. Sometimes just the nimble fingers are crucial, such as those of a fast-moving short-order cook or metal sculptor. Others put their whole bodies into their jobs, such as a gold miner or a hockey official. Physical work often isn't the best-paying way of making a living, as field hand on a Louisiana sugar plantation can testify. But some find a special satisfaction in it, and they take a great deal of pride in their handiwork or the services they perform. But for others— those who are ambitious for more status, for example, or for those who find the physical demands harder to keep up with as they grow older—working with their hands is considered a temporary livelihood on the way to something better.

1

At the Griddle

It is 7 a.m. on a weekday morning at the Flair Coffee Shop on Seventh Avenue near 40th Street, in the heart of New York's Garment District. The first customers of the day groggily file in, take their usual seats and grumble their customary orders. Waitresses scribble down the grumblings and lumber over to the kitchen counters to pass them on.

Poised behind one of the kitchen counters is Sam Hadden, short-order cook. He has been at work a half-hour and he already has a headache. As the orders come rushing in—two up, scramble two, a buttered English—his hands whisk back and forth and his head bobs like a pneumatic drill as he grinds out a steady procession of food.

The name of the game is hurry. Sam can make scrambled eggs in 45 seconds, a hamburger in two minutes, most sandwiches in four seconds. It isn't how good the food is that counts, but how fast it is made, though the best of the short-order cooks insist they make it good, too.

"I guess I'm not being very modest, but I rank myself as one of the best. I can really move that food," says 38-year-old Sam, a chunky man with a goatee and mustache. Mel Nudelman, Sam's boss at Flair, says, "He's a top man. He knows what it's all about, and he produces."

There are many ways to recognize a good short-order cook, and one of the best ways is by watching his hands at work. It helps to have large hands, but they must be fast, flexible hands. You can spot an experienced cook just by watching how he picks up a knife.

The average person grips a knife with all five fingers, making a fist around the handle. Sam picks up a knife delicately between his thumb and index finger, taking hold just where the blade begins rather than on the handle. That way he can slice bread like a buzz saw.

Another mark of a good cook is his temperament.

Short-order cooks put up with a lot. They put up with abuse from the customers, from the waitresses and from the boss. They put up with orders being returned because they are the wrong orders, or because they weren't cooked just so, or because the customer is just trying to be a wise guy. And they put up with periods that are busy enough to test the steadiest of tempers.

"You've got to always keep your cool," says Sam, who almost always does. "When the orders really start to pile up, that's the most important time not to hit the panic button. Just keep your head to the board and make sandwiches."

On a typical day, some 1,500 customers eat at the Flair, and quite a bit of the food is prepared by Sam, who is on duty from 6:30 a.m. to 2:30 p.m. with three other cooks—four others at peak hours. By the time breakfast is over, Sam will have gone through some 25 dozen eggs, 144 slices of toast, three pounds of bacon and four pounds of butter. At lunchtime he will dish out about 288 slices of white bread, 216 slices of rye, 18 slices of pumpernickel, 15 slices of whole wheat, a gallon of tuna salad, a half-gallon of egg salad, a quarter-gallon of chicken salad, 18 pounds of corned beef, 14 pounds of brisket, 10 pounds of pastrami, eight pounds of roast beef, 95 hamburgers, seven heads of lettuce and two dozen tomatoes.

With all those orders to contend with, Sam turns out the food much as a Detroit production line turns out cars— only faster. "The whole philosophy of a short-order cook is obviously speed," Sam says. "They don't come in here for a leisurely meal. They come in to belt something down and scram."

Quick hands aren't all that make Sam fast. There is also the system. Every short-order cook has a system, a method of arranging his ingredients and cooking implements so that they are optimally accessible.

At breakfast, Sam always cracks about 15 dozen eggs in advance and puts them in a big vat for future scrambling. He makes some toast ahead of time and heats up some muffins so that they can be quickly prepared when wanted. He always keeps his frying pan hot on the griddle. "You never put an egg in a cold pan," Sam says, "or else you're going to be stirring until the swallows return."

At lunch, Sam always keeps fast-movers nearest him. "Tuna moves best here, so I always keep that closest," he says. "Then I have the egg salad and the chicken salad. You always have the bread out of the wrapper, and the lettuce leafed. You start your hamburgers. You have to keep things in the same place so you can find them without looking. If you have to look around, the customer's going to be out in Rockaway before he's served."

Sam arrives at work at 6 a.m. to allow himself a half-hour to prepare his work area, which consists of a griddle, a long cutting board and 10 dishes to hold his food. He dumps some bagels here, cracks some eggs there, rips open a loaf of bread. It is a routine he has repeated countless times, and it comes naturally.

Sam's working conditions aren't comfortable. It gets steamy in the kitchen, the floor is rock hard and the temperature is blistering. Sam says he invariably acquires a headache within a half-hour of starting and his feet and neck tend to ache. "It's very hot and uncomfortable," Sam says, "but you acclimate yourself like someone working in central Africa. You become one of the natives."

Cafes like the Flair used to rely on waitresses shouting orders to cooks, who would have to do their best to remember them. Few restaurants, however, operate that way anymore. Instead they use slips of paper. At the Flair, waitresses often call out their orders as they hand in their slips, relying on a language peculiar to the short-order cook's world: a limey (an English muffin), a stretch (a Coke), whisky down (rye toast), Nova under snow on a sled (lox and cream cheese on an English muffin), wreck two (scrambled eggs).

As his orders arrive, Sam scans the slips quickly and memorizes up to eight of them. He will also group identical orders; if he is making a tuna sandwich and then two orders for pastrami arrive followed by another for tuna, he will turn out the second tuna before he starts on the pastramis. If Sam didn't employ such tricks of the trade, he might fall far behind, particularly when his backlog reaches the usual peak of 25 to 30 orders.

Whenever Sam prepares a wrong sandwich, which happens maybe three or four times a day, he does his best to get rid of it. He'll let it sit on top of the counter, hoping someone else orders one. If it's toasted, after a short interval he'll put a fresh slice of toast on top so that the sandwich will seem just-made. "Sometimes," he says, "I try to will it on someone."

Sam also knows a little egg trick. If someone orders boiled eggs and Sam makes poached eggs by mistake, he'll mix up the eggs so that they look boiled. "The customer thinks it's a boiled egg though it isn't. I'll tell you something: Most of the people who come in here don't know what the hell it is they're eating anyway."

There are also psychological tricks to make food seem better. When Sam makes, say, a liverwurst sandwich, he always heaps just about all the liverwurst in the middle of the bread. When the customer picks up the sandwich, and customers invariably pick up sandwiches in the middle, he feels a nice thick sandwich. He rarely notices that there is hardly any liverwurst around the sides.

"Another thing, you can't be afraid to use your hands in this business," Sam says as he scoops peaches out of a can with his hands. "Of course, you wouldn't do this in front of a customer. But what goes on in the back is different."

One of the things that goes on at the Flair is a constant war between the cooks and the waitresses. Waitresses are known to short-order cooks by many names, but mostly they are referred to as "the enemy." "We're sort of on the opposite side of the fence," Sam says. "They're not what you would call my buddies."

Waitresses are well aware that Sam is fast, but he never seems quite fast enough to suit them. So this waitress or that will march up to Sam every so often and say things like "My customer is halfway through the Indianapolis 500 and he would like to know if he could have his order before winter."

One waitress brings back an order of toast and drops in on the counter. "He wants well-done toast," she snaps. "Can't you read?"

"Can't you see?" Sam retorts. "Does he want well-done toast or well-burnt toast?"

"Would you give me some well-done toast?" the waitress persists.

"Pick it up," Sam says after toasting it some more. "One order of well-burnt toast."

You might wonder what Sam thinks of the food he prepares at the Flair. It is difficult for him to speak with any authority because he never eats at the Flair. In fact, he never eats at all during his working day, which, he adds, isn't because the Flair food isn't inviting. It's just that when you look at food all day, you tend to lose your appetite, Sam says. During his half-hour break, "I just go into the back and collapse," he says.

The only meal he eats is dinner, and since he can't stomach being in his kitchen at home, he allows his wife to do the cooking. She's not bad as a cook, Sam says, though it's plain he considers himself superior.

Sam isn't exactly fond of his job. Besides all the other troubles, he makes only $180 a week. "If I had to do it over again, I would have never gotten into this racket," he says. "I think this has got to be the worse job in the city. But once you get into it, you can't get out."

He got into it in 1957, when he came north from Anderson, S.C., where he was born. He landed a job as a dishwasher in a coffee shop, advanced to hamburger man after four months and then moved over to the nearby Flair in 1961 as a short-order cook. He lives in Coney Island with his wife and four children and commutes 45 minutes each way on the subway.

If things go the way he hopes they will, Sam won't be

spending the rest of his life turning out scrambled eggs in 45 seconds. Like all short-order cooks, he feels he is the poor man's chef, and he idolizes the gourmet chefs who get to prepare exquisite dishes, more or less at their leisure as Sam sees it. Sam has completed three night courses, in American cooking, catering cooking and Continental cooking. Now he hopes to land a chef's position.

Until that day arrives, if it ever does, Sam manages to extract some satisfaction from his work. "In a sense it's kind of an art," he says. "You're always trying to beat the man working next to you, and that's where the pleasure comes in. My satisfaction in this job comes from getting out a pastrami on rye in three seconds while the guy next to me is taking four."

—N.R. KLEINFIELD

Digging for Gold

In the "dry room" of the Giant Yellowknife Mine, the air is thick with the smell of caked mud and stale sweat as the men on the night shift straggle in for work. Their grimy hard hats, lumber shirts, overalls and rubber boots are suspended by chains from the ceiling, and the men lower them like victims of a mass hanging. The men suit up and drift out into the high, subarctic sun to sit and smoke at the base of the mine's tall, wooden headframe.

They are gold miners. They come from places like Korea and the Ukraine; they are wiry boys and barrel-chested men; they are wanderers and providers. And all of them have somehow found themselves at this speck of civilization in the Canadian wilderness, 275 miles south of the Arctic Circle, blasting gray rock in the frozen guts of the earth to satisfy the odd hunger for gold of faraway men in pin-striped suits.

Rusty-haired, ruddy-faced Jim Wylie is one of them. He is 46-years old with a brawny frame set on thin legs. His hands are puffy and stiff from hanging onto a 140-pound pneumatic drill. He has a wry grin, and he speaks softly, with the hint of an Irish lilt.

"The boys who wonder and speculate about gold, I feel very distant from them," he says, taking a drag on his Buckingham cigaret and hacking. "It's a very far-off subject to me. It crosses a person's mind, but at the end of the month all you get is your paycheck and the food to go on the table." Jim switches on the lamp hooked to his hard hat, crowds into the cage with the other miners and, after the hoistman rings four bells, drops into the black shaft to dig for gold.

World money markets and their daily twittering are mysterious to men like Jim Wylie and even to the men who manage the Giant. "We don't have much influence over the price of gold," says Mike Lane, an Englishman from Birmingham, who runs the mill, "so we don't stand to gain much by thinking about it." But it is true that the high price of gold is having its impact here. It is extending the life of the Giant mine, and that will translate into food on Jim Wylie's table.

The Giant is one of Canada's richest gold mines, but, except for its remote location, it operates much like any other in North America. By gold-mine standards, it is old having been started in 1948. Since then, more than 7.3 million tons of ore have been hauled to the surface, producing gold that sold for over $164 million. Until the gold price took off, it seemed as if the ore were close to being depleted. The company predicted that in two years the Giant would be mined out.

But the price jumped, and that means that extremely low-grade ore—well below ½ ounce of gold per ton—now can be mined at a profit. "As costs went up and the price stayed the same, we left more and more low grade behind," says D.J. Emery, the mine manager. "Now we're working the grade down as the price goes up." The mine produced less than its usual 200,000 ounces of gold in 1973, but at a far greater profit per ounce, but its profit will increase or at least hold steady. The high-grade ore will be saved for the future.

For the men, though, this strategic fiddling changes little. They still wrench 1,200 tons of ore a day from the Giant (all of which boils down to less than a single 50-pound brick of gold). They are paid the same and live the same rough but unassuming lives they did before the distant frenzy that has made the metal they dig out of the ground so much more valuable.

The Giant camp is three miles from Yellowknife, over a terrain of blue lakes and glacier-scarred volcanic rock grown over by stunted spruce, jack-pine, birch and poplar trees. There are 150 single men living in the bunkhouses near the shabby recreation hall and cookhouse that make up the camp—a huddle of frame buildings covered with dirty-white shingles and trimmed with green paint.

For $2.90 a day, the single men get a small cubicle with a bed, a closet, a desk and a chair. And they get all the food they can put away. The cafeteria serves up big spreads for ravenous appetites, with a table loaded down by salads, fresh breads and pies to go with the main course, vegetables and potatoes. One afternoon, the main course at lunch was thick veal cutlets. "Do you want two or three?" the counterman asked.

Thirty families also live in bungalows on the campsite. Others, including Jim Wylie and his family, rent company-owned houses in town. There was a time not long ago when the Giant camp was more self-contained than it is now. Dances are still held at the camp, and movies are shown there. There is a curling league in the winter, and there are baseball teams in the summer. But Yellowknife isn't just a mining town anymore—since 1967, it has been the capital of the Northwest Territories.

In 10 years, the population has doubled, to 7,200, and probably half the citizens work for the government. So even though Yellowknife is literally at the end of the road (the Makenzie Highway ends there), it is a cosmopolitan frontier city where it is hard to tell the difference between a miner and a bureaucrat—until you shake hands.

The Wylies live in a little six-room house on a residential street near the center of Yellowknife. It is a simple, lived-in place with a picture of an Eskimo on the living-room wall and a curling trophy awarded by Grimshaw Trucking displayed on a bookrack.

Jim makes about $14,000 a year as a contract miner, one of about 70 pros in the mine who actually break rock. The money has been enough (with some moonlighting helping the local mortician) to keep two children in provincial college at Edmonton, Alberta, throw a wedding party for an older daughter and keep 11-year-old Mary Anne supplied with ice-cream cones.

Since 1965, Jim has worked underground, first as a diamond driller boring rock samples and as a miner for the last two years. Until he was 29, Jim and his father were farmers in Saskatchewan. When his father died, Jim "took to wandering" with a survey crew in northern Manitoba—a job that kept him away from home for all but 11 days in 1958. "for a married man that's no good," he says. So he tried to start a small trucking business, but it failed. After that, he took up diamond drilling, and when the job appeared in Yellowknife, he took it.

Many of the professional miners in Yellowknife are family men like Jim. They don't drink much, ("At $1.40 a shot, I can't afford it," Jim says), and though you can usually find a game if you look, gambling isn't common. Jim is president of the curling club at the mine and is a past exalted ruler of the Yellowknife Elks Club. In the summer, he enjoys fishing on Prosperous Lake with his wife, Marion.

There is another kind of worker at the Giant Mine— the drifter who signs on for a few months at an unskilled job just to get a taste of the work and the North Country and then moves on. Most of these are long-haired boys in their late teens and early 20s. And while the Jim Wylies lend the mine its stability, the drifters account for an annual turnover at the Giant of more than 100%. (Still, the mines are happy to get the drifters, for there is an acute shortage of miners.)

Dave Kachur is a blond 22-year-old with the word "love" tattooed on the fingers of his left hand. He finished high school in 1967 and since then has traveled endlessly over Canada and the U.S., holding odd jobs for brief times. He fought forest fires in British Columbia, herded cattle in Texas and cleaned the beach at Fort Lauderdale. He mined for nickel in Thompson, Manitoba, and in mid-May he took a job as a powderman at the Giant.

The pay is $3.88 an hour for trundling explosives around the mine on the night shift. Dave says he came to Yellowknife because it was one of the things he "had to do." "A lot of men have died for gold," he says, "and here I am, digging out the wealth."

But the fascination won't endure. Dave wants to be in

the northern Eskimo community of Inuvik, looking for oil with a seismic crew. "Mining isn't the healthiest thing to do, and the money isn't that great," he says. "The miners are the only people who can make money, and I don't pass myself off as one of them."

Miners make money all right, but to make much of it they have to move the hundreds of tons of ore that qualify them for a bonus within the contract system. This means they work not only in some of the most dangerous conditions anywhere but also under constant pressure to break more and more rock.

Jim Wylie is a "stope" miner. His job is to scoop gold ore from a particular protrusion of the mineral body deep in the Giant's innards. (There are also "drift" miners, who dig the long tunnels to reach the ore, and "raise" miners, who blast vertical shafts; the latter is the most difficult job and is for only the youngest and strongest men.) Jim isn't young anymore, and the toughest part of his day has become the arduous commute to his stope—1,100 feet down in the cage, 9,500 feet north in a battery-driven train and then 215 steps up slippery, cold, wooden ladders through a pitch-dark raise.

Water dripping on his hard hat, gray mud coating his yellow, rubber gloves, Jim is grunting and breathing hard halfway up the narrow ladders. His breath is visible in the dank, 35-degree air (which, incidentally, is a lot more comfortable than mines in the South, where temperatures at depth easily run as high as 100 degrees). "My legs get so tired they can't carry any farther," Jim wheezes.

When he is nearly to his level, Jim and other miners in his "pool" (who work the same mine section) take a breather in the "lunchroom," a tiny heated cut in the rock. The 10 men are on mine captain Horst Wist's schedule to pull 1,500 tons of ore in a month, yielding 855 ounces of gold and a "profit" of $48,119 ("for the company, not for us," Jim says). The men work alone or with partners in the warren of stopes, where the air is choked with gritty dust and the scent of nitroglycerine lingers from the explosions that rip through the mine at the end of every shift.

After a smoke and a cup of milk from his Thermos, Jim and his partner Steve Beland make their way up the last ladders to their stope. Steve is only 19, one of the few young miners. His hair is long, and he wears a small gold earring in one earlobe. The stope is a room about 28 feet wide and 20 feet high. Its floor is covered with rubble from the previous day's blast. Steve grabs a hose and wets the rock to keep the dust down. Then he picks up the most dangerous tool in the mine: the scaling bar.

Standing on a pile of rock, Steve pokes at the ceiling with the beveled end of the long bar, prying off chunks of "loose," which fall to his feet with a frightening crash. More men are killed by falling rock than anything else in underground mines; two died in the first six months of 1973 at Giant. In 1972, Jim was out for a week after a rock split his finger. "Loose falls fast, and it hurts," he says.

While Steve works with the scaling bar, Jim revs up the "scraper," a heavy shovel attached to a winch that pushes the rubble down a mill hole into a waiting ore carrier with an enormous rumbling that sounds like breakers in a hurricane. For most of the night, Jim "slushes out the muck," as this is called, while Steve drills holes in the face of the ore with a pneumatic drill. Toward the end, the men fill the holes with pearled potash soaked in fuel oil, add a primer charge of nitroglycerine, attach the electric blasting caps and take their long trip back to the surface. When everyone is topside at 3 a.m., a key is turned, and fresh ore is blown free. The dust settles until the next shift comes on at 7 a.m.

Meanwhile, the mill begins processing the ore delivered during Jim's shift. The gray, gold-rich quartz is crushed and ground in mills and sent on conveyors and slurries through a maze of pipes and vats in the dimly lit wooden building until it emerges as an ashen powder, 10% of it gold.

The powder is brought to a small building, not much bigger than a two-car garage, ringed by a padlocked chain link fence. Two men dump the powder into a small furnace where it is heated to a molten, yellow-white liquid. The furnace is tipped and the slag poured off. Then Mike Tettenborn, a shift boss with the company 10 years, tips the furnace a bit more and fills a small mold with solid gold. The brick is cooled, cleaned, wrapped and sent—by ordinary parcel post—to the banks in Ottawa.

It is the last anybody at the Giant sees, or cares to see, of the metal that seems to evoke so much agitation in others. The next afternoon, Jim Wylie is in his 16-foot motorboat doing what interests him more than anything else in summer, trawling for trout. A bald eagle soars overhead, and Jim sips a rum and Coke as the boat moves slowly across the clear, cold water.

"You know," he says, almost as if he can't believe it himself, "I've been at the Giant for eight years, and I've never once gone over to watch them pour a brick." Then a 10-pounder strikes the line, and the subject of gold is dropped.

—BARRY NEWMAN

Bumper to Bumper

"Hi, I'm Gene, Fly me!"

The message, scrawled in the grime on the rear door of Gene Cox's delivery truck, seems particularly mocking as he sits deep in a Hudson River tunnel, trapped in rush-hour traffic behind a stalled car. The irony returns as he waits to get a slot at a Brooklyn company's loading dock—and again as he loses valuable time outside a Bronx plant waiting for the boss to move his Lincoln Continental from the receiving-door entrance.

So goes the down-to-earth life of the local freight-delivery driver. The tribulations he endures—not only traffic snarls but also dangers of crime and lack of customer cooperation—are generally growing worse. Deliveries of anything from food to jewelry tend to take more time and trouble nowadays, all the while gobbling up precious fuel. And though the consumer pays the extra cost in the end, the man at the wheel also pays, in tension and sometimes exhaustion. "Sometimes you can't eat you're so tense," the 49-year-old Eugene Cox says. "When I come home, I don't even look at a car if I can help it."

Still, Mr. Cox would rather fight than switch back to the intercity driving that marked the early phase of his 28-year trucking career. Flying high and wide on a turnpike is "monotonous," the wiry New York native contends. "All you see is highway, highway, highway. It's just a long, dreary ride."

By comparison, he adds, city driving "is a great challenge. You have to be more alert. You have to maneuver in and out of tight spots all day long. And you've got to use the old noodle in avoiding congestion...and dealing with people." Besides, he says, local trucking gives him more time with his wife and two children.

There are hundreds of thousands of short-haul drivers

like Gene Cox; by one industry estimate, they make up 70% of the nation's truck drivers. Together, they constitute a vital segment of the U.S. transportation network. The obstacles these drivers face, plus certain restrictions they operate under, are exacting a toll measured in gallons of scarce diesel fuel, in dollars and in hours.

Ludwig Parlavecchio, Mr. Cox's dispatcher at U.S. Trucking Co., figures many deliveries now take 20% longer than 10 years ago. During this 10-year period, the average daily overtime for the company's drivers has gradually crept up to "just over 2½ hours," laments Joseph Adams, president of U.S. Trucking, a Pittston Co. subsidiary specializing in local hauling. This, plus a 94% increase in the Teamsters' hourly wage, has caused the company's freight rates to double since 1964.

For his daily toil, Mr. Cox was drawing $6.22 an hour in 1974. With overtime, most U.S. Trucking Co. drivers earn $18,000 to $22,000 a year (only about 10% less than the average full college professor makes).

The driver's role is crucial, Mr. Adams says, "When that guy pulls away from your warehouse, he's the captain of the ship. Everything is in his hands, no matter how valuable the cargo" or how important the customer, he declares.

A day in the cab of a 25-foot truck with the hustling Mr. Cox offers a close-up of how a local driver uses his wits and skill to negotiate the obstacle course he faces. The preparations start early; Mr. Cox arises at 5:30 a.m. in the family's three-bedroom home in suburban Saddle Brook, N.J. After breakfasting alone on juice and milk, he leaves about 6:10 for the warehouse in Secaucus, N.J.

There, in the haze-covered lowlands beside the New Jersey Turnpike, Mr. Cox and other drivers get their day's orders from dispatcher Parlavecchio precisely at 7 a.m. The Teamsters contract requires that the regular eight-hour workday must begin between 7 and 8 o'clock, a rule that employers dislike intensely. This means a driver sent out at 6 a.m. gets an hour of overtime (at one-and-a-half times his hourly wage) before beginning a guaranteed eight hours straight time.

Another headache created by the uniform starting time becomes painfully apparent as Mr. Cox pulls out of the parking lot at 7:13 a.m. in his loaded truck. The adjoining back street is already clogged by rigs from nearby warehouses and terminals. The tide of trucks all at once set in motion stretches more than three miles to the Lincoln Tunnel—obviously slowing progress more than if starting times were staggered. (The delay also fritters away valuable fuel; consequently Mr. Cox's truck gets only six or seven miles per gallon of diesel fuel.)

"We've got a nice safari here today—a real safari," Mr. Cox mutters as he glances at the delivery orders for about seven tons of cellophane and other Du Pont Co. products going to nine locations scattered from the Bronx to the seaward reaches of Brooklyn.

(The cab atop the diesel engine is so noisy that conversation requires shouting, and there are few amenities. A shortwave set permits communicating with the dispatcher, but there's no other radio. "You can't concentrate on driving and on a radio," Mr. Cox reasons. He keeps his window open year-round to permit quick hand signals— and a steady rush of what he calls "fresh" air. And he doesn't worry about sunglasses: "There's so much smog around here you don't need them.")

Fifty minutes, eight miles and one tunnel tie-up after leaving the warehouse, Mr. Cox eases to a stop in a "no-parking" zone on Manhattan's East 23rd Street to make his first delivery; the company pays the fine for any parking violation essential to making a delivery.

Afterward, plowing north in a sea of traffic on First Avenue on his way to the Bronx, he is taut but talkative. "A lot of people say truckers sit on their ass all day. You may be sitting down, but it's mental anguish." He curses as a cab careens in front of the truck, carps about cars with diplomatic plates that "park anywhere" and complains that Volkswagen drivers are overly aggressive. Even some truckers "don't have the courtesy they used to have," he laments.

Heading back from the Bronx a while later, he observes: "There's no part of New York where you can go now and make a delivery without running into heavy traffic." His view at the moment: all six lanes of Second Avenue solidly packed with cars. "That's why we can't make deliveries—too damn many private cars coming into the city." On a side street, however, it's a double-parked panel truck that's holding up three other trucks. "It takes half an hour to do five blocks on side streets under these conditions," he says.

Rolling into Brooklyn a half-hour later, Mr. Cox encounters a different kind of traffic jam at a 100-year-old building near the waterfront where he delivers almost every day. There's often a delay because the company insists on loading its own trucks before taking any deliveries. Adding to the confusion this morning, the operator of a large semi-trailer has discovered his rig is too high to clear the entrance to the docking area and is trying to back out.

Spotting the problem, Mr. Cox eases his truck out of the way and goes up to help the semi-trailer driver maneuver clear. Then just as he jumps back in his truck to wheel back into line, an arriving laundry truck whips in ahead of him. "There's always one of those 'operators' around," Mr. Cox complains.

Eventually he eases his truck through the entrance with only two inches to spare on each side. "This place was built for horse-and-wagon deliveries," he grumbles. Adding to his woes, he finds the receiving clerk isn't at his usual post near the warehouse door.

Fortunately, Mr. Cox and the clerk get along well. (It was the latter who put the "Fly Me" slogan on the truck, and he gleefully retraces his handiwork each day to keep it visible.) Rather than wait, the trucker heads for a far corner of the warehouse, slips through a narrow opening and quickly re-emerges from the clerk's favorite hiding place—with the clerk in tow. The upshot: The truck gets unloaded perhaps 15 minutes sooner because Mr. Cox knows the people with whom he deals.

"One hand has got to wash the other," he says of his efforts to maintain friendly relations with receiving personnel. For his part, the clerk sometimes uses his forklift to help the trucker rearrange his load so it's easier to handle at subsequent stops.

It's Mr. Cox's turn to render a favor two stops later. He inches down a narrow street beside the Brooklyn bakery of Danilow Pastries Inc., which has requested that its regular shipment of cellophane arrive by noon. It's 11:38 a.m., and assistant manager Harry Oestreicher yells that he's about out of cellophane. When Mr. Cox hasn't managed to get an unloading slot be 12:05 p.m., he swings into action.

He grabs a cart, wheels it down the street to his truck and begins tossing on 37 cartons weighing 41 pounds each. Twenty-one minutes later, he pushes the cart inside with the aid of a conscripted bakery employe. Explains the perspiring Mr. Cox: "You're sort of a salesman for the company. So you've got to go halfway sometimes to help."

His attitude pays off for U.S. Trucking. Angered by poor delivery service, Mr. Oestreicher once threatened to shift to a supplier using another truck firm. "Then they saw to it that I got Gene all the time," he says. "He's the greatest, as far as I'm concerned."

With three widely scattered deliveries still ahead, the dispatcher directs Mr. Cox to skip his normal one-hour lunch break. Pleased to get the hour's overtime, plus a paid 20-minute eating period provided by the union contract, the trucker stops at Nick's All-Meat Hotdog stand for two quick ones loaded with sauerkraut.

After the snack, there is a stop at a nearby candy factory, followed by a trip through one of Brooklyn's tougher neighborhoods. "The jungle," Mr. Cox calls it. "They'll steal the eye out of your head," he says with a nod toward a group of teenagers standing on a corner. "Those kids will open the doors of trucks that have to stop and pull cartons out."

The problem of customer choosiness about delivery times pops up at the day's next-to-last stop. This company, like a growing number of other concers, refuses to accept goods that can't be inside its warehouse by 3:30 p.m. The need to meet this deadline was a big reason why Mr. Cox was directed to skip his lunch hour. As it is, the four one-ton pallets are safely inside by 2:30 p.m.

Then there is a trip to a remote section of Brooklyn; and by the time Mr. Cox turns his truck back toward New Jersey, the late-afternoon rush hour is in full swing. The day is ending, as it began, with bumper-to-bumper traffic, and a reflective Gene Cox admits the job's challenge can wear thin even when the pay hits $68.42 a day.

"The driving is tedious, not pleasure like it was years ago," he says. "The average man can't take 30 years of this racket. That's why you want retirement at 20 years."

—BYRON E. CALAME

The Subway Conductor

Frank Lozada is a chunky man of 43 with a chubby face and tousled brown hair, a pleasing grin and a spry manner. He is the sort of guy you instinctively like. Yet he says:

"Not a day goes by—not one—that somebody doesn't spit at me or curse me up and down, or somehow pick on me. It's like a war zone down here, and I'm on the front line. If a day goes by that someone doesn't spit at me, to tell the truth I'm a little disappointed."

Clearly while *you* might instinctively like Mr. Lozada, the people he meets every day don't. For Mr. Lozada is one of New York City's 3,200 subway conductors.

Probably every rider has cursed the subway at some time, maybe most of the time, either because it's slow or because it's uncomfortable or because it's noisy or because it's filthy, or all of the above. People travel on it not because they like to, but because they have to. Since it does no good to curse the subway itself, many riders curse or assault the conductor.

"I am every commuter's whipping boy," Mr. Lozada says. "Whatever goes wrong in the subway system, not only on my train, I get blamed for. People think I'm the god of the subways and if they yell at me I'll make things right. I can't do any more than they can."

Mr. Lozada's work world revolves around the fourth car of the eight-car, graffiti-plastered train he rides. Inside the four-foot-square conductor's cab are a small window, a control board to operate the doors, a public-address system and a collapsible seat that there is never time to rest on. About a quarter of the way up the window is a steel bar for the conductor to grab whenever someone on the platform tries to forcibly remove him from the cab, which happens.

Mr. Lozada is as much in charge of his train as a

captain is in charge of his ship. Along with the motorman who drives the train, he is responsible for its arriving safely and on time. The conductor's main function, however, is to open and close doors and, on trains with working public-address systems, to announce the stations and the transfer points.

To open the doors, Mr. Lozada inserts a key into a slot to activate some motors. Then he pushes some buttons. He opens all the doors at once, but he doesn't close them that way. First he closes the doors to the rear of his cab, then the ones in front of it. This makes it easier for him to avoid injuring people. He simply looks back before closing the doors behind him, then looks forward before closing the rest, to make sure no one is in danger of being crushed by the closing doors. Looking both ways and then closing all the doors at once wouldn't be so easy or so safe.

Transit Authority regulations requires that doors remain open at least 10 seconds. During rush hours, Mr. Lozada says, the doors often stay open as long as a minute because people hold them open. "Some jerk is always holding a door open for a friend," he says. "The friend is probably still out on the street, but the door's going to stay open until he gets here."

To make up the time lost that way, Mr. Lozada closes the doors more quickly at later stops. "I'll be closing doors so fast that people won't know they were even open," he says.

Once the doors are closed and the train starts, Mr. Lozada is supposed to lean out his window until three cars have cleared the station, checking to make sure nobody is being dragged. Some conductors cheat because they fear being assaulted. They glance out quickly or don't look at all.

Time after time, Mr. Lozada has had his cap knocked off when he leaned out his window. He has been pelted with spit, soda, newspapers, eggs, boxes, shoes, books, umbrellas. One man who had been fishing threw a fish at him. Another time, a man was casually standing on a platform with his back to Mr. Lozada. As the conductor leaned out, the man whirled around and, for no discernible reason, slapped Mr. Lozada as hard as he could. With no change in expression, the man walked away.

As soon as his train clears a station, Mr. Lozada is expected to step out of the cab and supply information and other assistance requested by riders. Here again, conductors sometimes cheat. They dawdle inside the cab, staring at the walls racing by (Or sometimes at the tenements. New York's subway systems have 137 miles of underground routes and, despite the name "subway," 72 miles of elevated runs.)

It isn't just fear. Trying to help passengers can be a headache. "In a job like this," Mr. Lozada says, "people expect you to be a psychiatrist, a mind reader and a donkey. The whole idea is to try to psych out the passengers because that's what they're trying to do to me. It's sort of a game. They want me to swear back, because then they can report me. But I fool them. I say nothing."

One rule of thumb is to answer questions slowly. "I hesitate a moment, like I'm thinking," Mr. Lozada says. "Then, if there's a crowd around, someone else will probably answer. Then he gets abused instead of me."

Some fellow conductors have suffered more abuse then Mr. Lozada has. Some have been killed or seriously injured. One lost an eye when he was shot with a zip gun. A number have had their hair pulled so fiercely that they have nearly been yanked from the cab. Many have been robbed.

Retaliatory action by the conductor can lead to more troubles. Not long ago a conductor was spit at by a teen-ager on the train. At the next stop, the same boy threw a flashbulb at the conductor. Incensed, the conductor chased the youth out of the train and down the platform, tugging at his hair in an unsuccessfull attempt to stop him. The next day, the youth arrived at the conductor's home with a patrolman and charged the conductor with assault.

The best (or least precarious) route to work on, according to Mr. Lozada, who has worked in the subways for four years, is the IRT No. 7 Flushing line, which runs between Times Square and Flushing's Main Street in Queens. "Most of the people are higher-class home owners, so they don't give you much problem," Mr. Lozada says.

The worst route, he says, is the No. 2 IRT line, which starts deep in Brooklyn, wanders through that borough, shoots up the West Side of Manhattan, passes through Harlem, makes stops in some scary and pathetic areas of the Bronx and finally winds up almost in Westchester County. "That train is crowded 24 hours a day with factory workers and school kids," he says. "School kids are a conductor's nightmare. All they do is dream up ways to torture us."

His own route is somewhere in between the worst and the best. His workday begins five blocks from his Manhattan home, at 6:42 a.m. on the downtown platform of the 168th Street station on a B train of the IND line. (There are three separate subway systems in New York—the IRT, the IND and the BMT—but all now are run by the same governmental agency.) His day ends 226 stops later at 2:36 p.m. on the same station's uptown platform on an AA train of the IND line. In between, it involves about 5,000 passengers.

On the first run, Mr. Lozada's train goes to Brooklyn's Coney Island and back. Then it changes from a B train to an AA train and completes three round trips between 168th Street and Chambers Street (which is near Wall Street) before Mr. Lozada is relieved for the day. Returning from Coney Island is Mr. Lozada's worst run. Jamming the train are more than 2,500 office workers, who don't pose much of a problem, and school kids, who do.

Besides abuse from passengers, Mr. Lozada must put up with the almost unbearable underground heat in the summer, the cold in the winter and the monotony of his job. He has little to do but open and close doors, stop after stop, run after run, day after day. "Sometimes," he says, "I play little mental games so it isn't so dull. I try to figure out how many people are in my car. I also sometimes try to guess what people do for a living, or where they live, or whether they're married. It isn't much, but it helps pass time."

Why does Mr. Lozada put up with all this grief? Money, for one thing. Conductors are paid about $200 a week plus fringe benefits. That isn't bad for unskilled work. The money makes a lot of sense to Mr. Lozada, who is married, has four children and lives in a six-room apartment at St. Nicholas Avenue and 163rd Street. He has never made more than $130 a week at anything else.

Mr. Lozada, a native of Puerto Rico, came to the mainland in 1950, settling in New York. First he worked for a machine maker in New Jersey for $40 a week, then moved to a Bronx record factory, then to a Manhattan diner where he was a waiter and cook, then to a Manhattan chandelier plant and finally in 1969 to the subways. He passed a Civil Service exam to get the conductor's job.

"When I first started," he says, "all the abuse and insults bothered me a lot. I'd have nightmares, and in the nightmares I'd be abused. But I've gotten used to it. When you get yelled at and spit at every day, it doesn't seem like much. I figure it's just part of the job. Football players get broken bones. Heavy-construction workers get hernias. Me, I get spit at."

—N.R. KLEINFIELD

The Field Hand

It is early-morning on Leighton Plantation, and the acres of lush, green sugarcane are waving in a breeze from across Bayou Lafourche. It is cool. But already Webster Adams is sweating. Since before dawn, he has been swinging a machete, cutting grass in the cane fields. It is hot work, and every few minutes he pauses to mop his face with the sleeve of his ragged shirt.

"Sugar work makes a man old before his time, that's for sure," he says with a sigh. "Every year I make a little more money at it, but I never seems to get my head above water."

Webster Adams, a quiet, gentle man of 49, is a field hand and tractor driver on this 2,400-acre sugar plantation just outside Thibodaux, La., on the rich delta of the Mississippi River. Like most of the state's 16,600 cane workers, he is black. And like most, he is struggling to get by in a world where progress is often difficult to discern. For despite substantial economic and social strides by many blacks in recent years, Mr. Adams and 7.4 million other black Americans remain trapped in the poverty they have endured for generations.

His annual income has more than doubled in the last decade, climbing from $1,338 in 1963 to $3,420 in 1973. But the rising cost of living has wiped out much of that gain.

In 1973, the typical Louisiana cane worker supported a family of six on a paltry $3,116. That was up from $1,560 about 10 years earlier, but was still $2,028 below the federal government's official poverty level for farm families of that size.

By some measures, Mr. Adams and his fellow workers have actually lost ground. During the last decade, while the median income of the nation's black families was inching upward from 53% to 58% of the median white-family income, earnings of the Louisiana sugarcane worker held steady at a fourth of the national white level.

"Every time the sugar worker climbs a few rungs, the whole ladder moves up, so he's always at the lowest level," says Sister Anne Catherine Bizalion, a French nun and executive director of the Southern Mutual Help Association, an Abbeville, La., group that seeks to improve the lot of cane workers.

Ironically, cane-worker poverty persists in a day when the sugar industry itself seems sweeter than ever. Because of a world-wide scarcity of sugar and increasing demand, American consumers were paying high prices for sugar in 1974. As a result, growers were expected to harvest a record profit. Despite Hurricane Carmen, which flattened 20% of the Louisiana crop in September 1974, the state's cane in 1974 was expected to bring a gross price of $383.6 million, or 149% more than the 1973 crop.

In the past, little of the industry profits, however, have filtered down to the workers. Witness the shoddy condition of the plantation housing, known as "quarters," in which most workers live. While Louisiana growers lately have spent considerable sums to improve the quarters—the number with indoor toilets, for example, has risen to 83% from 18% in 1969—deplorable housing still abounds in the state's 17-parish sugar belt.

The Adams family, for example, lives in a weathered, four-room shack about a half-mile from the plantation owner's spacious brick home, which is set in a grove of massive, ancient live-oak trees gracefully draped with Spanish moss.

Although the Adams home, which dates from Reconstruction, is the shabbiest place on Leighton Plantation, it is far from the worst in the area.

The Adams home, which the family lives in rent-free, has a front wall of unpainted cypress that is rotten in places and shakes in the wind. The only plumbing is one cold-water spigot in the kitchen. "At night, if you get up and

turn on a light," Mr. Adams says, "you find the kitchen
table be black with roaches."

To keep out summer mosquitoes and winter winds, the
inside walls are papered with pages of the Thibodaux Daily
Comet, the local newspaper. There aren't any closets;
clothes are hung on the bedroom walls and covered with
sheets of plastic to protect them from the water that drips
through the cardboard ceiling when it rains.

"So much rain fall inside this house, you might as well
be standing outside," says Mr. Adams' wife, Laura Victor.

For his part, the plantation owner, Fernand Price, says
the Adams house is "simply not worth fixing," It is one of
five located on land he sold to a housing developer, and it
will be razed. When that happens, the Adams family will be
moved into another plantation house, perhaps one of the 10
in which toilets and paneling recently were installed.

"I try to do the best I can by these people," Mr. Price
says.

Earlier in 1974, the prospect of record sugar profits
prompted efforts to improve the lot of plantation workers
through amendments to the 40-year-old Sugar Act. The act
sets quotas and subsidies for sugar production and author-
izes the Department of Agriculture to establish fair wages
and reasonable working conditions. But in a surprise move,
the House voted to let the entire act expire.

As it happens, Mr. Adams already receives some of the
benefits proposed by labor advocates. He is covered by
workmen's-compensation insurance, for example, and
since 1970 has been given a week's paid vacation annually.
Otherwise, however, his job has few rewards.

Occasionally, the work is hazardous. He spent one day
in the fields holding a flag to guide crop dusters and
repeatedly was sprayed with a chemical designed to kill
insects in the cane. "You got to wash that stuff right off
soon as you get home," he says.

Some days he cuts grass with a hook-bladed machete,
known locally as a "cane knife," or helps repair machinery
at the equipment shed. Usually, however, his work consists

of guiding a tractor back and forth across a field. During the late spring and summer, the season when the cane is planted and cultivated, his tractor pulls a drag-chopper, a machine that breaks and turns the earth. From mid-October through December, during the hectic harvest season, known as "grinding time," he hauls cane from the harvesting machines in the field to the raw-sugar mill about 100 yards from his front door.

He says the secret of his job, especially in the summer, is "to work as fast as you can early in the morning so you can fool around later in the day when the sun be beating down on you. That way the man can't say you ain't done nothing," he explains with a grin that reveals a half-mouthful of teeth, all decaying at the gum line. "You got to keep cool."

Following that admonition, he has cut vents in his battered, sweat-stained hats and doesn't always insist that Laura patch the holes in his faded shirts. "You got to let things breathe," he says.

A wiry man (he is five-feet, six-inches tall and weights 142 pounds) whose hair is just beginning to turn gray, Mr. Adams has worked in the cane fields since he was 10 years old and is fairly content with his lot despite its hardships. "Farm work ain't good, but it's better than it was, that's for sure. My daddy plowed with mules; I got a tractor," he says.

"Unless the mill is running, life is quiet here. I got a garden to raise me some okras and beans. If I went to town, I'd always be looking for work. And anyway, I'd just be driving a tractor for the Highway Department or something because all I can do is drive a tractor. Lord, I be driving a tractor the day I die."

Every weekday before dawn, Mr. Adams strolls a few yards down the gravel road to the equipment shed near the sugar mill, followed by a pack of scruffy cats that live under his porch. As he refuels his tractor, he chats with the other hands about the weather, their families and last night's television programs.

"Look like we in for another hot day," says Welmon Pharagood, a fellow tractor driver and father of 10.

"Yep," Mr. Adams says. "It do, it do. A hot one. That's for sure."

He swings his cooler of ice water onto the tractor, then climbs aboard and drives to the fields, drag-chopper in tow. Partly obscured by a cloud of dust, his tractor lumbers and bounces across the fields until 8 a.m., when he stops for breakfast—a bologna sandwich he has brought in a paper sack.

"Out in them cane fields, you ain't got time to think," he says, sitting in the shade of the tractor and sipping on ice water. "You just be turning them rows or chopping that ground, and you be looking to 4:30, when you be knocking off. You be half-hoping it rain and cool off and half-hoping it don't so you can get in them hours."

Mr. Adams is paid by the hour; if he doesn't work, he doesn't get paid. When it rains there is little work to be done on all but the largest sugar plantations, and Mr. Adams is idle much of the year, especially January through March, when the harvested fields are a swamp of brown cane stubble. During this period, the family gets by on food stamps and earnings from the harvest time. However, the harvest income isn't saved in cash; it is used to buy such staples as rice and beans in 25-pound sacks and canned goods, which are stored to feed the family during the lean months of late winter.

During the 1974 harvest, which began on Leighton Plantation in mid-October, Mr. Adams will be paid $2.50 an hour—the new wage set by the Agriculture Department and up from $2. "That money will help out a little bit, but food and everything has gone up so much, it still won't be enough," he says.

Each working day at noon, Mr. Adams returns home for his main meal of the day. When he arrives, his wife is in the kitchen, stewing okra and frying homemade flour cakes. She is 47 but looks much older. She suffers from a chronic circulatory condition that requires frequent trips to the closest charity hospital, in New Orleans, 60 miles away.

In the living room, which doubles as a bedroom, daughters Daisy Mae and Louise, who are both in their 20s, are arguing whether a young doctor on "Search for Tomorrow" should confess that he is the hit-and-run driver everyone is looking for. Except during cane-planting time, neither daughter works outside the home; both spend most of their days watching television. Louise is unmarried and lives with her parents. Daisy lives two houses away. She is separated from her husband, Willie, who was also a tractor driver on Leighton until he recently moved to another plantation. In a corner sits grandson Mickey, who is three years old but has just begun to talk.

Mr. Adams thumbs a little tobacco into his pipe and settles into a broken-down chair to watch television until his food is on the table. Although he fishes occasionally, television is his principal pastime. "Mostly, I like Westerns," he says, "but I sometimes does watch the news."

It is television news that has provided almost all his contact with recent black history. He remembers the civil-rights movement, for instance, as a series of film clips of sit-ins, marches and riots.

Still, the movement did make important changes in the lives of his children. When he was a boy, he recalls, he had to walk several miles, barefoot, over gravel roads to a one-room, all-black school. His daughters were taken to integrated schools by buses that stopped at their door. One of 14 children, Mr. Adams had to quit school after the first grade to go to work in the sugar fields to help support his family. Consequently, he can neither read nor write. Louise, however, completed the ninth grade; Daisy Mae, the eighth.

For Mr. Adams himself, however, the benefits of the civil-rights movement are less apparent.

Since the Voting Rights Act of 1965, for example, the proportion of registered black voters in Lafourche parish has increased 40%. But, Mr. Adams has never bothered to register. "I doesn't vote because sometimes you votes for the right man and sometimes you votes for the wrong one. And whoever gets in isn't going to care about me anyway, so what difference does it make?"

Legally, he now can live wherever he wishes. But, like almost all cane workers, he feels bound for economic reasons to the plantation housing supplied free by the grower. "I don't make enough wages to pay rent in town," he explains.

Today he can eat and drink in formerly all-white restaurants and taverns. But his family is too poor to dine out, and when he does go for an occasional beer, he prefers to sip it in what he calls "colored bars,"

"I tell you the truth," he says, "I think what that Martin Luther King did was good. That's for sure. But it never made much difference to me."

—RICHARD A. SHAFFER

Blue Corn, the Potter

Blue Corn takes a wad of ocher clay in her hands and kneads it into a ball. Slapping the clay with her fist and fingers, she slowly molds the ball into the rough outline of a bowl and lays it into the puki, a saucer-shaped base.

She takes another handful of clay and rolls it between her palms until it forms a ropelike coil. As she winds the coil around the top of the bowl, Blue Corn pinches it flat into fluted ridges, melding one bit of clay into the other. She makes several more coils and places them on top of one another until the shape of a pot emerges from her hands and the clay.

With wet shards of gourd and her fingertips, she smooths the inner and outer surfaces and gently massages them into symmetry. "There," she says softly, holding the still-damp creation at arm's length, "a pot." There is much more to do before she uses a polished stone to carve her signature and the name of San Ildefonso Pueblo, N.M., on the bottom, but the shape is there, the structure completed, the craft awaiting the art.

Blue Corn is a Tewa Indian potter whose strong hands and obsidian eyes continue a tradition begun before Christ in the cliff dwellings and kivas of the Southwest. Today, traders and buyers agree that native American crafts are more popular than ever with tourists, collectors and museums. A prolific, competent potter can make $25,000 to $50,000 a year, according to one local trader, with a single pot sometimes fetching $4,000.

Blue Corn, who probably earns on the high side of that salary range, has seen the price of one of her pots climb to nearly $1,000 from about 15 cents when she began some 25 years ago, but her motivation remains that of someone who enjoys her work. "Pottery, pottery—that's all I can think about," she says.

(Indeed, Blue Corn is far from ostentatious about spending her money. She has improved the interior of her home, bought three vehicles for members of her family to drive and is helping a son build a new home, but a sizeable portion of her earnings goes into savings or to help her tribe.)

As pots and potters flood the market, some experts fear a decline in quality. "Before this trend, only a few professionals were producing consistently," observes Anita Da, owner of a San Ildefonso studio. "Now mass production is depleting the authenticity of traditional designs—everybody wants to be an Indian." However, "there are still some great pieces being made," Rex Arrowsmith, a local trader, contends."Buyers are coming out here from Saks, Magnin and Macy's and camping on the potter's doorstep."

Sixteen of the 19 pueblos in Colorado, New Mexico and Arizona have made pottery since their founders migrated here before the Christian era, but three pueblos have produced the most famous craftswomen—San Ildefonso, Santa Clara and San Juan.

Like most northern New Mexico potters, Blue Corn works with the same materials in the same way as her prehistoric ancestors, the Mogollon Indians, who never developed the potter's wheel. Using the coil or ring method, they made storage jars, cooking pots and ceremonial vessels, the classic forms of pueblo pottery. Maria Martinez, now near 90, popularized the famous San Ildefonso burnished black matte ware during the 1930s. Currently, some potters have experimented with turquoise or beads imbedded in the clay, corrugated and multicolored pots and figurines.

Potters innovate in technique as well as style. A Santa Clara potter, for example, uses popsicle sticks and tongue depressors to smooth her pots. Other women dry their pots in electric ranges before firing. Stainless steel knives, tin-can lids, iron grates, commercial brushes and store-bought paints have replaced traditional tools in many pueblos. While using these modern methods, other potters have revived ancient tpes, such as *Potsuwi'i,* or carved designs, pictographic pots and religious figures. Blue Corn is credited with reintroducing polychrome pottery, a fine white ware made from a special, and secret, clay source. (One of her granddaughters is named Polychrome Flower.)

A genial, handsome woman of about 50, Blue Corn makes pots of several sizes and shapes, plates, figurines, bowls, ladles and wedding vases. Her work has won ribbons and prizes at numerous exhibitions, fairs and intertribal ceremonials. Richard Spivey, a prominent buyer for museums and Southwestern shops, ranks her among the best potters working today. Not only is she unique in reviving polychrome pottery, but also her work generally shows the graceful contours and disciplined lines common to the best kinaesthetic art.

She lives with her seven daughters and four sons, who in 1973 were aged three to 28, in a large adobe home near the kiva, or ceremonial chamber, on the plaza of this pueblo. Her husband, Santiago, died in December 1972 on the birthday of two of his daughters. Santiago, a Santa Domingo Indian, had helped carve, design and paint her pots, a job now assumed by Joseph, the oldest son.

Blue Corn gathers the materials for her pots—the clays, sand, plants for making paint and dried manure for firing—on the reservation. San Ildefonso lies among wind-chiseled buttes and arroyos about a mile from the Rio Grande and 11 miles from the Los Alamos atomic research laboratories. When she and two of her younger children walk through the pinon and cottonwood trees, the mesquite and creosote brush, they can see three snow-capped mountain ranges, as well as the haunting bulk of the sacred Black Mesa west of the reservation. "Come on," she calls to Caroline and Craig, "let's go look for some money." The children refer to the dried cow and horse dung as "cinnamon rolls."

Once she has dug clay from the earth and shoveled sand into a bag, she returns home to pound the clay into a smooth, porous mass and to sift both clay and sand until they are free from sticks or rocks that might blister the pot in firing. After the clay soaks in water, she mixes it with the flour-like sand until it has the texture and color she desires.

Ordinarily, Blue Corn works at a large table inside her single-story home, adobe mud brick on the outside but pine-paneled and furnished in modern style within. In one corner of the living room there is a glass-windowed cabinet containing some of the ribbons she has won in the past two years. Hanging from the walls are Indian rugs, blankets and baskets for which Blue Corn has traded some of her pots. Near a bookshelf in the workroom is a 1961 color photograph signed by Lady Bird Johnson, shown looking over Blue Corn's shoulder as she makes a pot in the plaza of her pueblo. Above one doorway is a shelf holding a few of the last pots and bowls designed by her husband.

On a summer day, Blue Corn works in moccasins, blue slacks and blouse and a floral print apron as she cuts excess clay off the pots with a paring knife, like peeling an apple. Then she begins to smooth the pot with sandpaper. As she rubs she talks about her work. "Girls today don't much want to make pots," she says. "They know it gets their hands dirty, and they don't want to mess up their hands. I told my son that he wanted a girl friend, not to take up pottery. Girls don't like rough hands."

Now the pot is ready for the slip, a liquid paint made from water and clay. The slip can be red, yellow or, in Blue Corn's case, athe polychromatic white. Using a piece of soft cloth, she applies several coats of the slip to the outside of the pot. While the slip is moist, she begins to polish the pot with one of several smooth, shiny stones. Many such stones are heirlooms, handed from one generation to another, and Blue Corn often uses a stone given to her by her grandmother. Frequently changing stones, she polishes every inch of the pot until it reaches a high luster. She stands while shaping and scraping the pot; but now she sits. Sweat forms on her forehead below the red bandana that keeps her black hair from her eyes. Her long fingers, already the same color as the clay, flex until her knuckles turn white around the polishing stone.

"My grandmother was blind," she recalls, "but she used to take my face and hands into her hands and she told me, 'Blue Corn, forget about school. Stay home and do pottery. Your hands are made for pottery.'"

After polishing, since this pot is to be decorated, Blue Corn traces the design with a pencil on the outside of the pot. When he was alive, Santiago designed and painted all the pots, and it has been difficult for her to resume a technique she hadn't practiced in more than 15 years. Today, she sketches the outline of Avanyu, the water serpent, measuring the distances with her fingers and constantly turning the pot to make sure her lines are true. Earlier, she boiled guaco, the juice of the Rocky Mountain bee plant, with sugar to make a thick black pigment. Now she takes an artist's paintbrush from which most of the bristles have been removed and slowly follows the pencilled lines of the serpent. Until 1971, she used the thin, looping fibers of the yucca plant, but now, like nearly every other potter, she uses a brush bought in a hardware store.

Pausing to push her glasses off her nose, Blue Corn says many of her designs come "from my head," others from illustrated books written by Anglo archaeologists about pueblo pottery. "Once they were digging a sewer through the village, " she says, "and they found a lot of old pieces of very old pots. I learned some designs from them and from the museum in Santa Fe."

After the paint dries and she has buffed the pots with a soft cloth, she clears her worktable and her daughters serve steaming platters of tamales and green chili wrapped in corn shucks, corn on the cob, bread baked in an outdoor oven and scalding coffee. While the children eat, Blue Corn sips a cup of coffee. She got up at 3:30 this morning to see if the weather would be good for firing, but it was too windy. She reminisces as she relaxes: "I remember once my husband and I went to San Diego to demonstrate on a television show. When we got out of the car, two men from the studio came and asked my husband where was our machine to make pottery. He pointed at me and said, "There is my machine—walking through that door.' When he told me what they said, I told them that I plugged myself into the wall in the morning, made pots all day and then unplugged myself at night to go to sleep."

Today there is a corn dance in the pueblo honoring the crop planting and St. Anthony. On the north plaza, two lines of men, women and children from San Ildefonso, in their flowing mantas, moccasins, headdresses and bells, sway to the rhythm of a ceremonial drum and the hypnotic chants of the tribal elders. Blue Corn has danced in many of these, but today she is anxious to finish enough pots to fire and sell to the traders and tourists who flock to her door.

The evening is too windy. She rises about four on Sunday morning and looks out into the darkness. It is quiet. No wind is blowing. Behind her home, she builds a grill from several pieces of iron and slides shredded cedar under it for kindling. Joseph is up now, and as first light breaks over the mountains he helps her place the week's 14 pots upside-down on the grate. Then they surround the post with sheets of tin until they are completely enclosed. Next, cakes of dried cow and horse manure are stacked all around the square tin kiln. They light the kindling, and soon the dung smolders and burns sweetly. A grey feather of smoke rises into the calm air. Somewhere a dog barks.

Firing is the last, and most crucial, step in making pottery. A potter spends days shaping, drying, polishing, carving and decorating her pots, but she may lose one, or all, of them during the firing. An errant draft can cause the fire to scorch and discolor the pots. Insufficient heat may warp a pot; too much heat can break it. Blue Corn remembers well the day she fired two large, intricately patterned plates that she hoped to enter in the New Mexico state fair: "I usually sold them for about $885 each. They were in the fire, and I heard a large *crack!* One of the plates had broken in the middle, and manure had fallen onto it. The other was also damaged. I sat down and cried. I gave up pottery for a week—I just couldn't do it. I didn't even enter anything. I heard that all these people were asking for my pots, and I was home crying."

Today, the firing is successful. Blue Corn and Joseph move around the smoky fire prodding the dung cakes and cedar and peering with weeping eyes at the pots visible behind the flames. "Joseph once bought me—what do you call them?—those things you wear swimming—goggles— for me to wear when firing pots," she says with a smile. "But I got so sweaty and couldn't see anything. I think that is why so many potters must wear glasses because the smoke damages our eyes."

After about an hour, they begin delicately to remove the manure with a rake and small shovel. When the kiln is clean, Joseph dons a pair of gloves and gingerly lifts the tin pieces from around the grill. His mother wipes her hands on her apron and bends over her pots clustered below. "I think they are okay," she says. "Oooh, I like the color of that one—it's almost orange. But I don't like that yellow—it looks too commercial." As they wait for the pots to cool, Blue Corn and Joseph sit near the grill and drink a cup of coffee. "I am so glad," she says with a sigh.

Blue corn was born in San Ildefonso and attended school at the pueblo. Then she went to Santa Fe Indian school, 24 miles from home, and while she was there her mother and father died, a year apart. She couldn't attend either funeral nor that of the grandmother who had encouraged her to "forget school and become a potter."

At about 17, she went to Southern California to live with relatives and worked as a domestic in Beverly Hills.

She married Santiago, also called Sandy Blue Corn, at age 20. Like many Santa Domingo Indians, he was a silversmith and plied his craft briefly at a Santa Fe curio shop. During World War II, Blue Corn worked in Los Alamos as a housecleaner for J. Robert Oppenheimer ("He was very quiet and very nice," she says). Shortly after Joseph was born, she decided to take up pottery again. She had begun it once in the early years of her marriage, but "then it was so hard to get materials and so rough and dirty a job, so I quit it."

She soon found her calling. "Ever since I got away from school," she says, "my mind was on pottery, pottery—where to get my clay, how to mix it, how to fire. My husband and I thought it was our best resource in raising our children, so he quit his job to help me with it." Blue Corn recalls the time early in her new career when they moved from San Ildefonso to Albuquerque: "We had no car, so we had to hitchhike. Here we were, walking along the highway, with my husband carrying Joseph on his back and a box of pots under one arm, and me carrying Michael on my back and a box of pots under my arm."

Those times seem long ago. Today her work is known and demanded nationally. Blue Corn doesn't have to leave her home to sell her pots; traders and tourists knock at all hours asking to buy. She doesn't even have a sign in front of the house. "If they want my pots bad enough, they'll find me," she says.

Yet it's obvious that she takes her craft—and her art—seriously. Sitting one late afternoon with her chafed, blistered hands in her lap, she gazes out the window of her workroom. "Every night," she says softly, "before I go to bed, I come out here and look at my pots."

—MIKE THARP

The Sculptor

"Now there's a beauty," says Peter Weil, climbing the side of a hill above an old sawmill to a capsized 1925 Essex, its body rusted to a burnished, velvety texture. He hops onto a fender and rocks on it, trying to pry it loose, and he wriggles underneath to grapple with the crumpled hood.

"We'll have to put the torch to that," he says and then bounds down into a heap of gnarled scrap. Oblivious to a cloud of black flies buzzing around his dark, bearded head, he heaves his finds onto the dusty road: a saw blade, a barrel, a hoop, a sled runner. When the hair of scrap subsides, he studies the take with some satisfaction. "That's pretty good pickings," he says.

Peter is a metalworker—a welder and a craftsman— who will very likely transmogrify that pile of litter into rough-hewn little sculptures of a winged elephant, a pig with a flower in its mouth, a turtle on wheels or a bicycle-riding Dox Quixote, as well as assorted candle cages and pot hangers.

There may be some lobstermen and blueberry farmers in Steuben, Maine, who consider the 40-year-old one-time Washington bureaucrat an oddity. But Peter Weil, who came to Maine in 1970 and lives with his wife, Jan, in an old house on the serene town square of Steuben, has a method to his eccentricity.

Buffeted for the first 35 years of his life by standards of achievement he could never bring himself fully to accept, he like many others, has turned the pressure off by retiring to the relative isolation of a craft. And while he protests that he isn't part of any "trend," he doesn't deny that the American craft revival of the last few years is helping him make a modest living at welding bits of metal into funny animals or items of more practical use.

"I absolutely don't see myself as part of the back-to-nature movement or anything else," he says. "I'm probably a frustrated auto mechanic. I love the process of working with my hands—the glow of hot metal, the sounds of the tools.

"Maybe I'd like to be a creative artist, making one-of-a-kind pieces. But people don't have to think half as much about paying $50 for some craft work as they do about paying $750 for a work of art. Plenty of people are willing to buy."

Judging from the number of people selling their crafts, the number willing to buy is growing without letup. In the past decade, the American Crafts Council has doubled its membership of craftsmen and others interested in the crafts to its current 33,000. In 1967, the council counted 510 craft shops in the country; there were 800 in 1973. In 1969, 116 colleges were offering undergraduate degrees in the crafts; 204 were offering them in 1973. In the late 1960s, the council says, there were fewer than 30 craft fairs in the country. Now there are over 100 three- or four-day fairs a year where craftsmen go to hawk their creations.

All these people aren't rustic folk artisans coming out of the backwoods to cash in on a quirk in modern culture. Many are urbanites or former urbanites. It's true they usually have an infatuation with the methods of the past and an aversion to mass production. But they are nevertheless shaping their clay, wool, metal, wood, plastic, glass, enamel and what-have-you into what might well be called contemporary folk art.

Making money at this sort of thing, though, is a craft few have mastered. Peter Weil figures he has pulled in about $20,000 selling his work, mostly since 1968. In 1972, he grossed $3,800 and his wife made another $4,000 running a local nursery school. When he is actually producing, Peter works about six hours a day at his welding bench, six or seven days a week. "After expenses," he says, "I'm probably making $2 to $2.50 an hour, horrible as that is to contemplate."

Churning out his wares is just the beginning. The toughest part is finding a market for them. Peter travels to three or four craft fairs a year in search of retailers who will put his contrivances on the shelves of their galleries and shops. There's a museum in Omaha, where his father lives, that has some of Peter's things for sale. So does a gallery in Florida whose owner took a fancy to them at a Maine fair. Peter and a dozen other local craftsmen have opened a craft co-op in an old hardware store in nearby Millbridge. The total investment was $80, mostly for paint.

But there isn't much of a market in Maine. Peter tried to interest some natives in a few things at a fair sponsored by his wife's nursery school. Nobody bit. "What got sold were cakes and pies and stuff to make patchwork quilts with," he says. Finding takers is easiest in Washington, D.C., where most of Peter's acquaintances are. He had a Sunday sale at the home of a good friend there. "Not that many people came, but the sales were incredible," he says. "I made $700 in one day. Of course, though, that only happens once a year."

(The items retail for anywhere from $10 to $175 each, mostly in the $30-$50 bracket. None is much longer or taller than a foot, and if Peter makes 30 of any one design he considers them mass-produced.)

Despite the sales problems, Peter does have some advantages over other craftsmen. For one thing, there aren't that many welders around. About 400 craftsmen showed up at the big Northeast Crafts Fair in Bennington, Vt., a few years ago. Of those, Peter says, only five besides himself were metalworkers; 200 were potters. This makes it hard to get lost in the crowd.

Metalworking, moreover, involves practically no overhead. Most of Peter's raw material, about 1,000 pounds of scrap metal a year, is free. "There are so many junked cars and washing machines and boilers in the woods of Maine, I could never run out," he says.

Capital investment for Peter means a $10 anvil from an antique shop, a $50 grinding wheel, a $125 torch and a few pliers. His biggest expenses are renting two tanks of gas for $15 a year each and paying about $450 a year for the oxygen and acetylene that goes in them.

Perhaps the most significant advantage over other modern craftsmen is the fact that Peter lives up here. Steuben is in one of the poorest counties in Maine, and though land prices are booming, Peter bought his 140-year-old house and three flowered acres along Tunk Stream for $6,500. He sold some stock and borrowed some money to fix the place up, keeping all the original floors and even the original plaster with its horsehair binder. Then he bought an even older house next door and is converting the downstairs into a workshop and the upstairs into an apartment he hopes to rent.

Even with these expenses, he can run two cars and eat his fill of fresh boiled lobster (which doesn't do his touch of gout much good). "Living what is by some standards a subsistence life isn't a religious or ethical thing for us," Peter says. "This is just a poor place. I've never been on the make. Obviously, that's why I didn't get anywhere as a civil servant. This is a better life; Maine has opened me up."

Today, Peter is active in local politics (he was tax assessor last year) and is assistant chief of Steuben's volunteer fire department. With the houses to renovate and his metalworking, he says he has "enough work to last a lifetime—more than a lifetime."

But getting to where he is now took some doing. For years after graduating from Antioch in 1956 he was in and out of schools and jobs as an academic-flavored bureaucrat. First he took a master's degree in conservation at the University of Michigan. Then he spent a year and a half in Chicago researching a book for someone else that was never published. ("I did a lousy job," he admits.)

After that he went to Washington to gather statistics for the President's Commission on Outdoor Recreation. (One project was to measure the public's opinion of recreational areas. "The Bureau of the Budget said it couldn't be done," Peter says, "and we proved them right.") Three years later he joined the Organization of American States to help make economic maps of Latin America. And, finally, he went to Johns Hopkins for two years of classwork toward a doctorate in geography. He never wrote a thesis.

"Every time a project finished or a course ended," Peter says, "it was a matter of not knowing what the hell else to do."

Through it all, as something of a reclusive bachelor, Peter was learning crafts. In Chicago, "lonely and bored to tears," he took a course in pottery. In Washington he met two sculptors who were willing to teach him how to carve stone. "It was some sport," he says. "I was knocking out a piece about once a month and I was a success in some juried shows. But it was a hobby. I wasn't thinking of it as a career at all."

As a favor to a friend who didn't want to travel alone to a class in a tough section of Washington, Peter attended a course in welding at Bell Vocational High School. "I never finished the thing," he says. "I just went long enough to learn the technique, bought some equipment and went to work." In a garage behind his apartment house, he began to weld little animals and cartoon people. "Slowly," he says, "I began to make money at it."

Knowing he could earn a smidgen at metalwork, Peter started cutting down on his more conventional pursuits. He worked only part-time in his last months at the OAS, and he did a lot of welding while studying for his doctorate. Meeting Jane, who is 33, changed his life still more, and she soon "dragged" him to Maine, he says.

The tensions of his pre-Maine years still seem to weigh on Peter. He paces nervously while he talks, and he munches peanuts or sips strong espresso coffee or strikes matches to relight his pipe. But Maine and Jane have mellowed him. "I'm told that when I was younger," he says, "I was really vicious."

The move to Maine convinced him at last that he didn't need a fixed routine "to hold me together." And his unfocused past, combined with a pointedly cycnical sense of humor, has provided him with grist for the work of a full-time craftsman. "Out of all the pain and travail of my career and all the false starts and bypaths I've gone down," he says, "I've gathered an awful lot of material in my mind that I can put into my work. There's something vastly ridiculous, isn't there, about a pig with a flower in its mouth?"

Peter sits at his dining-room table and lets his ideas pour out on sketch paper. Then he puts on a sweatshirt pocked with burn holes from flying sparks and two pairs of similarly swiss-cheesed pants and descends into the tiny dirt-floored furnace room he uses as a his shop. The project is a bird on wheels.

He pulls on his round smoked-glass goggles and fiddles with the gauges on his gas tanks. The fumes begin hissing out of the cutting head, and with the flick of a flint the yellow flame jumps out. He adjusts it down to a hard blue cone and balances a flat piece of pitted steel on firebrick. Resting the torch on a bridge of knuckles like a billiard cue, he cuts.

Under a shower of sparks, the four-inch-high profile of an open-beaked sparrow emerges. When it's complete, he cuts a square from another steel plate; it becomes the torso. "I can cut a pretty straight line just eyeballing it," Peter mumbles. He snaps caked slag from the edges of the steel with a pair of pliers but doesn't do anything about the deep-gray coloration along the path of the torch. "I just lie back and like it," he says.

Peter switches on the grinding wheel and presses the pieces to the carborundum. The edges smooth out with a piercing screech. (Peter wears goggles for grinding. He didn't for a long time, and he says he had his share of splinters dug from his eyes.) He grabs the torso with his pliers and pounds it with a sledge on the anvil until a neatly curved tail appears. "I'm just guessing about the curve," he says. "Very often, the pieces just develop as I'm working on them."

Back at the welding bench, he unscrews the cutting head from the torch and screws on a welding head. With a thin length of welding rod in one hand (one of the few raw materials he buys) and the torch in the other, he melts tiny U-shaped wires onto the underside of the torso, slips an axle through them and fastens to it the small, spoked wheels he already has made. "You really need three hands at this point," he says. "One to hold the torch, one to hold the rod and one to hold the piece."

To the topside of the torso, he "tacks" the sparrow's head. Then he welds it in place at the base of its neck with small droplets of molten welding rod that quickly solidify into delicate gray swirls. The bird is finished. He plunges it into a cooling bucket, pulls it out and playfully rolls it across the firebrick. "That's fine," he says. "I think I'm going to like it."

—BARRY NEWMAN

Man in the Middle

The Philadelphia Flyers have just beaten the St. Louis Blues, 1-0, and John D'Amico is one of the last off the ice, skating slowly, his head hanging.

He has just helped officiate another two-and-a-half hour game, and in the process he skated some five miles, broke up two fights, prevented four others, and blew his whistle a dozen times to halt play after various rules infractions. His head throbs from a goose egg left by a ricocheting puck. Still ringing in his ears are the boos of more than 19,000 National Hockey League fans.

But John D'Amico is happy. "That was a good hockey game" with "a lot of scrambling," he says, pulling off his black-and-white-striped jersey, plastic shin guards and sweat-soaked long underwear in the small dressing room reserved for officials. He isn't really tired, he says after a hot shower; "the game wasn't really that tough."

Certainly not as tough as the one a few years back, when it took 16 stitches to close a gash across his chin—a gash put there by the curved end of a player's stick. Or the one in which a New York Ranger's wild punch broke a bone in John's jaw. Or the one late in the 1972 season in Toronto when a collision with a player left John laid up for 10 days with torn ligaments in his left leg.

Professional ice hockey is one of the fastest and roughest sports there is, so it isn't surprising that a hockey official's job is probably the most physically demanding of any sports officiating job. "It's rare that a hockey official will go through an entire season without some kind of injury," says Scotty Morrison, the league's referee-in-chief. Unlike pro football or soccer referees, hockey officials can't escape to the safety of the sidelines when the action gets rough. The sidelines on a hockey rink are three-foot-high board fences, dangerous spots to get sandwiched between a couple of heavily padded players fighting for a puck.

Even when all goes well, officiating a pro hockey game is grueling. Players usually sit on the bench about half of each game, but there's no respite for the three officals. And if one of them gets hurt badly enough to have to leave the ice, as happens four or five times a season, the other two simply have to skate that much harder to keep up with the play.

Off the ice, the job is even more taxing. NHL teams are scattered among 16 American and Canadian cities, and the league insists that the officials keep moving constantly from one to another—partly to prevent players (and, sometimes, unruly fans) from becoming too familiar with any one of the 45 NHL officials.

The St. Louis game was John's third in four nights— the other two were in New York and on Long Island. The next day, he had to be up at 5:30 a.m. to fly to a game in Chicago. That meant traveling 1,000 to 5,000 miles a week to officiate in four games. "When you have four games on four nights and you're getting up at six every morning, it's really tiring," he says.

Despite the rigors, there's no shortage of job seekers. The NHL hired four new officials in 1973 from scores of candidates. Fifteen of the best prospects were invited to try out for the jobs by competing in skating drills and officiating preseason exhibition games.

John, who's 35 years old, has been in the league 10 years and is one of its best officials, according to players and other officials. "He's got extremely good rapport with the players," which helps in breaking up fights, and "he's on top of the plays," says Mr. Morrison, his boss. John has been selected eight times to officiate the final playoffs for the championship Stanley Cup; only four linesmen a year are picked for those games.

As one of the two linesmen assigned to officiate each game, John's responsibilities are to patrol half of the ice spotting rules infractions and breaking up fights. Every time play is whistled to a halt, a linesman retrieves the solid rubber puck and drops it between two opposing players to start the game again. The head official is the referee, usually several years more experienced than the linesmen. He skates all over the ice, follows each play as closely as he can and is the final arbiter of such ticklish matters disputed goals and penalties called for tripping, fighting or sticking an opponent.

John's fairly typical of the NHL officials. He is an expert skater and is able to recite chapter and verse of the league's 82-page rule book. He also works at keeping his 5-foot-9-inch, 190-pound frame in top physical condition. He does daily calisthenics, even during the off season, in order to be ready for the NHL's rigorous 10-day preseason training camp, which all officials must attend. He's anything but a flamboyant personality. The NHL wants no colorful characters on the ice in black-and-white stripes. "People come to see the hockey games, not the officials," explains Herb Ralby, publicity director of the Boston Bruins.

For John, the job's biggest appeal is simply the opportunity to be involved in big-league hockey. "I really love the game," he says. Like most officials, he grew up in Canada and would have liked to become a pro player himself. "I wasn't good enough to be a player, so the second best thing to me is to be an official," he says. He hopes to officiate until he's 45 or 50, even though he knows most linesmen and referees quit in their early 40s, worn out from skating alongside 20-year-olds and catching planes four times a week. "If I had to leave the business today, I don't know what I'd do," he says.

He'll probably be a linesman until he retires. The NHL tried promoting him to referee in 1965 and it didn't work. He spent two years refereeing in the minors, then a half-season in the majors before he asked to be reassigned as a linesman again. "I'd get one game over with, and I'd be worrying about the next one," he recalls. He broke out in psoriasis from the constant pressure and had red blotches and flaking skin over his whole body at times, he says. It wasn't an easy decision to go back to being a linesman. Refereeing pays $8,000 to $12,000 more than the nearly $17,000 he gets as a linesman, but three months after he left the referee ranks his psoriasis was gone.

John picks up an extra $3,500 a year officiating the playoff games, and in the summer he picks up a little more near Toronto, teaching at a school for referees and officiating at a hockey school for youngsters.

He has acquired the usual trappings of success, including a ranch style house with swimming pool in a Toronto suburb. But he has little time to enjoy them or to be with his three children. His wife, Dorothy, is "both a mother and father to the kids," he says. Being away from home so much bothers him a lot.

What bothers him least about it is the risk of injury during games. "The last thing I think of is getting hurt," he says. "If I worried about being injured, I'd be psychotic." He accumulates some 30 bruises a season from ricocheting pucks, collisions with players and wildly swung hockey sticks. Most are quickly forgotten. But he lost two of his rear teeth early in his career when a player stabbed at an opponent with his stick and caught John instead. In 1971 in Boston he was hit in the eye by a stick and rushed to a hospital, but his eye wasn't damaged.

John considers the torn ligaments in his left knee in 1972 his worst injury. He missed six games and had to wear a leg brace for the last few weeks of the season. Until then, he had missed only four games in his career, all with pulled muscles. Such stress injuries to his legs are the ones John fears most—they're the kind that can shorten or abruptly end officals' careers. "You can always skate with stitches and bruises" but not with muscle and ligament problems, he says.

Born and raised in Toronto's "little Italy" section, John started skating when he was 11 and from age 12 to 20 played hockey in youth and amateur leagues. At 16, he recalls, he was suspended for five games by his amateur league when, while fighting with other players, he became so furious he shoved a referee.

A youngster who is considered a pro prospect usually starts hearing from scouts when he's 16 or 17, says John, but by the time he was 20 no one was knocking at his door. A friend persuaded John to officiate some youth organization games, and from there he went on to officiate in an amateur league, all in addition to his regular job as a construction worker. In 1963, when he was 25, a rare opening came up for a linesman in the NHL, which then had only six teams, and John beat out about 70 other prospects for the job. "I was just floating on clouds" at the time, he recalls. "Here's a guy who was digging ditches suddenly rubbing shoulders with Gordie Howe and Jean Beliveau."

The abuse linesmen frequently receive from fans quickly brought him back to earth, though. During his second year on the job, after throwing a New York Ranger out of a game, irate fans surrounded his cab outside Madison Square Garden and rocked it back and forth. Until 1969, when the officials' dressing room in the Boston Garden was moved to a spot less accessible to fans, officials were regularly barraged by eggs, cigaret butts and beer on their way in and out of the dressing room. "They (the fans) were real scavengers," John says.

Even today, he occasionally must leave a bar rather than risk getting into a fight with a drunk or unruly fan after a game. On the ice, there are constant taunts and insults. "What bothers me most is when they attack my nationality and call me a stupid dago," he says. For the most part, however, the insults "go in one ear and out the other" during a game, John says.

Probably his most sensitive duty is to break up fights. "You're a peacemaker in a sense," he says. Often he spots trouble before fists and sticks start swinging, and he skates in to avert a brawl with a little gentle coaxing.

"He'll try and talk you out of a fight," says Keith Magnuson, a Chicago Black Hawk. "If it's a 3-to-2 game, he'll say, 'Hey Magy, you don't want to hurt the team now. You'll do more harm than good in the penalty box,'" Mr. Magnuson says.

If diplomacy fails or if John arrives too late for talk, he and the other linesman simply grab the fighting players around the chest or shoulders. Often John winds up on the ice in the midst of a wrestling match, and that's when his own considerable strength comes in handy.

"I've been known to grab a guy pretty hard," he says. Occasionally, if players seem evenly matched, John lets them slug it out. "Sometimes a fight cools things down," he explains.

Between games on the road, John spends most of his time sitting in hotels, working out at a local YMCA and browsing through downtown stores. "We have so much time we can find all the bargains," he says. In Montreal, he frequents a tailor shop where he can buy a custom-made sportcoat and a pair of slacks for $80. In Boston, he buys shoes at half price at a little store specializing in "seconds." In Chicago, he regularly stops by a liquor store he claims has the lowest prices in North America.

In cities like St. Louis, where he can't find bargains, he spends a lot more time sitting around hotels. "I sometimes think I should have taken some correspondence courses," he says. (He dropped out of high school when he was 16.) "I probably could have gotten a few degrees by now."

On the road, he always dresses in a suit or sport jacket and tie, his grey flecked hair is trimmed short, in conformity with league rules. "Hockey is a business" and officials should "travel looking like business people," a league official explains.

On the day of a game, he acts much like an athlete in training, eating little and relaxing a lot. "You really can't work well with a full stomach," he explains. "I might get hit and throw up." He psyches himself up for the game by leafing through the little notebook in which he chronicles his own performance. The idea, he says, is "to be prepared physically and mentally for the upcoming game."

—DAVID GUMPERT

The Rural Wife

The tractor's roar breaks the silence of the sunny Iowa day. Ignoring the din, the driver concentrates on plowing a muddy cornfield. Suddenly, the tractor become stuck in a quagmire of manure and mud. The driver shifts the throttle, raises the plow and twists the steering wheel about.

But the tires grind deeper. The stench is overwhelming. Finally, after lip-biting effort, Donna Keppy frees the tractor. "I knew that as long as we kept moving, we'd make it," she says.

The statement fairly sums up 37-year-old Mrs. Keppy, too. In her busy, expanded role as a modern farmer's wife, she helps her husband Allen run a prosperous hog and grain farm here. Mrs. Keppy is much more than a field hand, however. Though the roles of America's two million farm wives vary widely, Mrs. Keppy perhaps typifies a new breed. She's her husband's business partner, involved in nearly all aspects of their complex farming operation— from planting to harvesting their 235 acres and from breeding to marketing 2,000 hogs a year.

Some agricultural experts believe the long-term outlook for family farms like the Keppy's depends on whether more food producers have partners in marriage who are also partners in farming. Mrs. Keppy represents "the type of farm wife we're going to see a lot more of in the future," says Keith Hefferman, a friend of the Keppys and director of agricultural promotion for the Iowa Development Commission. "That's the only way the family farm is going to make it."

The role of the contemporary farm wife is a far cry from that a generation ago. Back then, homemaking, raising children, growing and canning produce and possibly feeding chickens consumed most of the farm wife's time. Heavy farm chores were "men's work," as were business decisions such as crop plantings, marketing or equipment purchases. And a farmer's wife who "kept the books" was more likely to handle family photograph albums than farm bookkeeping.

Today, "farm wives are working more with their husbands and at a more sophisticated level," says Calvin L. Beale, who directs population studies for the U.S. Department of Agriculture's Economic Research Service. A poll of 12,000 Successful Farming magazine readers confirmed his view; it found, for example, that three-fourths of the wives participate in farm business decisions.

Effects of these changes are rippling throughout agribusiness. Farm-equipment makers say that wives' greater role in field work is one reason tractors are being made easier to operate and more comfortable, with such options as power-assisted clutches and air-conditioned, carpeted cabs. Many equipment dealers, now catering to female customers, are setting up ladies' waiting lounges stocked with women's magazines. And some farm wives have become political activists, promoting agriculture and pushing, before legislators and television cameras, for what they consider fair crop prices. In November 1974, several regional groups formed American Agri-Women, the first nationwide coalition of farm women.

The widening horizons of farm wives reflect, in part, changes in agriculture generally. More and more family farms have reduced their hired hands, gone heavily into debt to expand and mechanize, and emerged as high specialized businesses. As the number of such operations grows, more of the total food supply is being produced by large farms; in 1973, farms with $100,000 or more in annual sales accounted for nearly half of the nation's food and fiber marketings, up from only 17% in 1960.

Growing complexity and replacement of brute force with managerial talent are contributing to farmers' greater reliance on their wives. In turn, farm women have more time to help farm because modern household conveniences and smaller families have simplified "traditional" home-making duties.

A day in the life of Donna Keppy illustrates these changes. The clock radio clicks on at 5:15 a.m. on day in early May 1975 in the Keppy's small white ranch house, where they have lived for three years. Previously, for 10 years, they rented a 143-acre farm from Mr. Keppy's father. Both Allen's and Donna's parents and grandparents lived in eastern Iowa, near where the family presently farms with only part-time assistance from Mr. Keppy's brother. The home is full of evidence of the Keppy's livelihood: posters of smiling hogs, piggy banks, "Pigs Are Beautiful" buttons and pig-shaped soap holders.

Mrs. Keppy dresses quickly for her chores: corduroy jeans, black rubber boots, gloves, a beat-up ski jacket and head scarf. By 6 a.m., she is working outside with her husband. She shovels manure and feeds, waters and checks the health of the animals in the farrowing house, an old barn where pigs are born and raised for six weeks.

Her duties as "sanitation supervisor," as she jokingly refers to herself, represent the most physically demanding of her chores. "Sooey!" Mrs. Keppy yells, slapping the puppy-sized pigs out of the way so she can pitch 30-pound forkfuls of manure-laden straw out of the barn.

Future projects are the Keppys' main topics at breakfast this brisk spring morning. The four Keppy daughters, aged seven to 15, serve the meal as Mrs. Keppy and her husband discuss selling hogs to cover feed-corn purchases and to meet a payment on the farm. But hog prices are rising; so they mull taking out a loan rather than selling hogs at lower prices now.

They decide to sell just a few and hold the rest in the hope that hog prices climb further. (Weeks later, they find their timing was right; hog prices increased $5 a hundred pounds. "We paid back the 30-day note to the bank and made money at it," Mrs. Keppy says.)

Breakfast at the Keppys is a simple fare of cornbread, sausages and orange juice. Mrs. Keppy says she can't take time to fuss with meals. An exception is the noontime dinner, for which she usually bakes and prepares steak or a ham. It isn't unusual for supper to consist of frozen pizza. By contrast, her mother-in-law still cooks five complete meals a day for her farmer-husband. When Viola Keppy's seven sons were growing up, "my responsibilities were centered around the home," she recalls. "(Donna's) responsibilities are spread out more."

Breakfast is also when "Donna gets her assignments for the day," Mr. Keppy says. While he regards his wife as his business partner, he gives the work orders in their traditional household. "He's the boss," Mrs. Keppy concurs.

This doesn't diminish her importance, Mr. Keppy, a strapping 200-pounder, hastens to add. "Without Donna, I'd need an additional full-time man here," he observes. "The timeliness of having a wife in the house to take phone calls, or run a tractor or help load pigs is much more valuable than her trying to add $3 an hour to the family income with a regular job." In fact, when the Keppy daughters were infants, he found it cheaper to hire a babysitter than to replace his wife with a paid field hand.

By 7:30, the farm couple is back outside, inspecting the muddy fields. Mrs. Keppy expresses doubt that they're ready for plowing and concern that if the pace of field work doesn't pick up soon, planting will be delayed. "I agree that the fields don't look quite fit," he tells her. "But I think we should go ahead anyway."

She plows nearly three hours. Her ruddy face and stocky, five-foot-eight-inch, 150-pound frame indicate that she has done her share of farm work since learning to drive a tractor at age 12. As she plows, pop tunes and the morning commodities report blare from the vehicle's radio.

The work seem monotonous and bone-wearying. Yet the dark-haired woman drives the vehicle with the careful attention of someone who loves the land. "I get satisfaction from turning over the old to start the new," she says.

It's now 10:30. Mrs. Keppy bathes and changes clothes

because she must take 36 hogs to market. Mr. Keppy's brother has helped him tramp through mud to select and herd the squealing, 250-pound animals onto a hauler's truck. This messy job of "running the gate" is Mrs. Keppy's when she isn't plowing.

"You know, marketing is our bread and butter, the final end of the product," Mrs. Keppy observes as the truck pulls away. "It's good to know this group (of hogs) made it through without being sick." Once year, a dysentery-like disease killed 20% of the Keppy's pigs.

She delivers the hogs to an Oscar Mayer & Co. meat packing plant close to Davenport, 25 miles away. At the plant, her friendly kidding with the weighing-office workers suddenly ceases when the hogs prove overweight. That usually means they have too much fat. Lines crease her forehead. But because Keppy animals enjoy a reputation for having a high proportion of valuable lean meat, the packer pays her the full price. She leaves happy.

Since genetics and nutrition are key factors in maintaining livestock quality, Mrs. Keppy keeps informed of latest hog-breeding developments by reading industry publications. This know-how comes in handy each fall when the Keppys shop for a boar, which can cost $5,000 or more, as well as every few weeks when they choose certain young female hogs to breed rather than market.

A no-nonsense attitude characterizes Mrs. Keppy's approach to farming. She refuses to use the phone for idle social chats, and she gets angry at equipment dealers who lack needed parts. Dealers "aren't business-minded enough around here," she complains. "Our philosophy is that time is money and money makes money."

So, as the empty truck lumbers past grazing hogs, she wonders how farmers can succeed with such old-fashioned pasture feeding (the Keppys own a $62,000 automatic feed-grinding facility). "Their end product isn't much different from ours," she muses. "It's just not as efficient a way to get the hogs to market."

Mrs. Keppy knows what she's talking about. Their

farm's annual hog sales exceed $140,000, and last year Mr. Keppy was named Iowa Pork All-American—meaning that he's regarded as one of the state's best hog farmers.

Following midday dinner, Mrs. Keppy returns to plowing and then harrowing. Her work ends at 6:30, more than 12 hours after it began. "It's been a slow day," the farm wife says, wearily climbing down from the tractor. Her fatigue and an aching back make her edgy with her daughters, who are playing softball after having finished their evening chores. "Tie those shoelaces right away!" she yells at seven-year-old Colleen. Without waiting to see if her daughter obeys, she turns and walks slowly into the house.

Even though field work wears her out, Mrs. Keppy's farm heritage has instilled in her a strong sense of purpose. "Farming is hard work, but it's got its rewards, and they're not all monetary," the usually soft-spoken woman says forcefully. "There's a lot of self-satisfaction, too."

Mrs. Keppy's work frequently continues through the evening. When the weather gets warmer and the ground dries, she plows until 9:30 at night. Otherwise, she may spend her evening working on farm records, preparing animal entry forms for state fairs or typing business letters.

In view of the modern efficiency of most of their farming, the Keppys are surprisingly ill-prepared for record keeping, Mrs. Keppy believes. Her "office" consists of a desk in the master bedroom and a file cabinet in the kitchen. To get peace and quiet while discussing grain prices on the telephone, which is located in the busy main hallway, she frequently steps inside the bathroom. Thus, one of her high priorities is a full-fledged office. "We need one if we're going to run this farm like a business," she says.

The winter of 1974-75 found Donna Keppy involved in yet another job: state president of the Porkettes, a women's auxiliary of the National Pork Producers Council. Her leadership has helped it evolve into a group of promotion-oriented "pork pushers," as she calls them. For example, along with other Porkettes and their husbands, the Keppys traveled to supermarkets in several states early in 1975, handing out pork recipes, chatting with shoppers about farmers' problems and appearing on television talk shows.

Her hectic, broadened and more public role as a farm wife developed without any assistance from the women's liberation movement, Mrs. Keppy says. She thinks feminists don't realize how difficult equality of the sexes can be. "You know, we say that a woman's libber never lived on a farm," she observes. "I do a man's job when I'm out there scooping manure or lifting 50-pound-bales of hay in the summer." But then she adds with a smile: "Maybe we're the first generation of women's libbers."

—JOANN S. LUBLIN

Part Two

WORKING WITH THEIR WITS

The essential ingredient in some kinds of work is the ability to think fast on one's feet. Be it a comedian's patter or a salesman's chatter, words are frequently the means by which the quick thinking manifests itself. In other instances, such as lawyers' courtroom tactics, the practitioners' wits often are expressed in action as well as words—and, quite often, in somebody else's money.

The Saleslady

The deal was a snap. Real-estate agent Joan S. Thomas drove the young couple past a few houses in Westfield, N.J., a comfortable suburb of New York. They saw one they liked. The husband went through it in 15 minutes; the wife took 25. Result: the quick sale of an $80,000 home.

That's the way it often seems to go in the real-estate business in spring. Balmy weather brings people out looking for bigger and better quarters. And it's a season when many transferred employes are searching for homes in new locales. So despite higher prices and financing costs, real-estate people in sought-after communities like Westfield find customers so eager to buy that some homes are sold within hours after coming on the market.

All this would seem to add up to palmy days for people like Mrs. Thomas, who make their money by bringing buyers and sellers together. Because real-estate commissions are tied to a house's selling price, they are escalating along with property prices. According to the Westfield Board of Realtors, which also serves the neighboring towns of Fanwood, Scotch Plains and Mountainside, the average sale price of a home in the area in 1973 was was $54,962, a 9.7% increase from the $50,094 average price in 1972, and 73% above the average price of $31,760 as recently as 1967. Based on the usual commission rate of 6%, that means the average fee for selling a house has jumped to about $3,300 from $1,906 in a little over six years.

But to Mrs. Thomas and others whose livelihood depends on how many houses they sell, it isn't as simple as it sounds. Home selling, they say, has become an increasingly competitive business in which frustrations are commonplace and rewards depend on hard work leavened with luck. Times of tight money can send the market into a tailspin and create weeks-long sales droughts. Even a booming seller's market can have its drawbacks. Then, some homeowners decide they don't need to pay for the services of a real-estate agent and put out "For Sale" signs themselves.

Mrs. Thomas has experienced most the discouraging aspects of the business—at one time she went a month and a half without a sale. But in her six years as a saleswoman for the all-female Nancy F. Reynolds Associates agency, she has become one of the more successful in her field. In 1973, by selling more than $1 million worth of properties, the 45-year-old divorcee became one of only 163 salespeople of some 5,000 in the New Jersey Association of Realtors who did as well.

Mrs. Thomas sells on the order of 20 homes a year, and for her efforts has an annual income approaching $30,000. Some of her sales are as easy as the $80,000 house that took less than an hour of showing time. But to achieve her aim of at least $1 million worth of sales a year, Mrs. Thomas admits to being "on the run" most of the time. She spends at least 50 hours a week on the job, much of it at odd hours and on weekends. That leaves her with little spare time to spend with her five children, who range in age from 11 to 16. She celebrated Mother's Day in 1974, for example, by showing houses to customers.

What keeps Mrs. Thomas running is an influx of new salespeople into her 21-square-mile, four-town territory. The requirements for getting into real-estate sales in New Jersey have never been especially stiff (a minimum of an eighth-grade education is one qualification). And particularly in recent years, the idea of earning money by showing people through houses has attracted a wide range of talent, from bored housewives to executives fed up with a life of commuting.

William Maidment Jr., executive secretary of the Westfield Board of Realtors, estimates there are 325 "reasonably active" real-estate salespeople in the area now, compared with 215 five years ago. Part of that increase comes from real-estate offices outside the area that have joined the Westfield board in an effort to have more houses to show. The board had 59 member agencies in 1974, compared with 37 in 1968, when outsiders weren't accepted.

Salespeople in Westfield, Fanwood, Scotch Plains and Mountainside mostly show the same products, because the bulk of the homes sold in these areas are offered through the Westfield Board's multiple-listing service. To make sure its member agencies have an equal chance to sell a house once it goes on the market, the board dispatches a courier to hand-deliver detailed information about each day's new listings between 5 a.m. and 6:30 a.m.

Mr. Maidment of the board estimates that about 100 house listings are available at any one time. But Mrs. Thomas figures this often isn't enough to give customers a wide choice, because prices can range from $40,000 to over $200,000 and styles of houses and locations vary considerably. At one point, when 120 homes were in the list, she could find only four that seemed to fit the requirements of one young couple for whom she was trying to get a house.

"A lot of luck is involved," Mrs. Thomas says. "You have to have the right house at the right time." If she doesn't, customers turn to the competition. Perhaps 35% of her customers are transferred executives, and those who move frequently are "schooled in looking," she says. "Sometimes these people will visit three real-estate offices in three different areas in a single day." Experienced home buyers sometimes go to more than one real-estate office in a given area, on the chance that one will be offering a house unavailable to other agencies, or simply to enlist more free help in their search for a home. (It is the seller of a house and not the buyer who pays the real-estate agent for his services.) Mrs. Thomas claims this ploy has its disadvantages. "If customers are loyal to you and aren't going to someone else as well, you'll work twice as hard for them," she says.

To better fit houses to customers, Mrs. Thomas spends lots of time keeping track of the rapidly changing inventory of homes for sale in her area. Consider one spring Thursday, normally a big day of the week for new listings. Mrs. Thomas and Alice Fife, one of her associates, set out on a two-and-a-half-hour tour during which real-estate agents can walk through the latest homes listed. This day 20 houses are being shown, but the tour isn't encouraging. Before the morning is over, they encounter four homes with "Sold" signs already on the door.

The other offerings are unimpressive. "That's a most unmemorable house," Mrs. Thomas says after a perfunctory dash through a dark-gray split-level in Scotch Plains. She doesn't even get out of the car when they pull up to an older frame house in Westfield obviously in need of repair. It is priced at $53,000. "They'll probably get $45,000," Mrs. Thomas says as she drives off.

Despite what she calls "a very uninteresting day," Mrs. Thomas spots one $71,500 split-level in Scotch Plains with possibilities, and makes a note to call one of her customers about it. But before she has a chance, she learns back at the office that the house has been sold a few hours earlier.

Even amid the stiff competition and fast tempo of the Westfield housing market, Mrs. Thomas adopts a low-key approach to selling property. "She was the least pushy of all the real-estate people I've ever dealt with," says Mrs. George Petty, who bought a home in Westfield in 1973. "We told her we wanted to spend so many dollars a month for housing and she respected that. Many realtors say you can afford much more."

Mrs. Petty also was impressed with the amount of time Mrs. Thomas spent giving special attention to her family's needs. "We were concerned about getting in an area with small children," Mrs. Petty says. During a visit to one house, she asked Mrs. Thomas how many children lived in the neighborhood. "She ran over and rang the doorbell of the house next door and asked them," Mrs. Petty says. "We've never had a salesperson do that."

Mrs. Thomas economizes on her time by sizing up customers quickly. "I don't show that many houses for those I sell," she says. As important as "knowing the product and the area," she claims, is "understanding what people are looking for. You can almost get vibrations from them after seeing several houses." For this reason, Mrs. Thomas shies away from the common practice of presenting batches of pictures to customers and letting them pick the houses they want to visit. "Often they will tell you they only want to look at center-hall colonials and they wind up buying a split-level," she says. "Most houses are bought on emotion. When people walk in the door, they say 'This is it.'" Not long ago one of her customers refused to enter a house he had been driven by three times, because he didn't like its exterior. But after listening to what he wanted, Mrs. Thomas insisted that he at least take a walk through it. He bought the house.

Few sales are that easy. Mrs. Thomas has been searching for months for a house for a Westfield woman who wants a place with more room. "I think I've shown her 30 houses," she says. In some cases, it's impossible to match up a buyer with a house. One of Mrs. Thomas' recent customers had a single inflexible requirement for a house: the basement had to be no smaller than 40 feet by 23½ feet. The man was building his own airplane and needed at least that much space to work on it. He eventually bought a house in another town.

Mrs. Thomas insists she doesn't lose many sales, however. On those she does, she keeps a record "so I don't make the same mistake again. In fact, I keep records of everything. I used to be a bookkeeper, you know." One precaution she takes it to make sure she always has a blank sales contract form in the glove compartment of her car. She's also careful not to miss the signals when a customer is seriously interested in a house. "When they start finding fault with a house, that's when you know they are ready to buy," she says. "On the other hand, when they say a house is 'so nice,' that means they aren't interested."

Mrs. Thomas has good reason not to let a deal slip through her fingers. Her income depends entirely on commissions from sales and from home listings she brings to the agency or has assigned to her. A house that sells for $60,000 in Westfield will typically produce a real-estate commission of 6%, or $3,600. (Though the Justice Department has been after the nation's real-estate boards since 1969 to make commission rates more competitive, a single, established rate is commonplace in many communities, Westfield included.) Mrs. Thomas doesn't pocket the entire commission, however. Roughly 25% and sometimes much more goes to the real-estate office that listed the house, even if that office isn't the one that finds the buyer. And if Mrs. Thomas sells a house to a customer who is referred to her from a real-estate office in another area or from a special referral service, their share of the commission can be as much as 30% of the total.

After deducting other expenses, Mrs. Thomas shares half of what's left with her own agency. As a result, says Nancy Reynolds, owner of the agency, "the salesperson might wind up with not much more than the listing broker."

Mrs. Thomas has considerable expenses of her own, too, such as maintaining an up-to-date, full-size, air-conditioned sedan in which to shepherd customers about. And because she deals with the public, her clothing and dry-cleaning bills are unusually high. The Nancy Reynolds agency provides her with desk and telephone, keeps her up to date on changes in listings, picks up the tab for license fees and provides a back-up car to use in emergencies. Such amenities, Mrs. Thomas says, aren't necessarily typical of real-estate agencies. "In some offices," she says, "sales-people have to bring in their own pencils and paper."

—ROGER B. MAY

Bucking the Tide

A lot of edgy stockbrokers stay glued to their desks waiting out the market slump and hoping that the phone will start to ring again with orders from customers who actually want to buy and sell stocks.

But don't try to call Stephen H. Karelitz at Shearson Hayden Stone Inc. in Boston on Wednesday afternoon. His secretary will say he is in an important meeting and can't be disturbed. But he is really miles away, watching wrestling matches at Milton Academy, the prep school his two teenage sons attend.

The lean, fast-talking, 40-year-old stockbroker can well afford to duck out of his plush downtown office to watch his sons compete in the sport that 20-odd years ago earned him the nickname "Crusher." For in 1974, when some 3,000 stockbrokers had lost or left their jobs, and most of the 33,000 who remained felt lucky to earn between $10,000 and $16,000 in commissions, Steve Karelitz still prospered—though on a more modest scale than in the past.

He expected to earn $90,000 to $95,000 in 1974, his cut of a little more than 35% of the firm's gross commissions on the buy and sell orders he handled. That was down from $103,000 he netted on a $225,000 gross, and it is well below his peak year of $225,000, earned in 1969, on $600,000 of gross commissions.

Mr. Karelitz feels the pinch of the pay decline. He says he swallowed hard before paying the 1974 $12,000 prep-school tuition bill. He and his wife, Jane, cancelled a planned trip to Europe, pared their entertainment budget and spent less on clothes.

Unlike many brokers, however, he isn't worried about losing his job. He is consistently one of the 25 top revenue-producers among the 1,500 retail salesman at Shearson Hayden. And even with securities firms consolidating furiously through mergers and staff reductions, job opportunities are plentiful for Mr. Karelitz. He spurns at least 25 job offers a year, he says.

Mr. Karelitz's 35% commission rate is premium pay in the industry and can go as high as 40% on shares of some new issues and 50% on mutual-fund shares. Most brokers net about 30% on commissions from retail customers and, before negotiated fees came into being in May 1975, about 20% on sales to institutional investors like banks, insurance companies and mutual funds. About 90% of Mr. Karelitz's business comes from individuals, most of whom have incomes of at least $35,000 a year. "I don't like to feel I'm taking a guy's last dollar," he says. "These people can afford to have ups and downs."

His customer list, some 2,000 names of people who have brought or sold stocks through him sometime in his 14-year career, spans the U.S. and includes 30 company presidents, 30 big farmers, six judges and a wide range of other occupations. He adds 10 to 15 names a month to his list, and he makes it a point to contact every person on it by phone or by mail at least four times a year.

Except for Wednesday afternoons, he is in his office from 10 a.m. to 6 p.m. most weekdays. At home, when he isn't playing gin rummy with friends or watching his three TV favorites, "Dating Game," "Treasure Hunt" and "Kojak," he usually reads research reports, studies stock charts and plans the next day's phone calls. "I think, think, think, about who I'll call tomorrow and who hasn't called me lately," he says. "It drives me crazy sometimes."

His status as a top salesman at Shearson Hayden brings certain prerequisites besides premium pay. Mr. Karelitz's richly appointed corner office has a better view of Boston harbor than his boss's has, for example. He insisted on the red-shag carpet, dazzling autumn-foliage draperies, teak desk and credenza, leather chair, black and white sofa and two white telephones when the firm wooed him away from Walston & Co. in 1971. "People like dealing with a successful person," he says, and he thinks his office—along with his $350 suits, Gucci belts and big cars—favorably impresses potential customers.

The $6,500 spent to decorate the office was worth it to make Mr. Karelitz comfortable and happy, says W. Godfrey Wood, who until he left the firm in November 1974 headed the 40-broker Boston office. "Steve's proud of being a broker when that's nothing to be proud of today," Mr. Wood says. "He's always on top of the world and his spirit helps morale."

Brokerage-office morale has needed all the boosting it could get in 1974, as the Dow Jones industrial average skidded to a 12-year low and trading volume remained sluggish. The 1974 market was one of the most volatile in history, and even a sharp rally in October of that year enticed disappointingly few investors back into the market.

The duration and depth of the bear market took its toll on even the ebullient Mr. Karelitz. His weekend golf game suffered, and toward the end of the year he began throwing away the second half of his sandwich at lunch. "The market makes me sick to my stomach," he said. "It's the worst I've ever seen. You've got to hold everyone's hand and you've got to be creative or you'll starve."

Mr. Karelitz's lengthy customer list usually brings him at least 15 buy or sell orders a day, no matter how bad the market gets. He makes and gets more than 100 phone calls daily and sends out prodigious amounts of mail to attract new customers. Copies of a Shearson Hayden investment brochure sent to 800 oral surgeons listed in the local yellow pages drew responses from 20 doctors asking for additional information. A letter to 2,400 attorneys telling them he could quickly liquidate stocks in estates brought 75 responses and 20 new accounts.

He phones regular customers frequently: "This is your friendly broker calling about Syntex. It should have been down, but it's holding," he tells a pediatrician. ("Just to make him feel the world isn't coming to an end.") A few days later, the doctor calls him back to buy 400 more shares. "Who do you think I am, Houdini?" he asks an orthodontist who calls to find out why his stock is going down while the market is up. "Give it a chance," Mr. Karelitz advises.

His conversations contain good-natured bantering, but are schoolboy polite. "Thank you for the order, times are tough," he tells a New York executive buying 3,000 shares of PepsiCo and paying $950 in gross commissions. "He's a loyal customer," Mr. Karelitz says. "He could have gone to 10 brokers in New York, but he went out of his way to come to me."

His customers keep coming because he is attentive to their needs. Malcolm Finks, a Boston attorney, says, "Steve treats me like one of his most important customers, which I'm sure I'm not. When I need back quotes, he'll put his girl right on." Mr. Karelitz says that although Mr. Finks doesn't have a big account, "he is always willing to toot my horn, which makes him just as important."

Often, the extra service pays off. Mr. Karelitz made a quick appraisal of some stocks in an estate as a favor to an attorney. Not long afterwards, the lawyer sent him a new customer who invested $90,000, mostly in high-yield bonds and utility stocks. (Mr. Karelitz says more of his customers are doing the same lately. Bond dealing has increased from "practically nothing" to 10% of his business, he says.)

He worried about what the industry's planned switch to negotiated commissions on all transactions, scheduled for May 1975, might do to his business. (Brokers and customers prior to that negotiated commissions on trades over $300,000 and under $2,000; customers paid fixed fees on other transactions.) "It's an aggravation I don't need," he says. "I call some clients five times a day without making a single trade. How can I give them that type of service if I have to stop and worry about rates?"

Many customers have decided what they want to buy or sell before they call Mr. Karelitz. But when one does ask his advice, the broker recommends the two or three stocks he has been following closely in recent months and is buying for his own portfolio. His stock-market strategy has always been to limit his own holdings to large blocks of a few stocks that he has researched himself.

Since July 1974 he has been buying and recommending Damon Corp., which fell as low as $6 a share in October of that year but later recovered to some extent. He says he has been watching the company for years, ever since he met its president at a party. Damon makes medical diagnostic-test equipment, and Mr. Karelitz thinks the company could grow rapidly.

He called doctors and medical laboratories to ask their opinions on Damon equipment and how it stacks up against competing brands. He also visited the company and talked to some of its executives. "And I checked out the parking lot at 6 p.m.," he says. "If it's full, you know they're hustlers."

Another stock he was buying in late 1974 was an old favorite, Buttes Gas & Oil Co. Between 1968 and 1972, he bought 600,000 Buttes shares for himself and customers at prices between $10 and $17 a share. In 1972, he got edgy over rising Mideast tensions and unloaded 80% of the stock, taking $5 million in profits for himself and customers, he says. In 1974 he was buying Buttes shares again, paying about $14 to $16 a share. "It's got good earnings and good cash flow," he told customers. "It's a much better company today."

The other stock he was buying for himself and recommending to customers was Damson Oil Corp., and oil-and-gas exploration stock that he considered highly speculative.

A year earlier his three favorites were Studebaker-Worthington Inc., STP Corp. and Bolt Beranek & Newman Inc. The three stocks nosedived so sharply that he and customers to whom he had recommended them sold out at combined losses of about $2 million, Mr. Karelitz says. His own portfolio, which contained stocks with a market value of nearly $1 million in 1972, was worth only $600,000 in mid-December 1974, he says. Stock holdings made up 60%

of his own investments, down from 80% in 1972, and put more of his own money into oil wells, a mobile-home company, a New York apartment complex and a computer time-sharing business.

Mr. Karelitz's financial savvy surfaced early. He has been interested in the stock market since age 12, when his father, an attorney in Haverhill, Mass., bought Tennessee Gas Transmission stock and it doubled. In prep school, young Steve concocted mock portfolios and wrote to investment-counseling firms seeking free advice. (A couple of salesmen soon appeared to tell "Prof. Karelitz" that his holdings were too heavily concentrated in natural-gas stocks.)

At age 17 he put his $700 savings into a Canadian uranium stock, Consolidated Denison Mines (now Denison Mines Ltd.), and sold out a year later for $18,000. He finished his education at Hobart College, Geneva, N.Y., in 1956 with a $22,000 profit on 400 shares of South Carolina Electric & Gas Co. stock.

Mr. Karelitz hated his first full-time job, buying materials for his new father-in-law's showmaking company. He quit in 1960, after making a $100,000 killing on NAFI Corp. (now Chris-Craft Industries Inc.), which he bought at $18 and sold at $64.

He bought four new suits and went to work as a trainee in the Boston brokerage office of Hornblower & Weeks-Hemphill, Noyes & Co., where he grossed $80,000 in his first eight months selling. The firm gave him a psychological test to try to find out why he did so well, he says, but they never showed him the test results.

At Hornblower other brokers "used to call five of us—two Jews, two Italians and an Armenian—the 'Gaza Strip,'" he recalls. "We did more business than the rest of the office combined." But the firm didn't promote him, so he left in 1965 and soon became a senior vice president at McDonnell & Co.

There he won a new nickname, "The Bomber," while riding the crest of a high-flying market with big gains on, among others, Comsat, EG&C and National Equipment Rental, which has since merged into American Export Industries Inc. In 1969, when McDonnell closed down its Boston office, he joined Walston & Co., where he stayed until 1971, the year he joined Shearson Hayden.

—LIZ ROMAN GALLESE

Aiming High

At the age of 29, Kim Kelley was already something of a legend around Honeywell Inc. "He's the one who cried when he made his sale, isn't he?" a fellow Honeywell salesman asks with a chuckle.

Indeed he is. Kim stood there in his customer's office in June, 1973, and bawled like a baby. And for good reason. Kim has just shaken hands on an $8.1 million computer sale to the state of Illinois. He had gambled his whole career on making that sale. He had spent three years laying the groundwork for it, and for three solid months he had been working six days a week, often 14 hours a day, competing against salesmen from four other computer companies.

It was a make-or-break situation for Kim Kelley, and, standing there with tears of joy and relief streaming down his cheeks, he knew he had it made. A bright future with Honeywell was assured, and he had just made an $80,000 commission—more money than he had earned in all four of his previous years with the company.

Looking back on it now, Kim says: "It was pure hell." And his wife, Sandy, agrees emphatically: "I'd never want to go through it again." Such is the life of the "big-ticket" salesman who pursues multimillion-dollar contracts while others sell in bits and drabs. Lured by fat commissions (1% of the equipment's total value in Honeywell's case), they devote months to delicate planning and months more to the heat of battle, all to make one big sale.

"You're playing for big stakes, and what you ante is your life," says Dick Kuszyk, a Honeywell computer salesman in Pittsburgh. He "gambled three years" of his life, he says, to sell a $4.5 million computer to Jones & Laughlin Steel Corp. Before he finally clinched the deal, his home life got so hectic that his wife packed up and went home to her mother for seven weeks.

A Honeywell salesman in Denver, Don Sather, was so wrapped up in trying to sell a $250,000 prototype computer system to Mountain States Telephone that he barely found time to slip away when his wife gave birth at 1:08 a.m. on Aug. 15, 1973. "I stayed through labor and delivery, and then went back to the office," he says. He made the sale.

Kim Kelley thrives on such high-stakes action and always has, according to his mother in Davenport, Iowa, Mrs. Dorothy Rynott. He was aggressive even as a paper boy: He pulled in $150 in Christmas tips one year. After a year at the University of Iowa he spent a year in California cooking pizza, selling shoes and hustling at pool. He returned to Iowa, married his high school sweetheart in 1965 and prepared to follow the career of his late father, who had been a tire salesman. For four years he wandered from one retail sales job to another. Finally, in 1969, he landed at a Honeywell sales office in Peoria, Ill.

He was sent to Springfield, Ill., in 1970 and told to keep four or five big sales simmering but to put only one at a time "on the front burner." Kim wasted little time picking his target, the state government, the biggest potential customer in his region. His long-range strategy was to devote at least half his time to pursuing the state, and to use the balance to scratch out small sales elsewhere to meet his annual quota of $500,000 worth of new equipment.

For three years, he patiently made daily rounds of key state offices, pausing a few minutes in each one to drop off technical documents or just to chat. He pursued the bureaucrats further at after-hours hangouts like the American Legion hall.

"People don't buy products, they buy relationships," Kim believes. To that end, he even molded his personal life to suit his customers' preferences. He bought a big Buick and expensive suits, even though he could barely afford them. "People like to deal with a winner," Kim reasons.

"They don't buy $8 million products from some guy who's worrying can he pay his rent." On the other hand, he says, it doesn't pay to appear *too* prosperous; for that reason, he quit his country club when he sensed that state employes resented his being able to afford it.

Thanks to a succession of nonstate sales, Kim's income was steadily, if unspectacularly, expanding, from $18,000 in 1970 to $22,000 in 1971 and $25,000 in 1972. The state bought hardly anything. In those three years, Kim made less than $3,000 in commissions on sales to the government.

But when the break finally came, Kim was ready. Toward the end of 1972, the Illinois secretary of state asked for bids for a massive new computer system. Five manufacturers responded: Honeywell, Burroughs, Univac division of Sperry Rand, Control Data and International Business Machines.

In the ensuing three-month scramble, Control Data was eliminated because of "high cost," according to Noel Sexton, head of a technical committee assigned by the state to evaluate the bids. IBM was never in strong contention, says Hand Malkus, who was then division administrator in the secretary's office. "IBM doesn't tailor its equipment to a customer's need. They just say, 'Here's our equipment, you make your system fit it,'" Mr. Malkus contends. (An IBM spokesman, asked to comment, says: "IBM feels it offers an extremely broad range of products. . . .We strive to combine all these products in each proposal to provide a prospect the best possible solution to his data-processing requirements.")

That made the contest a three-horse race between Honeywell, Burroughs and Univac. "The equipment was close," says Patrick Halperin, executive assistant to the secretary of state. "But the staff felt far more comfortable with Honeywell because they felt Kim had been more thorough in his marketing."

Indeed he was. Kim dealt solely with the committee. "Some of the other vendors put more emphasis on selling to the front office and tried to play on previous friendships," Mr. Sexton recalls.

Kim fed the committee information, not persuasion. "When we asked to see customers," says Mr. Malkus, "Kim just gave us a list of Honeywell users and said, choose." Univac, on the other hand, annoyed committee members by discouraging them from interviewing users.

Kim flew in Honeywell experts and top marketing officials from Boston, Minneapolis, Phoenix and Chicago to answer technical questions on engineering, financing, installation and service. "He showed the ability of his firm to cooperate," says Mr. Halperin.

"Incredible attention to detail" helped, too, Kim thinks. The committee was asking for new bits of information daily—things like how much air conditioning his equipment would need. Kim answered every question within two days, always hand-delivering replies to each committee member. "That gave me five minutes more selling time with each one," he explains.

Kim hates to fly, but he flew the six committee members and their bosses to Atlanta to meet Honeywell users, to Phoenix twice to see performance tests at a Honeywell facility there, and to Houston to interview another user. When he could, he used Honeywell's "slow propeller plane," carefully chosen, Kim says, to allow more selling time in the air. Kim and his secretary arranged everything—hotel and plane reservations, rental cars, meals, meetings, even the committee's spare time.

For the Houston trip Kim even made a dry run by himself beforehand, so he'd know the best flights, how to find the Hertz counter, good restaurants and ways to avoid rush-hour traffic. The committee had picked up a rumor that Tenneco Inc., in Houston, was dissatisfied with its Honeywell computer. Kim knew the rumor to be false, but wanted to let Tenneco itself tell that to the committee. He persuaded Tenneco to give the committee a bargain rate at a hotel it owns, and while scouting Houston, he learned that two companies there were having trouble with a competitor's equipment. He dropped hints about them to Pat Halperin, who took the bait and spent his time in Houston talking with a disgruntled customer of another vendor. "I left nothing to chance," Kim says. "Detail is what sells computers."

Kim's hot pursuit of the sale, meanwhile, was taking a toll on his family. Sandy Kelley says the "tension" was dreadful. Kim "snapped" at their three-year-old daughter, Brook, and had only a few hours on Sundays to spend with her. "Every morning she asked if Daddy would be home tonight," Sandy says.

"I'd keep lists of things I wanted to talk to Kim about," Sandy says. She resented having to manage the family alone, even the new house they were building. "When Kim walked into the new house for the first time, he was like a stranger." Had this happened earlier in their marriage, she says, "it might have reached the point of breaking up." As it was, what she did most was worry. "I'd wake up in the middle of the night, and wonder what I'd do if Kim didn't get the order. I knew he'd be crushed, and I didn't know how it would affect our lives."

Kim was worried sick himself. When Hank Malkus gruffly ordered him down to the state capitol in June, 1973, Kim knew it was "decision day," but he didn't know who had won. He paused only long enough to vomit into a wastebasket before hurrying to Mr. Malkus's office. Minutes later, Mr. Malkus was grinning, his secretary was hugging Kim, and Kim was crying.

By now, Kim had recovered his poise and made his peace with Sandy and Brook. He's busy supervising installation of the equipment. How well he handles this job and how smoothly the equipment performs later are important in keeping his new customer happy and in paving the way for future sales to the state.

Kim is still a bit astonished when he thinks back on what he endured to make his first big sale and when he looks at his current bank balance. He got 40% of his commission or about $32,000, when he signed the contract in August of 1973. He'll get the rest when it's all installed.

Kim traded in his 1972 Chrysler (which he bought after driving the Buick awhile) for a new $9,250 Lincoln Continental (paying the $5,430 balance in cash), turned Sandy's old Ford in for a $2,200 used Volkswagen and paid cash for a $2,000 dining-room set. But the Kelleys have no plans to continue their spending spree. "A year from now our lives will be the same, except that I'll have $60,000 more in cash," Kim says.

And he likes that just fine. In fact, when Honeywell recently rewarded Kim by promoting him to sales manager, he requested "demotion" in order to avoid going on straight salary. Honeywell refused but did allow Kim a special status where he runs an 18-person sales office but stays on commission. His salary is $12,600 a year; he expects more than three times that much in commissions in 1975. Kim says he expects to move high in management eventually, but right now, "I can't afford the pay cut."

—THOMAS EHRICH

The Comedian

In the parlance of the trade, it is known as "going into the ground." Which is exactly what comic Eric Cohen is doing this evening in 1972 on this tiny, isolated stage at a tiny, isolated nightclub before a bored, benumbed audience of six.

To deal with the drug problem in Vietnam, Mr. Cohen cracks, the Army has announced that "a $100-a-day habit on the streets of New York would only cost $10 on the streets of Saigon." His conclusion: "The Army is trying to recruit junkies. You know, Uncle Smack wants you.

Silence. Dead silence.

Perspiration, as Mr. Cohen likes to put it, forms "beads of blood" on his forehead, and he plunges ahead with more samples of his sardonic humor.

And is greeted with more silence.

It is an ego-smashing experience, one that faces almost every apprentice comedian and one that Eric Cohen knows painfully well. Most often the ego is smashed at "the toilets"—small nightclubs with usually drunk, usually hostile crowds—or auditioning in a fetid, sweaty cubicle before a disinterested club owner or performing gratis at 3 o'clock in the morning at clubs that set aside a few hours a week for new performers. Awaiting the graduate of such agony is television, Las Vegas, movies and great sums of money. But the course is long and perilous, and the dropouts by far outnumber the graduates.

And lately, there's been some question whether the school can keep going. Traditionally, the "school" for young comics like Mr. Cohen was the small nightclub. But as the economy flags and television blares forth from every living room, the small clubs are disappearing. For that matter, the large clubs are, too. Once-successful niteries like the Blue Angel and Cafe Society in New York, the Cork

Club in Houston and the hungry i in San Francisco have folded.

The owners of those clubs still around agree that television, crime in the streets, and empty wallets are all eating away at their business. Los Angeles' famed Cocoanut Grove was dark from March to October in 1971 because, as one official put it, "We didn't feel the economy could support a superstar supper club." The Grove has reopened, but no one knows for how long. In New York, the Latin Quarter has also taken to closing seasonally.

In Los Angeles, Robert Adrian struggled for about a year to make a go of it at the Bitter End West by booking name performers, but he finally threw up his hands and sold out. "It's a rich man's business," he says wearily. "You can keep putting dollars in, it's just a question of how hard you want to work for nothing."

Furthermore, club owners say that with all their problems, they don't want to take the risk of billing comedians instead of singers and bands. Some club owners have even come to believe that America is now too somber a place for humor to survive in. At the Upstairs and Downstairs, two New York rooms operated under the same roof, owner Irving Haber, who books mainly comics and satirical revues, says revenues have been sliding ever since the assassination of John F. Kennedy in 1963. Mr. Haber laments that "nothing has seemed funny since then," and he says he may drop the revues in favor of jazz music.

All this has led to speculation that the comic, already a dwindling breed, may dwindle right out of existence. There is no exact count, but the number of comedians in the American Guild of Variety Artists has been declining relentlessly in recent years. "The places to work are less, so the numbers are less." says William Swan, Guild secretary-treasurer. "The clubs priced themselves out of business. You go there, you get a well-watered drink for $2. Who needs it?"

Into this malaise rides Mr. Cohen, eager to etch his name alongside all the brash Lennys, Jackies and Buddys of the Jewish comedic pantheon. Young and long-locked, Mr. Cohen specializes in a disdainful, irreverent, sometimes heavy-handed kind of satire that derives largely from such personal heroes as Woody Allen and Lenny Bruce. A typical Cohen look at the news: "I see that Papa Doc Duvalier was removed from office by Haiti's last remaining democratic institution—death."

Mr. Cohen has been trying to hone that humor for at least as far back as high school, when, as editor of the school paper, he conducted a "win-a-date-with-Eric-Cohen" contest. Second prize was two dates with Eric Cohen and 1,000 cubic centimeters of penicillin.

At the University of Southern California, he was the resident campus satirist with a regular column in the student newspaper and editorship of a satirical magazine. Twice, he ran unsuccessfully for student body president. In his first campaign, he promised "A Return to Machine Government" on the ground that "If it's good enough for Chicago, it's good enough for U.S.C." In his second try, he urged agrarian reform for the campus, promised the establishment of a military dictatorship and endorsed pollution in an attempt to encourage Union Oil and General Motors to contribute campaign funds.

Since leaving school in 1970, Mr. Cohen has spent a year and a half performing on one small stage or another. He is still unsure of himself at times and often has difficulty judging his audience. (Once he did an antidrug routine in front of a hip, young crowd and received icy stares in return.) But show business people who have seen him perform, most often at the Ice House, think he shows promise. Promise of what, they aren't saying. "He's very talented and does funny things," says comic Louis Nye. "He has a good chance to be some kind of thing."

TV producer Ernie Chambers, who hired Mr. Cohen to write a comedy album, believes he is "one of the few good comedians to develop in the past couple of years" but wonders what's to become of him. "So where's he going to work?" he asks. "All the hungry i's have closed, he's not good enough yet for Vegas. They want to put him on college concerts, but face it, the kids who go to those just want to hear music. TV is the only business left in show business. Everything else is limping."

Agent Jack Rollins, who has shepherded the careers of Woody Allen and Dick Cavett, concurs. "Years ago, when the Catskills hotels were swinging, the Borscht Circuit was a great minor league, but even that's cut out now."

Another traditional avenue to stardom, the record industry, which made comics like Bob Newhart, a few years ago, is also virtually closed off to young comedians. "We don't cut comedy albums anymore," says an RCA spokesman. "You tell me where the market is." (In fact, there has been a modest resurgence in comedy record sales recently but the big-selling comedy album is still considered a rarity.)

So the main hope for a young comic lies in the chance that someone important may be so taken by him that he wins a spot on a TV show. That's what happened to comic Rodney Dangerfield. After a 12-year retirement, Mr. Dangerfield made a show business comeback at age 40. Three years later, he was still working in Greenwich Village clubs for nothing. Then, overnight, a series of spots on the Ed Sullivan Show made him a star. Today, he is the proprietor of Dangerfield's, one of New York's few booming clubs—booming primarily because Mr. Dangerfield performs there himself.

Despite that, Mr. Dangerfield warns of television's dangers. "The young comic wants to get right into TV," he says. "If you rush into it and flop, you're stamped. It'll be a long time before you get another chance." There is another danger. As Mr. Chambers puts it, "TV has a gluttonous need for bodies. If anybody shows any spark at all, he's thrown right into the big time. It's like coming up to the Yankees too soon; he usually can't hold it."

The answer, all agree, is simple—suffer. And then suffer some more. "You've got to work the joints, the dungeons, work for nothing," says Mr. Dangerfield. Still, a man must make a living while he suffers. Mr. Cohen's sporadic public appearances earn him perhaps $125 a week—when he works. So he writes for other comics and for a while worked as the director of tour guides at a museum. The writing is beginning to pay off—besides the album work, he has done material for the Smother Brothers, Louis Nye and another young comic named Gabe Kaplan. In all, he earned nearly $10,000 in 1971.

Meantime, Mr. Cohen lives with his brother, a rented piano and dozen blankets in a crumbling relic of an apartment in south-central Los Angeles. He isn't sure his neighbors like him. He cites occasional encounters with an elderly woman who, although she left Eastern Europe 50 years ago, has mastered only one English phrase: "Go to hell, crazy Jew." And, of course, he continues to scratch for performing jobs. Like an appearance on a drug-abuse telethon in Phoenix. ("I hope to break into the major diseases soon," he quips.) Or yet another appearance at the Ice House, where Bob Stane, the owner, has booked him for five week stands.

In the wee hours of the morning, Mr. Cohen stands on the stage of the Ice House before that sleepy crowd of six, tossing out routines that have brought laughs on better nights but bring nothing on this night. The idea is that drug companies, having deodorized armpits, feet and almost everything else that smells bad, will have to invent new body odors.

"Hi, I'm nine out of 10 doctors," goes the pitch. "And this, this is a diagram of your inner ear. During a day of active listening, tiny particles accumulate in your ear . . . ear plankton . . . This causes audiosis, or (cupping his hands around his mouth), Eee! Eee! Oh!—Embarrassing Ear Odor! But when you use this simple spray—L-O-B-E— Lobe, ear plankton dissolves and flows gently into your head. So remember: If he whispered in your ear once, will he whisper again? Use Lobe and you'll hear things you never heard before."

On another night, at the Troubador, Los Angeles'

most successful club, Mr. Cohen works "the hoot," a night set aside for new performances. He has suffered through several teeth-gnashing experiences at the Troubador. On this night, he follows a crashingly loud rock band with many friends in the audience—who depart when the band finishes, leaving a room half-filled with an audience half-deaf.

The flight of the Jews from Egypt and the engulfing of the Egyptian army as the parted Red Sea unparts can be "viewed from two perspectives," he tells the crowd. "The Jewish perspective—that is, the death of the Egyptian army, or the Arab perspective—the birth of the Egyptian navy." A noisy, unbroken hum drowns out much of his monologue, but he pushes on. He tells of famed used-car dealer Ralph Williams strapped like Captain Ahab to one of his "clean, late-model used cars," while vigilantes in a consumer rebellion plot to do away with him.

Ralph Williams "begins bargaining desperately," intones Mr. Cohen. "Says he'll throw in free accessories—engines, tires . . . " The audience drones on, all but oblivious to the man on the stage.

That experience came right after a particularly successful stint at the Ice House and, Mr. Cohen admits, it unnerved him a bit. "When I left the Ice House, I was mulling over the screen version of my life," he says, "'A Star Is Born.' I thought I was the messianic comedian. After the Troubador, I thought perhaps a star was stillborn."

Since then, he has done better at subsequent Troubador hoots. But not well enough for a booking there. Troubador owner Doug Weston considers comics "time-fillers" who "haven't added much to the show." He says he has succeeded by booking big-name rock stars like James Taylor and Elton John and persuading record companies to pay the fat promotion and advertising bills. "The profits are not as great as you would like to believe," he says. "The club business has never been healthy. Clubs need to be subsidized by big fish like record companies to some degree." (Mr. Stane, of the Ice House, who like comics and is one of the few club owners who has succeeded booking nobodies, considers such tie-ins disastrous. "Someone always has a lever over you," he says).

If stage appearances are trying for Eric Cohen, so are auditions. At one club, he is ushered into a small room, confronted with a massive man smoking a cigar and drinking rum and Coke and told to be funny for a few minutes. "The only sound," in such a situation, he recalls, "is your voice cracking. So you settle for other things—you pause when he clears his throat, play off the clink of the ice cubes in his drink. When he shuffles some papers, it's the equivalent of a belly laugh." His worst audition, he says, was the time a club owner paid detailed attention throughout the whole routine—not to the routine, but to the tuna fish sandwich he was eating.

Why does Eric Cohen put up with all that? That's a question that often occurs to Eric Cohen. He says club owners are "the most tyrannical group of people you'll ever meet," and standing on a stage trying to make a bunch of drowsy boozehounds laugh is "the hardest level of comedic performance. I guess exhibitionism is a factor. There's a certain element of didacticism. You like the idea of having a platform for your ideas."

Ideally, he will not have to stand on the stages of clubs for the rest of his life. He says he would prefer the cerebral pursuits of the writer or director of plays or movies. "Nightclubs are the first rung, or writing for other comics. You have to do that before you get the artistic control of a Mel Brooks, Woody Allen or Mike Nichols."

Until then, Eric Cohen continues the battle for laughs and for reassurance. "Listen," he tells a pessimistic companion before marching out to confront yet another indifferent audience, "all I want to hear from you is, 'You're gonna kill 'em, sweetie baby.'"

—HAL LANCASTER

For the Plaintiff

Seated at his desk surrounded by modern art objects, lawyer Phil Corboy is in a buoyant mood. The day before, he obtained a $725,000 settlement for an auto mechanic who had lost an eye in a work accident, and the congratulatory calls are pouring in.

He grabs his chrome-plated office phone to take a call from a lawyer friend. "Yes, I'm very happy with the settlement," he tells the caller. "You know, that's the most I've heard of for one eye in Illinois."

Such handsome recoveries aren't at all unusual for Mr. Corboy. During his 20-year career, the jut-jawed attorney has filed suits on behalf of thousands of victims of auto accidents, airplane crashes, medical malpractice and defective products. He has won millions of dollars for his clients, often from major corporations and insurance companies with vast financial resources and teams of defense lawyers.

Mr. Corboy is a tort lawyer, or, as he prefers to be called, a plaintiff's lawyer. Under the law of torts, which derives from medieval England and the much older Judeo-Christian notion of individual moral responsibility, people are entitled to collect compensation from anybody they can prove responsible for harming them. Not only can plaintiffs in tort actions collect for past and future lost wages and medical expenses, but they also can frequently obtain far more money for such intangibles as mental anguish and pain and suffering.

But to collect, plaintiffs generally must retain a personal-injury lawyer like Mr. Corboy. The profession runs the gamut from marginal and often shady practitioners, living off small auto accident claims, to highly paid specialists like Mr. Corboy, who because of their reputations draw the major cases.

Tort lawyers have become increasingly visible in recent years. In 1971, they were involved in more than 500,000 auto accident claims, double the total of 10 years earlier. Riding the wave of consumerism, they are filing 10 times as many product-liability suits as a decade ago, seeking damages for everything from exploding beverage bottles to drugs with allegedly harmful side effects. The number of malpractice suits against hospitals and doctors is soaring with the easing of legal barriers to such actions.

At the same time, tort lawyers and the whole tort system are coming under growing attack. Critics charge that the tort requirement of fixing fault before allocation damages leads to mounting court backlogs, spiraling insurance costs and unfair delays in the compensation of injury victims. "The tort system is about the most costly and inefficient way imaginable to compensate accident victims," insists Prof. Guido Calabrese of Yale Law School, who has written extensively on economic aspects of the tort system.

A 1970 New York Insurance Department survey showed that more than half of every premium dollar paid for auto bodily injury insurance is eaten up in litigation and administrative expenses, with only 44 cents ultimately reaching injury victims. Accident victims in such areas as New York, Chicago and Los Angeles often have to wait as long as five years before their cases come to trial.

Critics also claim that personal-injury lawyers, key figures in the tort system, swell its costs by filing inflated and sometimes fraudulent claims on minor accidents, exploiting insurance companies' willingness to settle small claims to avoid costly litigation. A Philadelphia Bar Association probe and a Chicago federal grand jury report disclosed numerous instances where lawyers bribed doctors and insurance adjusters to aid in faking accident claims; policemen were also bribed to steer clients to them.

The investigations revealed that some lawyers employed "runners" who cruise city streets in cars equipped with police radios in order to rush to auto accident scenes to solicit business. Others pay "finders' fees" to policemen, tow-truck operators and emergency-room orderlies to steer injury victims to them.

As a result of this criticism, several states have enacted no-fault auto-insurance laws. No-fault largely eliminates the need to sue by making some compensation automatically available to accident victims, regardless of who was to blame for a mishap. Some no-fault laws prohibit tort suits unless the injured person's medical costs exceed certain limits or he suffers permanent disability of disfigurement.

Other major areas of tort litigation also are being threatened. Some experts even are predicting the eventual demise of the entire tort system and its replacement by a national social insurance program.

The returns so far on no-fault auto insurance lend support to the contentions of tort critics. In Massachusetts, bodily injury insurance premiums have been cut by 43% and court case backlogs have been reduced dramatically since no-fault was enacted in January 1971. Moreover, the dollar amount of bodily injury claims in the state in 1971 fell 50% from the year before, leading observers to speculate that many of the claims filed under the old system were spurious or inflated.

Despite such evidence, however, personal-injury lawyers remain adamant in their defense of the tort system. "When you limit the size of victims' recoveries, as no-fault does, you are tampering with basic human rights," contends Marvin Lewis, a San Francisco tort lawyer who is a past-president of the American Trial Lawyers Association, the tort lawyers' primary professional group. "Who has the right to arbitrarily say what a missing arm or leg is worth? Potential defendants like manufacturers and physicians would exercise much less care than they do now if the threat of tort litigation was removed."

The lawyer's position isn't surprising, of course; no-fault has already put a number of them out of business in Massachusetts and threatens to do likewise in other states as it spreads. Yet in most areas, tort lawyers, sustained by the perils of modern life, are busier than ever.

Such is the case with Phil Corboy. Relaxing in his plush office overlooking Chicago's steel and glass Civic Center, the scene of many of his courtroom triumphs, he smilingly acknowledges that business has never been better. To handle the crush of cases, Mr. Corboy's six-lawyer firm has to turn down two out of every three prospective clients. "He takes only the good stuff—cases where the injuries are serious, the negligence clearcut and the party responsible well-insured," says an envious fellow lawyer.

Mr. Corboy says that tort lawyers play an all-important role in representing the underdog against stingy insurance companies. "It's not that insurance companies or large companies generally are necessarily cold-blooded, but to them an accidental death, a missing limb or a horrible scar is just an accounting problem," he says. "The plaintiff's lawyer injects humanity into the system by reminding them or a jury, if necessary, that an enormous personal tragedy has taken place and by getting fair compensation for his client."

Mr. Corboy's interest in the size of clients' recoveries springs from more than a burning sense of justice. Like other personal-injury lawyers, he works on a contingency basis rather than on hourly fees, taking anywhere from one-quarter to one-third of his client's recovery, whether by pretrial settlement or jury award. This is fairly typical for tort lawyers generally—although some take up to 40%.

Critics charge that contingency fees encourage lawyers to exaggerate clients' injuries. Mr. Corboy defends the practice, contending that it gives even the poor access to top legal talent and insures that lawyers do their best for clients, because if the case is lost the lawyers collect nothing.

He declines to disclose his annual income, but persons close to him estimate it at more than $500,000 a year— roughly $495,000 more than he earned in his first job, a political patronage post in Chicago's corporation counsel's office. Whatever the exact figure now, the son of a policeman is clearly affluent—as evidenced by everything from the gleaming Cadillac he drives to the Picasso lithographs and Steuben glass figurines that grace his office. He, his wife, Doris, and five children live in a commodius home in Chicago's North Shore suburbs. He has extensive real estate holdings.

As one of a handful of top tort specialists in the U.S., Mr. Corboy obtains most of his prospective clients from other lawyers, who refer to him cases they find too difficult to handle themselves. In return, Mr. Corboy pays the referring lawyers up to one-third of his fee, depending on the amount of work the other lawyer puts into the case. The remainder of his clients come to him directly, drawn by his reputation or steered by satisfied former clients.

Publicity attracts new business, too, and Mr. Corboy relishes public exposure. He regularly addresses local bar groups, legal seminars and other professional gatherings. In addition, following a large recovery of damages, his secretary routinely distributes press releases to local newspapers, a type of promotion that, unlike ambulance chasing, is deemed to be ethical. Indeed, his status in the Chicago legal community is indicated by his election to the presidency of the Chicago Bar Association in 1972.

It's courtroom victories, though, that ultimately attract clients, and Mr. Corboy has had many triumphs. Lawyers who have watched him over the years say his success is mainly a result of his prodigious pretrial preparation.

To prepare for a major case, Mr. Corboy and his assistants spend months interviewing witnesses, taking sworn statements and consulting experts and technical publications. A trim 160 pounds, Mr. Corboy also carefully watches his diet and runs a mile a day at the Chicago Athletic Club to maintain his stamina for the grueling court session and 60-hour weeks that his practice entails.

Careful jury selection is crucial to his success. "It isn't enough to get jurors who will find the defendant liable; they must also be willing to give the plaintiff big money," he says. Thus Mr. Corboy generally shuns retired people because they frequently are on fixed incomes and are "too tight with the buck." Blacks and Jews, on the other hand, tend to make good plaintiff's jurors because "they have tasted discrimination and therefore tend to identify with the underdog plaintiff," he says. He also prefers blue-collar workers because "they empathize more with victims because their own bodies are their livelihood."

To wring large sums of money from juries, Mr. Corboy relies heavily on courtroom dramatics. "The biggest sin a lawyer can commit is to bore the jury," he says. For one thing, he always holds off presenting his accident victims until late in the trial. "I want the jury to be properly shocked, especially if my clients is a paraplegic or an amputee," he explains. "I learned early in my career that if a jury gets overexposed to a plaintiff, it begins to accept his injury as commonplace."

He also makes ample use of color photos of injuries, of skeletons, and of frank display of his client's injuries. In one case, the color slides of a burn victim he showed were so gruesome that a female court reporter fainted. Needless to say, that didn't hurt his cause with the jury.

In court, Mr. Corboy is quick on his feet. In one recent trial, the defense lawyers attacked the credibility of his client, an injured construction worker Mr. Corboy had described as a "total vegetable," by showing the jury a movie of the worker changing a tire on his car. After recovering his composure, Mr. Corboy ripped the defense for invading his client's privacy by hiring a detective to tail and photograph him. He brought out that the film had been doctored so as not to show the worker's struggle with the tire. After brief deliberation, the jury awarded his client $500,000.

All of these talents were on display in a trial in which Mr. Corboy represented Italo Procaccini, an auto mechanic who had lost an eye in 1966 at the Chicago garage where he worked when a chip of steel flew from a punch he was using and lodged in his eye. The accident left him completely blind because he was already blind in the other eye. In 1967, he filed suit against Sears, Roebuck & Co., where he had purchased the punch, and McPherson Huff Tool Co., its manufacturer, charging that the tool was defective.

Because of the backlog in Chicago's courts, the case didn't come to trial until May 1972, five years after the suit was first filed. In the meantime, the 48-year-old Mr. Procaccini was forced to support his wife and two children on his workmen's compensation and Social Security benefits, expending his life savings the process. The day before the trial, Sears and McPherson Huff offered him $300,000 to settle the case, but Mr. Corboy advised him to hold out for more.

Mr. Corboy and several assistants spent months preparing for the trial. During that time, Mr. Corboy steeped himself in metallurgy by consulting over 20 books on the subject. He had the punch in question tested by a number of experts, even flying it to California where it was examined under a special electron microscope large enough to permit viewing of the entire tool. Some 20 lengthy depositions, or sworn statements, were taken from various experts, witnesses and other persons connected with the case. He had more than 100 exhibits prepared, including a number of poster-sized blowups of the chip and tool. The preparation cost more than $20,000, which was to come out of the client's share of the recovery.

Jury selection took two days, with both Mr. Corboy and the defense using all their allotted eight preemptory challenges before picking a 12-member jury. Among the prospective jurors Mr. Corboy excused were a pensioner and a metal-forging plant foreman, who Mr. Corboy feared might "offer phony expertise to the jury."

The crux of Mr. Corboy's case was the claim that the tool was defective. He brought in an industrial metallurgist from Chicago and a professor of metallurgy from Long Beach State College in California, who testified that the chipping occurred because of a lack of uniformity in the tool's chemical composition and several flaws in its internal structure. The defense answered with its own expert, a metallurgist from Illinois Institute of Technology in Chicago, who contended that the tool wasn't defective.

The defense's key argument was that Mr. Procaccini was responsible for the mishap because he wasn't wearing safety glasses. To counter this, Mr. Corboy produced four mechanics, including one who had taught thousands of mechanics in the Navy, who testified that mechanics don't customarily wear safety glasses when using punches. The lawyer also brought out that Sears had started to issue such warnings only after the client's accident.

Mr. Procaccini was the lawyer's last witness. It was his first appearance, though the trial had run two weeks, and his entrance was staged to produce the maximum impact on the jury. Moments after Mr. Corboy asked permission to bring on his last witness, the doors of the court swung open and in came Mr. Procaccini, wearing sunglasses, led by his 20-year-old son and a seeing-eye dog. The decision to include the dog had only been reached late the previous evening by Mr. Corboy and an associate. They decided that the poignancy of having the dog lying at his master's feet was worth the occasional barks and recesses that the dog required.

For two hours Mr. Corboy examined his client on his life as a blind man. Pausing frequently to daub his eyes, the slender, baldish mechanic told of empty days, sleepless nights and the constant pain of his injured eye. At one point, the lawyer led Mr. Procaccini in front of the jury box and had him remove his sunglasses, exposing his scarred, milky eyes. By the end of the testimony one female juror was in tears. The defense then asked only two perfunctory questions and excused Mr. Procaccini. "You don't kick around a blind man in front of a jury," a Sears lawyer explained later.

The climax of the trial was Mr. Corboy's closing argument. After reviewing the evidence and the law in the case, Mr. Corboy "pulled out all the stops," dwelling for more than an hour on the horrors of his client's blindness.

As the jury sat in rapt attention, he emotionally described how the accident had robbed his client of even life's simplest pleasures, such as "remembering what his wife and children look like, or taking a walk to the corner store, or even smoking cigarets for fear of starting a fire." He added that "in the kingdom of the blind the one-eyed man is king" and concluded with a wringing plea for justice for his client who "had been doomed to a life of perpetual midnight."

After the trial, while the jury was still deliberating, the defendants agreed to meet Mr. Corboy's settlement demand of $752,500, more than double what they'd offered before. Of this, Mr. Procaccini ended up with approximately $540,000 of tax-free income after deducting lawyers' fees and expenses.

Such out-of-court settlements are typical. Less than 10% of all personal-injury suits reach a jury verdict. Even a trial specialist like Mr. Corboy settles approximately four cases to every one that he tries to verdict. "But in every one of them I'm always prepared to go all the way," he says.

—JONATHAN R. LAING

For the Defense

Attorney Max Wildman cuts a less-than-impressive figure as he walks into a court in Chicago. He's dressed in a baggy tweed jacket with elbow patches and badly frayed sleeves. One of his scuffed shoes is separating at a seam. He carries a battered briefcase.

Mr. Wildman, however, isn't some down-at-the-heels lawyer scratching for business. He boasts a six-figure income and a blue-chip clientele that includes many of the U.S.'s biggest insurance companies and corporations. He specializes in defending them against personal-injury suits. In that capacity, the sandy-haired attorney has battled hundreds of victims of automobile crashes, work accidents, product mishaps and medical misadventures seeking millions of dollars in damages for their injuries.

His shabby courtroom attire is one of the many ploys he has used successfully during his 25-year career to gain the sympathy of juries and thus to aid the cause of his clients. "Why should the other side have a monopoly on sympathy?" he asks with a smile.

Under the law of torts, injury victims are entitled to collect compensation for losses and attendant mental anguish from anybody they can prove responsible for harming them. The vast majority of these lawsuits are settled by insurance companies before they reach trial—usually without the intercession of defense lawyers. But in the major cases, where the damages are large, insurance companies and other tort defendants generally fight plaintiffs in court, and for this they hire highly paid defense lawyers like Mr. Wildman.

In recent years, defense lawyers have been busier than ever because of a surge in damage suits caused by such forces as consumerism and growing public litigiousness and a number of legal changes that have made personal injury suits easier for plaintiffs to win. For example, plaintiffs in product-liability cases today can sometimes collect for injuries caused by a product without proving negligence on the part of the manufacturer.

Max Wildman certainly is busy. He proudly takes a visitor on a tour of the new offices of his burgeoning firm of Wildman, Harrold, Allen & Dixon, which occupies an entire floor of Chicago's new IBM building. Mr. Wildman founded the firm in 1967 with five lawyers. It since has expanded to 32 attorneys, most of whom are occupied solely with personal-injury defense work.

Mr. Wildman declines to disclose his annual income, but persons close to him place it at well over $250,000. That's a far cry from the $3,600 that the son of a country doctor in Peru, Ind., earned in 1948, when he joined Chicago's biggest law firm of Kirkland, Ellis, Hodson, Chaffetz & Masters (now Kirkland & Ellis) fresh out of the University of Michigan law school. He, his attractive blond wife Joyce, and their three children live in a $250,000 chateau-style home in the northern Chicago suburb of Lake Bluff.

Colleagues say that Mr. Wildman is among the best in the U.S. in his specialty. "Max is one of the toughest defense lawyers around," says John J. Kennelly, a well-known personal-injury lawyer who has won a number of million-dollar awards. Echoes Nat Ozman, a Chicago plaintiff's lawyer who has faced Mr. Wildman in court many times: "What makes him so dangerous is his ability to use emotionalism, and other plaintiff-lawyer tactics against the plaintiff. Juries seem to lap up that Hoosier country-boy act of his."

The bulk of the Wildman firm's cases come from insurance companies that send suits too large or too complex for their own claims agents and lawyers to settle. In a given year, such major clients as Aetna Insurance Co., Travelers Insurance Co. of Hartford and Medical Protective Co., Fort Wayne, Ind., may refer several hundred cases each to the firm. The remainder of the firm's cases come from corporations that either don't carry liability insurance or, for a variety of reasons, insist on having the final say in defending tort suits.

Out of 1,500 or so cases that pour into his firm annually, Mr. Wildman personally handles only the half-dozen biggest ones, which often take as long as a month to try in court. "He gets the kind of cases where the plaintiffs are so horribly injured and the liability so clear that the insurance company has little chance of winning," says a fellow lawyer. "They want Max because they know that there are few defense lawyers better at holding down the size of the jury verdict. And sometimes Max even wins the cases."

Mr. Wildman's courtroom success doesn't come easily. It's built on weeks and sometimes months of dogged preparation by him and his associates. In preparing for a major case they will interview scores of witnesses and technical experts, consult numerous technical manuals, conduct in-depth legal research and take as many as 60 sworn statements.

During his career, Mr. Wildman has taken private cram courses in everything from bacteriology to metallurgy in readying himself for trials. In one case in which he successfully defended a cigarette company sued for $500,-000 by a smoker suffering from throat cancer, his firm even conducted secret background investigations of 200 veniremen from whom the jury was to be drawn, to determine each individual's attitude towards smoking and the prevalence of cancer in his family.

Mr. Wildman also routinely investigates plaintiff injury claims—sometimes with interesting results. One such case involved a worker who sued Mr. Wildman's client, Pennsylvania Railroad (now the Penn Central), for $200,000, claiming incapacitating back injuries in a switching-yard accident. Skeptical of the claim, Mr. Wildman hired a private detective agency to tail the switchman. The surveillance proved fruitless until one evening when one of the detectives managed to pick a fight with the railroad worker in a tavern. In the ensuing battle, the switchman quickly knocked down the detective, but not before a confederate of the detective, hidden behind a door, captured the struggle on film. "Needless to say, the jury gave us a not-guilty after seeing movies of the fight," Mr. Wildman says with a chuckle.

Jury selection also is all-important to Mr. Wildman's success in court. "You have to find people able to resist the natural impulse to give the plaintiff the moon, and that's not easy," he says. Mr. Wildman prefers retired people living on fixed incomes and older blue-collar and middle-management workers. "They are accustomed to shifting for themselves and are usually conservative with awards," he says. He shuns young jurors because of their "tendency to have a social-worker, do-gooder mentality." To sow dissension in the jury he often tries to exploit racial tension and class conflict in his selections. "A disunified jury rarely grants large awards," he explains.

To keep down the size of verdicts, Mr. Wildman frequently resorts to artifices and ploys. "You can put on the strongest case in the world, but if you don't use your ingenuity and pull tricks you'll get murdered by the jury anyway," he says. "After all, in this day of consumerism and distrust of the establishment, a lawyer defending corporations doesn't have a hell of a lot going for him, so he has to make his breaks."

For one thing, Mr. Wildman makes frequent use of his knowledge of semantics, in which he has taken courses. "Take the word 'accident,' which is at the bedrock of all tort litigation," he muses one afternoon in his office. "To a lawyer it means an occurrence, while to the laymen sitting on a jury it means a mishap where no one is at fault. I can't tell you how many cases I've won exploiting that confusion in meaning.

Mr. Wildman also employs nonverbal communication to bolster his presentation. "Everything I do in front of a jury, whether done in court, during recesses or in the corridors outside court, is calculated to create a certain impression with them," he says. "The facial expression, the physical gesture, the mannerism are often more important than what a lawyer actually says. It's absolutely fatal for a defense lawyer to convey arrogance, prosperity or insouciance about the plaintiff's injuries."

Thus, Mr. Wildman dresses poorly. He never smokes his cigars, which he has custom-made, in front of a jury. During a trial he makes a point of always eating in the courthouse cafeteria with the jurors rather than at his usual haunt, Chicago's posh University Club. In one case which is now a legend in Chicago legal circles, Mr. Wildman leaped to his feet and solicitously offered a handkerchief to a plaintiff's lawyer who had burst into tears during an emotional closing argument. "That gesture turned potentially dangerous pathos into bathos and resulted in a skimpy jury verdict," he recalls.

To counter the dramatic impact of the injured plaintiff, Mr. Wildman tries to have the defendant or a company official, if his client is a corporation, with him at the defense table throughout the trial. He feels that the presence of a "goat," as Mr. Wildman calls him, is essential in personalizing the defense.

"I want to create the impression with the jury that the goat's head is on the block, so that when they retire to the jury room to decide the case, their sympathy for the plaintiff will be offset by their concern over the fate of the goat."

Some of his ploys are less than subtle. In one trial in which Mr. Wildman's client was charged with negligence by a middle-aged businessman whose wife died in an auto wreck, he had his attractive blond secretary come into the courtroom at the end of the trial and sit next to the widower. Following Mr. Wildman's instructions, she asked the man an innocent question, smiled, patted his hand and quickly left. "Just one look at the cold expressions on the lady jurors faces was enough to tell me that we were home free," Mr. Wildman recalls with a smile. "When the jury came back with a not-guilty, the plaintiff's lawyer never knew what hit him. You see, the entire interchange took place while he was facing the jury in the midst of his closing argument."

Mr. Wildman's defensive skills were recently put to the test in a trial in which he defended Coath & Goss Inc., a Chicago building contractor that was being sued for $1.2 million by the widow and three children of a 27-year-old elevator mechanic's helper who was killed at one of the company's construction sites. The accident occurred when a one-ton elevator platform, held aloft only by safety shoes, plunged four stories, crushing the mechanic who was working below.

The trial presented Mr. Wildman with a number of problems. First, under an Illinois law called the structural work act, Coath & Goss, as general contractor, was liable for damages arising from any accident at its construction projects. Also the damages in the case were likely to be high because of the mechanic's long work-life expectancy and his trade's high pay level (Chicago elevator mechanics earn about $22,000 a year).

The dead man's attractive, 27-year-old widow, who sat primly dressed at the plaintiff counsel's table throughout the week-long trial, and the three young children appeared to make favorable impressions on the jury. Furthermore the widow's lawyer produced a parade of witnesses including a safety engineering expert from Illinois Institute of Technology, Chicago, and several officials of the Elevator Constructors Union, who testified that the elevator platform was unsafe because, contrary to prevailing industry practice, it wasn't cabled to the building in addition to being secured by safety shoes.

To counter this, Mr. Wildman argued that Westinghouse Electric Corp.'s elevator division, the mechanic's employer and a subcontractor on the job, was to blame for the accident and not Coath & Goss. He contended that not only was Westinghouse as legally responsible for insuring the safety of the elevator as the general contractor but that Westinghouse had improperly installed the unit, thus causing the accident. "The argument was partly sophistry, but I was trying to plant enough doubts in the jurors' minds on the liability question to keep down the size of the verdict," Mr. Wildman explains.

In addition, Mr. Wildman resorted to several of his favorite ploys. As the goat, he used the Coath & Goss general superintendent from the job where the fatal accident occurred. The superintendent sat at the defense table dressed in work clothes during the trial. He was Mr. Wildman's only witness and the focus of the lawyer's emotional closing argument in which Mr. Wildman implied that the superintendent and not his company was being charged with responsibility for the fatal accident.

Mr. Wildman also had a claims supervisor from Liberty Mutual Insurance Co., which had retained him in the case, watch the entire trial to create the impression that the widow had a boyfriend. On Mr. Wildman's instructions, the man chatted amiably with the widow in front of the jury on a number of occasions when her lawyer was absent.

At the end of the trial, Mr. Wildman was brimming with confidence. Earlier he had turned down an offer by the plaintiff's lawyer to settle the case out-of-court for $300,000 because he expected an even lower jury verdict.

After three hours of deliberations, the jury returned a verdict of $424,000. Sitting in his office, Mr. Wildman accepted the news philosophically. In a voice tinged with disappointment, he observes to a visitor, "Well, I did everything I could think of to keep the plaintiffs from ringing the bell. And you know, were I to try the case all over again I wouldn't do anything differently."

—JONATHAN R. LAING

Part Three

DEALING WITH PROBLEMS

Some people wouldn't have their jobs at all if everything ran smoothly. But because the world is an imperfect place, there are jobs dedicated to problem-solving. Some of these jobs are familiar and obvious, such as the park ranger. Others are less frequently in the public eye—the social worker and the union committeeman, for instance. And there are those that are downright obscure and technically demanding, such as a trouble shooter for a machine company.

The Park Ranger

"Grab the kid in the yellow hair," crackles the voice over the walkie-talkie, and Walter Dabney, anchoring his Smokey-the-Bear hat, is off at a run through the waist-high grass of a meadow In California's Yosemite National Park.

Ahead of Mr. Dabney spirits a long-haired, barefoot youth, clad in tattered blue-jean shorts. Mr. Dabney gains steadily, but, after a half-mile run, the youth plunges into the fast-moving Merced River and swims across. Suddenly, two uniformed men mounted on horses gallop out of the woods on the bank opposite from where Mr. Dabney stands and quickly apprehend the youth as he emerges from the river.

"Nice going over there," Mr. Dabney pants into the radio, grinning broadly. "That horse patrol looks good. I thought sure that would be the first one to get away, because I sure wasn't going to swim that river after him."

The one that didn't get away in this case was a minor suspected of alcohol possession and the chase was all part of a night's work for Walt Dabney in his role as a ranger for the National Park Service. For as supervisor of the night shift in the Yosemite Valley, Mr. Dabney is frequently seen running down suspected criminals and making arrests on such charges as narcotics violations, intoxication, disorderly conduct, theft and assault—all in addition to performing such relatively standard tasks as answering endless tourist questions about fishing spots, cautioning city-born campers about bothering wild bears, and rescuing careless vacationers who get lost in the mountains or fall into rivers.

"A lot of people think a park ranger is a guy off in a cabin in the woods," observes Mr. Dabney, a 27-year-old Texan who is in his third summer as a ranger here. "But it isn't like that at all."

It most certainly isn't. As such urban problems as crowding, drugs and crime have moved into the once-tranquil wilderness of the country's 38 national parks, the lives of the nation's 1,872 permanent rangers have changed drastically. Since 1970, for example, nearly all of the rangers have been required to complete at least 400 hours of law-enforcement courses. "The old days of hunt, fish and trap and live in a cabin are past for the ranger," laments one Park Service veteran.

Nowhere in the system are these changes more evident than in the Yosemite National Park, where a staff of 35 permanent rangers is supplemented by 200 seasonal rangers to handle summertime crowds. In 1972, more than two million people visited the 1,190-square-mile reserve sprawled in the Sierra Nevadas. More than one and a half million stayed overnight, and most of this group parked their campers, pitched their tents or rolled out their sleeping bags within the seven square miles that constitute the valley proper. On a typical summer night, a restless city of 20,000 strangers camps among the towering pines between the sheer cliffs of the valley walls.

Yosemite Valley, in fact, is the most heavily populated seven square miles of wilderness in the national park system, and the strains of accommodating such crowds have become increasingly evident. In the last decade, the number of visitors to Yosemite increased 51%—but the number of major crimes shot up 253%. In 1972 alone, the park was the scene of three homicides, three forcible rapes, seven robberies, 18 assaults, 142 burglaries and 624 thefts (including 10 automobiles). And the ranger hats, gray shirts and green trousers of Walt Dabney and his fellow rangers are the only law-enforcement uniforms in the area. (Out of uniform, the bushy-haired mustachioed Mr. Dabney looks more like an urban swinger than a ranger.)

"I've never, ever checked a fishing license," Mr. Dabney says. "I haven't had time to."

Yosemite is particularly prone to the urban crush because of its location—just four hours by car east of San

Francisco and a six-hour drive northeast of Los Angeles. But the crime rate is rising for reasons other than sheer crowd numbers. Ranger Rick Smith explains: "For the past few years, we've been getting what I like to call nontraditional campers. They're a young urban constituency that doesn't see a national park as a national park so much as a place to party."

Take the case of the buses. A few years ago, Yosemite introduced a system of double-decked shuttle buses for the purpose of reducing traffic congestion. And traffic congestion *was* reduced. But the buses created their own brand of problem when young people discovered that the vehicles were ready-made rolling party centers. Youths drinking alcohol and smoking marijuana began to take over the double-deckers at night, forcing other passengers off. In fact, the parties became so riotous during the early summer of 1973 that rangers on several occasions had to close the upper decks of the buses.

"It was so bad it was disgusting," Walt Dabney recalls. For this reason, among others, Mr. Dabney is helping to direct an ambitious new campaign aimed at reducing such turmoil while avoiding physical confrontations with young people. Part of this campaign involved placing plainclothesmen on the buses and warning the passengers to refrain from disruptive behavior. One evening, for example, Mr. Dabney, in uniform, boarded one of the buses and declared to a boisterous crowd on the upper deck that "the buses are for everybody." He added, his voice booming with authority: "They aren't for just a few people to take them over and party, so if you get out of line, you'll be arrested."

Such threats are by no means idle. On the Fourth of July holiday in 1973, Mr. Dabney and two other rangers climbed aboard a particularly noisy bus and arrested three shaggy, intoxicated young men. The trio had been pointed out by the rangers' undercover operative, a crew-cut young man in blue-jeans and denim jacket who said he had been offered a marijuana cigaret by one of the three—all of whom were charged with disorderly conduct (one was also charged with possession of LSD and another with possession of marijuana).

There were five arrests on buses that night, but the number has run as high as 20. "These kinds of people just ruin things for everybody else, absolutely destroy things," Mr. Dabney says, spitting violently from his ever-present cud of tobacco.

Another part of the rangers' campaign is focused on Yellow Pine, a wooded, hike-in area in the pines several miles downstream from the park's main campgrounds. Yellow Pine was introduced as an alternate camping location in 1971 in an effort to lure rowdy young groups away from camping families. But control proved difficult, Mr. Dabney says—so difficult, in fact, that on the Fourth of July in 1972, "We lost it . . . There were 400 people in there, and we just had to pull out and watch."

Despite his occasional toughness, particularly with repeaters, Walt Dabney often shows considerable restraint in dealing with the park's youthful visitors. "I don't like to arrest people," he told two of the park's concession workers and three visitors, all of whom he found smoking marijuana, "but you and I both know what the law is. I'm just going to give you a warning this time, but next time you'll be out of this park." He then recorded the names of the workers, all teen-agers, and the five, obviously frightened, turned over the remaining marijuana.

"My philosophy is to use the least stringent means that will get the same result," Mr. Dabney told a night watchman after this incident. "I'll use a verbal warning, a written warning, a citation and an arrest—in that order." (Like most of Yosemite's permanent rangers, Mr. Dabney carries a concealed 38-caliber police revolver and a canister of Mace; he has never used either.)

On another night, called to a gift shop where security guards said they had apprehended a shoplifter, Mr. Dabney found a 12-year-old boy who had pocketed four key rings worth about $1 each. He returned the boy to his parents who were camped nearby, telling them, "I'll let you handle it this time."

"We're supposed to take them in and book them," the ranger said later in his deep, Texas drawl, "but 12 is a little young to have a record, and I just can't feel right about doing that. I remember that when I was about that age I took a roll of BBs. My grandmother caught me, and I didn't do that again.

"I didn't even have a BB gun," he adds.

Thefts, many involving valuable items, occupy a considerably amount of Mr. Dabney's time. In one July 4th week, for example, a vacationing doctor from New York reported the theft of a pack containing a rare silver flute worth $500, 100 syringes and three bottles of insulin that he carried for his own use. "It didn't even enter my head that somebody would rip off a backpack in the mountains," the victim lamented. "In the city maybe—but in the mountains?

Yes, in the mountains. Increases in thefts and burglaries accounted for most of the 15% rise in major crimes at Yosemite from 1971 to 1972, burglaries increased 51% and thefts 11%. In May and June of 1973, some $5,400 worth of property was stolen in 102 car burglaries. (Somewhat surprising, however, in light of Yosemite's transient population and wilderness setting, the park boasts an arrest rate of 25% for major crimes, well above the national average of 20%.)

Despite the trials and tribulations of his job, Walt Dabney maintains that the diversity and the prospect of the unexpected fascinate him. Take the day that included the drug arrest at Yellow Pine and the confiscation of marijuana from concession employes. The day's work begins at about 3:30 p.m., when Mr. Dabney and his wife, Mary (who works as a night radio dispatcher for the rangers) walk to the headquarters from their one-bedroom apartment. After a briefing session with the dozen rangers on the shift, Mr. Dabney heads for a light green station wagon, which is equipped as an ambulance, for a stint on road patrol.

"It's hotter than Texas in here," Mr. Dabney remarks, climbing into the car. Almost as soon as he reaches the road, work begins. "You're going the wrong way," he informs a driver whom he has flagged down. "This is a one-way road, so you'd better turn around." Later, as he walks down Yosemite Village Mall, the valley's main thoroughfare, a German girl asks where the post office is, a woman questions him about fishing spots and a young man from Texas asks about hiking trails. "People follow a ranger to the bathroom up here," he drawls wryly. "They think we know everything."

Day turns into night. A man asks assistance in finding a lost nephew who left hours earlier to ride the buses. A woman thinks her husband has gotten lost driving the family camper. Several persons complain that bears have wrecked their campsites looking for food.

And so the days and nights go, rarely less busy, and often more so. On one Saturday night, Mr. Dabney for two hours simultaneously coordinated a river rescue, a boat recovery, a helicopter rescue of a youth suffering an asthma attack on a high trail and a search for a fleeing robber, while a fire alarm (later proved false) almost disrupted his carefully orchestrated efforts. (Rangers also make up the park's fire department.)

On less chaotic nights, Mr. Dabney might share soup and sandwiches in the communications center with his wife, a slender, dark-haired Texas woman. (The two met in 1966 at a state park near Austin, Texas, where Walt was a ranger and Mary was camping with her family.) Then, it's usually back on patrol until midnight, when the shift officially ends. Finally, there is the lengthy paperwork detailing arrests, suspicious persons, missing objects and rescue incidents—meaning that it is sometimes close to dawn by the time the ranger's night is ended.

Indeed, rangers in Yosemite devote nearly every waking hour to their work. That means putting in a work week of about 60 hours, running daily to maintain peak condition and devoting days off to giving testimony in U.S. Magistrate's Court or to perfecting such ranger skills as first aid, marksmanship, fire-fighting, climbing, diving and cross-country skiing.

"It's a commitment," Jim Brady, the valley's head ranger, says of the job. "A blend between avocation and vocation. These guys just won't let the park go to hell."

For such attention to duty, Mr. Dabney, a 1970 graduate of Texas A&M, is paid about $12,000 a year. (Ranger pay varies from $7,694 for a recruit to more than $20,000 for a chief ranger.) He rents his apartment from the government for $73 a month.

And he is happy. "I really like the job I'm doing," he says. Nevertheless, he admits that a Yosemite ranger's work exacts a toll and believes that three years is the maximum time that a ranger would want to spend in this park. For despite discussions at Yosemite concerning the reduction of rangers' law-enforcement duties in the future and such long-range plans as an elimination of cars from the valley, Walt Dabney nevertheless hopes to move to a less crowded and less turbulent park, perhaps Yellowstone.

"I really just want to do something out of doors," he says.

—ROBERT L. SIMISON

The Social Worker

With seven troublesome children to look after, the mother just can't find the time to give young Carlos Romero all the care and training he needs. So Carlos, dressed in his diapers, simply sits on the floor and drinks from his bottle. He has never tried solid food.

This wouldn't be so worrisome, perhaps—except that Carlos is seven and a half years old.

But there now is at least a glimmer of hope for Carlos, thanks to the efforts of Susan Bellinger. Miss Bellinger, an energetic young social worker, who serves his poverty-stricken neighborhood on the Lower East Side of Manhattan, is coordinating a complex effort to solve the family's many problems, including getting the mother to feed her children solid food. In the Romero family (not their real name; all cases in this story are somewhat disguised), the father is dead, the mother may have cancer, her lover is in jail on a drug charge and every child is at least somewhat retarded.

Such is the world of the social worker, the individual who copes with society's problems at the level where they turn into real people. In the past decade, programs to deal with the nation's social woes have proliferated; their payoff in actual cases often depends on the individual social worker who deals with the specific problems one by one. Thus, increased interest in prison reform means a burgeoning demand for social workers in rehabilitation programs. Proliferating programs for drug addicts rely heavily on social workers. The growing effort to move mental patients out of long-time confinements in state institutions depends on social workers who can supervise out-patient cases in the community.

According to government figures, the nation employed more than 170,000 social workers in 1972, up sharply from

116,000 in 1960 and only 45,000 in 1940. The Bureau of Labor Statistics estimates that the country will need an additional 100,000 social workers by 1980. Today, social workers directly reach millions of Americans ranging from the drug addict and the derelict to the suburban couple trying to glue a marriage back together.

But as social workers gain importance, they become increasingly controversial. To some they are heroes. But to others they are merely ineffectual do-gooders who serve mainly to get more people on the welfare rolls. Yet very few people really know what social workers actually do. A look at Miss Bellinger's work provides some answers.

The 34-year-old social worker is no stranger to the problems she handles. The daughter of a railroad clerk and a devoutly religious mother, she grew up in a fourth-floor Central Harlem walk-up tenement. "Those were the days when people were being thrown off rooftops in gang fights," she recalls. "I can remember in the third or fourth grade seeing blood gushing from a man who had been stabbed in our hallway."

Today, however, Miss Bellinger lives in the two worlds of the middle-class social worker, earning $16,400 a year for working with society's losers. She lives in a pleasant residential section of the Bronx, takes Caribbean vacations once or twice a year, attends the theater and modern dance performances, collects African and modern jewelry and passes out an occasional leaflet for a liberal politician.

But each morning, she rides the subway to the world of Carlos Romero. There she works in a converted apartment in a public housing project as chief social worker for a small mental-health unit operated by the Hamilton-Madison settlement house. (Like many social agencies, this unit didn't even exist a decade ago. But spurred by governmental grants, such facilities have proliferated in the last seven years.)

Serving 200 to 300 clients a month, the facility's part-time psychiatrist, part-time psychologist, three social workers and seven assistants to use a combination of counselling, psychotherapy and concrete services to help troubled people cope with their myriad problems. "My greatest goal is to help people see that they have some jurisdiction over their own lives," Miss Bellinger says.

This is often a tough task, and progress can be slow. Take the work with Carlos Romero's brother, Juan, a highly withdrawn 12-year-old, born with only one eye, who spends most of the day at home drawing pictures of monsters. His eyelid hangs grotesquely over the empty eye socket, contributing to the boy's abyssmal self-image.

At this stage, one of Miss Bellinger's assistants visits him at home regularly and simply draws pictures with him. Miss Bellinger hopes the boy will eventually join a therapy group, but merely getting him to "trust just one person," the social worker, may take "months," she says.

Meanwhile, Miss Bellinger plans to get a glass eye for Juan to improve his appearance and self-image. Such concrete services can be crucial to mental health, social workers increasingly believe. Carlos' 16-year-old sister is a crippled and retarded girl who never went outside, except when the famly moved. Simply getting her a wheelchair— which she had never had before—markedly improved the girl's life.

Tough as they are, cases like the Romero family offer a chance for real rewards. With some basic training, Carlos could become a self-sufficient member of society in a sheltered workshop, Miss Bellinger believes. Without help, of course, he is headed for a lifetime of complete dependency.

Sometimes social workers radically change lives. In a seemingly routine case a few years ago, a school referred to Miss Bellinger's office the Miller family, whose children seemed to cut class often. Indeed, when Miss Bellinger visited the family in its public-housing apartment at 10:30 one morning, she found the mother still in bed and the youngsters hanging around aimlessly.

She soon learned that the alcoholic Mr. Miller had died of liver disease and his widow seemed to be fast following suit. An 18-year-old son was in prison for armed robbery. Another son had been arrested for car theft, the 11-year-old son was sniffing glue, the nine-year-old boy liked to flood the housing project and break up park benches, and even the seven-year-old had a police record. On top of all this, Mrs. Miller had previously thrown another social worker out of her apartment, saying she was "tired of being called a bad mother." This is what social-work textbooks refer to as a "multi-problem family."

To cope with all these problems, Miss Bellinger coordinated an effort that eventually involved 13 different social and governmental agencies. The social workers first determined that the basic problem was a mother so overwhelmed with troubles that she couldn't function.

As a start, the workers persuaded Mrs. Miller to visit a clinic for her liver condition. This saved her life. Then Miss Bellinger and her colleagues placed the most disturbed, criminal children in special homes for treatment and placed the other youngsters in various after-school activities. They taught a 16-year-old daughter to help care for the younger children, and they took Mrs. Miller to a dentist to fix her almost totally rotted teeth.

Later, Miss Bellinger encouraged Mrs. Miller to join a group of mothers with problems. "It's very important for them to see that other people have their problems—that they're not the only ones afraid of the school principal," she says.

Then the workers helped Mrs. Miller get a part-time job as housekeeper for an old lady. Besides bringing in money to supplement Social Security survivors' benefits, the job has vastly improved Mrs. Miller's self-esteem. "She knows this elderly woman really depends on her, and she's tremendously proud of this job," Miss Bellinger says. Mrs. Miller also has stopped drinking, and the children stayed out of trouble with the police.

But not all cases end so successfully, and some can be downright dangerous. Early one evening, Miss Bellinger was alone in her office with a teen-aged suspected drug pusher, a court referral who came for counselling against his will. Suddenly the youngster became enraged at the counselling, leapt to his feet, knocked over his chair, whipped out a switchblade knife and thrust it toward Miss Bellinger.

"So what are you gonna do about *this?*" he shrieked.

"I just sat and looked at him," Miss Bellinger recalls. "He threatened, and I shrugged." As the youth waved the knife in front of her face, she coolly pointed out that others knew he was in the office, that he couldn't get away with stabbing her and that the whole incident showed how he did things that hurt him more than the "victims." Eventually the boy threw the knife on the table and stormed out. He soon thereafter landed in a home for the criminally insane.

Miss Bellinger says she is rarely afraid when visiting clients in tenements. But others say fear is common. "I worked three years visiting people in Harlem, and frankly, I was scared stiff every day of the week," says a white social worker—who now works in a center for young children. Adds a New Jersey social worker: "In some buildings, I always make my calls before 11 a.m. That way, you're gone before the real addicts wake up."

Social workers say they put up with all this because their work offers a chance to help people who need it. "I grew up believing we're responsible for other people," says Miss Bellinger. Her family's very active membership in a Harlem Presbyterian church that stressed social service strongly reinforced this belief, she says.

Of course, for many workers, benevolence isn't the only motivation. Like teaching, social work is a major vehicle for mobility into the middle class. (Salaries for social workers in the field range between $8,000 and $20,000 a year, and some administrators earn well over $30,000 a year, according to the National Association of Social Workers in Washington.) Among numerous psychological factors, some people find the authority over the client population gives them a sense of superiority, reports one New York social worker. Still, the main motivation really is "doing good," he says.

But "doing good" can be tough. Miss Bellinger says her work results in a "dramatic improvement"—a radical change in a person's way of life—in not more than 10% of all cases. In about 40% to 50% of the cases, there is a "noticeable improvement," she says. "It can be awfully frustrating. Sometimes, I feel I'm just giving out Band-Aids," she says. "Many of these problems are so long-standing they'll probably always be there," she adds.

Few social workers think their activity can slash welfare rolls significantly. At the private Hamilton-Madison House, where Miss Bellinger works, Joseph Tronolone, adult-services director, says his office has helped "a dozen or so" clients in one year get off welfare and into jobs. At the same time, the office also helped 100 people obtain welfare benefits they weren't receiving, largely through ignorance of what they are entitled to, he says.

"If more low-skill jobs were available, most of the people we see would take them—though some are just incapable of work because of emotional or behavioral problems," Mr. Tronolone says. The situations that cause people to go on welfare—shortage of low-skill jobs, old age, disability, broken families—are often "just beyond the scope of social work," he says.

In her own work, Miss Bellinger says that in one year she helped seven welfare recipients (with about 30 dependents) get jobs. She says she also persuaded 15 dropouts to go back to school (though not all stayed there) and persuaded another 25 not to drop out in the first place.

One might argue that such activity helps social work "pay for itself." (Miss Bellinger's mental health unit has a budget of $151,000 a year. Private contributions to the settlement house pay half the bill, and New York City pays the rest.) But Miss Bellinger says work and self-sufficiency concern her because they save tax money. "The main responsibility is to the dignity and well-being of the individual client," she contends.

Of course, many social workers have little contact with welfare cases. And even in Miss Bellinger's work, not all clients are indigent by any means. For instance, Miss Bellinger is seeing an Irish policeman who suffers from timidity. He has made only three arrests in the last four years—and two of the suspects arrested were dead drunk.

Miss Bellinger is using psychotherapy one hour a week to deal with this policeman's lack of confidence and other problems. With a master's degree in psychiatric social work from Boston University, she is considered professionally qualified to offer this therapy. Indeed, social workers provide a large share of the psychotherapy that is given to affluent as well as poor patients.

Besides dealing with individuals, Miss Bellinger and other social workers also conduct group sessions for clients who can gain strength from discussing their problems with others in similar situations. For instance, she recently conducted sessions for a group of trouble-making, under-achieving teen-aged girls who all liked to get high by sniffing glue. (After two months, they all stopped sniffing glue—and started drinking. In another few months, they stopped drinking, too.)

Like many social workers today, Miss Bellinger sometimes takes part in community organization, too. In a previous job, she once helped organize 40 New York parents who demanded meetings with a school principal and pressured the school to correct some blatant racial discrimination. Some social workers organize pickets, consumer boycotts, demonstrations, rent strikes and similar actions.

Such activity increasingly pits the social worker against established authority and creates conflicts. Established authority, which pays the bills for social work, is thus placed in the position of financing protests against itself. Established authority finds this ironic, at best. Thus, the activist minority social workers frequently encounter considerable pressure from their bosses—and sponsors—to go easy on the protests.

Many social workers shun social activism entirely. But increasingly, the younger workers, especially, think they must not only solve individual problems but also change the society that, they feel, created those problems.

"What I am really doing (in casework) is helping people adjust to a system that I consider unjust," says Miss Bellinger. "So to some extent, it really is a cop-out. I haven't become a bomb-throwing radical, but I think I do identify with people who want to break down the system." She says that out of despair, she has at times even considered becoming a revolutionary.

But in the end, most social workers realize that they are committed to "making the system work," that indeed, they themselves are part of the established authority. "If I felt I were not helping change the system, I would get out," Miss Bellinger says. "But obviously I haven't given up on the system—or I wouldn't be a social worker."

—ROGER RICKLEFS

The Foreman

When two workers on the giant assembly line at the Ford Motor Co. plant in Wixom, Mich., were recently assigned some extra work, a war of nerves ensued. The workers, who balked at the tasks, had trouble keeping up with the pace of the line and called in their union representative to protest the situation. The union man argued that the workload was too heavy. But a company official, who makes time studies, insisted that there was plenty of time because the line speed had been slowed.

The hassle went on for several days, with experts from the union and the company continuing their bickering. The workers continued to protest. Then, in the face of threatened discipline, the workers backed down. A full-fledged crisis had been averted.

It was then, and only then, that Ed Hendrix breathed a sigh of relief. Mr. Hendrix is a foreman in charge of a 300-foot stretch of the Wixom assembly line, and, as such, he is very much the man in the middle in such crisis-threatening disputes. As Ford's man on the spot, it is up to Mr. Hendrix to battle the union, please his bosses and keep the pressure on his workers so that the company's Thunderbirds and Mark IVs will keep rolling off the line. And even after disputes are finally settled, and the union and top company officials have long forgotten the details, it is Mr. Hendrix who often must live with the consequent bitter feelings.

"The foreman is the punching bag," the 29-year-old Mr. Hendrix says. "You get your ears beat off from both sides of the fence."

But such are the facts of life for Ed Hendrix and the rest of the 8,000 or so assembly-line foremen in the 44 huge auto factories scattered across the country. They are men who are caught in the center of a system of tight discipline and relentless pressure—a system upon which the auto companies rely to keep the lines moving day and night, five or six days a week.

The system is getting harder and harder to maintain. Given the choice, many—perhaps most—workers on auto assembly lines would rather avoid the mechanical repetitive tasks that constitute their jobs. "You do this 250 to 350 times a day," says a bushy-haired young man screwing control panels to car doors. "It isn't a hard job. Just boring as hell."

The pressure on Ed Hendrix begins and ends with management's desire to achieve maximum production and profit without sacrificing quality. Specifically, Mr. Hendrix feels the pressure—indeed he expects it—from several sources: the general foreman, who is his immediate boss; the superintendent, who can promote him or fire him; other foremen, whose own workers are affected by the output of Mr. Hendrix' men; and the two inspectors who oversee his "zone."

But Ed Hendrix also applies his own pressure. "I drift along the line," he says. "I check the installations. If there is a problem, I talk to the operator." And he accepts no excuses from his workers. If prodding doesn't work, he calls in the union man. If discipline is necessary, he applies it. Yet he seems careful to always seek a balance—pushing hard enough to get the work done, but never so hard that he'll incur backlash from his men and the union.

Mr. Hendrix well understands the limits of his powers over his men. (It's easy to make a foreman look bad," says one of his workers. "Just screw up.") Although as a foreman he can prod and discipline, he can't fire, transfer or even grant a worker a day off for personal business without clearing it with someone higher up. What's more, the union representative with whom Mr. Hendrix deals can go over the foreman's head—and often does—with the result that some of Mr. Hendrix's decisions are overturned. "It happens," the foreman says. "No committeeman likes to see his man get disciplined."

One reason for a foreman's constant watchfulness is that hundreds of things can go wrong during an average day. There is the constant danger of industrial accidents. Workers may be absent, or late, or leave early without permission. Or they may run out of parts, a particularly crucial problem. On one occasion, for example, Mr. Hendrix himself ran to get some missing parts, even though he was risking a contract violation because the rules say foremen aren't supposed to do physical work. And, more often than not, one crisis will lead to another—an accident can lead to a worker shortage, which can lead to a supply problem.

And all the while, car after car after car goes by, for only in extreme emergencies does Mr. Hendrix hit a button and stop the line. He tries to avoid that action at all costs, explaining that it means idling 1,600 workers up and down the line—at $5 an hour each. Consequently, during his five years as a foreman, Mr. Hendrix has hit the button only a few times, preferring where possible to have workers chase after cars.

Nevertheless, Ed Hendrix is considered a better-than-average foreman by the men under his supervision. "He's reasonable and fair, and that's all I expect of a guy," says Tim Schoening, a worker in Mr. Hendrix's zone. Says another worker: "If you do your job, he leaves you alone."

Indeed, Mr. Hendrix says he tries not to get too close to his workers (one reason his home phone is unlisted). "I don't drink with them very often," he says. "Sometimes it is hard to be a friend and a foreman." And while he does talk to his workers while on the job, it is mostly about their parts supply and their tools. "I used to be scared of the men," he says. "But after a while, you get a thick skin. When you come through the door, you say, 'I've got a job to do. They've got a job to do.' You get so you can look 'em square in the eye."

That he does. For example, when a worker has trouble installing a screw and wants to skip it, Mr. Hendrix says: "That's a lot of crap. You don't walk to the next car as far as I'm concerned." Nor does he tolerate sloppiness, such as a worker leaving extra screws in the cars. "A penny apiece. That adds up," he says.

It is instincts like these that Ford admires and that have helped Mr. Hendrix shine in the eyes of C. Van Snyder, his superintendent. Mr. Snyder has 19 foremen working for him, five of whom, he says, are "moving around because they show potential for advancement." Ed Hendrix is one of the five.

Despite his progress the pressure still seems to get to Mr. Hendrix. He smokes constantly. He drinks black coffee all day long. When the line stops at 4:30 p.m., he can't click it off in his mind. "I carry it home," he says. "Some nights I don't sleep at all, worrying about where I'm going to get the men (the next morning). I let my wife listen to me. Sometimes I take it out on the kids." And he still wonders whether his job is secure. "You feel they may come down here and fire you because you can't run your own area," he says.

The shifts at the Wixon plant vary in length from eight to ten hours, depending on activity. When Mr. Hendrix works the day turn (he switches shifts every four months), he sometimes must get up as early as 4 a.m. and then doesn't get home again until 5:30 or 6 p.m.—usually dog-tired.

"Maybe one night a week I'll hit the rack at 8:30 or nine to catch up on my sleep," Mr. Hendrix says, adding that he was so tired driving home one Saturday that he fell asleep and collided with another car.

With all the disadvantages, why be a foreman? The answer, at least for Mr. Hendrix, is money. His salary in 1973 was about $13,000 a year, several thousand dollars more than he would make as an hourly worker. He also picked up an extra $5,000 from overtime, boosting his total annual income to more than $18,000.

He needs this money, Mr. Hendrix says. He has a sick daughter, which prevents his wife from working and has resulted in a pile of medical bills. Furthermore, the

Hendrixes like the possessions they can afford on a foreman's pay—part interest in a camper, a second car, two hunting dogs, a snowmobile, a new motorcycle.

But another reason that Ed Hendrix became a foreman was the chance to escape the line and become a part of management. "It was boring, stagnant, I wasn't creating anything," he says of his first job in an auto plant (as a paint sprayer for GM). Later he got a job as an inspector at the Wixom plant and subsequently was offered a chance to become a foreman.

"I felt I wasn't trained for it," says Mr. Hendrix, who is a high school graduate. But, he recalls, "they said they'd help me." Training consisted of one week's instruction (Ford requires two weeks now). However, Mr. Hendrix says that experience has been his best educator and that life as a foreman "never worked the way" the instructor said it would.

One thing a foreman soon learns is that no two days are exactly alike, yet there is a certain sameness that permeates Mr. Hendrix's working life. For most of the first hour of most days, he grapples with manpower problems. He needs 34 people to run his area and has a pool of four to six workers to tap when workers are missing.

His zone runs smoothest, of course, when he had his work slots filled with trained people. To maintain quality on days when trained workers are missing, he sometimes has to assign two substitutes to one job—one to keep track of the parts, the other to do the actual work—and then explain later why he exceeded his budgeted manpower. But on some Mondays, the manpower shortage becomes so acute that the plant closes down a half-hour in the morning and another half-hour in the afternoon so that the workers can get the six minutes an hour of relief time specified on their contract.

How should unexcused absenteeism be dealt with? Sternly, Mr. Hendrix believes; indeed if he had his way, he'd impose a one-day disciplinary layoff for unexcused absences rather than starting with 12 minutes off without pay, which he asserts is "much too slow."

Working within the rules, Mr. Hendrix nevertheless tries to be tough, calling an "AWOL" to his desk the morning the man returns to work. "I talk to him about why he was absent," Mr. Hendrix says, after which he says he calls the labor relations department to check the man's record. If the worker has missed one or two days, the foreman calls the union. "I have the committeeman talk to him to tell him he is heading for a disciplinary layoff," Mr. Hendrix says.

In one typical case, he planned to be tough with Rick, a 19-year-old installer of rear-window molding who had missed two days in a row and had been disciplined only a month earlier. In a hearing in the superintendent's office, Mr. Hendrix laid out his case against the pony-tailed worker, who seemed unimpressed by the proceedings. "They (company officials) do what they want anyhow," Rick grumbled at one point.

The union representative defended the worker, arguing that a disciplinary layoff wouldn't help to change Rick's attitude. In fact, even Mr. Snyder, the superintendent, seemed to think Rick should get another chance. And so, feeling somewhat undercut, Mr. Hendrix pocketed the discipline—an 18-minute penalty—but nevertheless kept in the back of his mind that the penalty could be served later in case of a further infraction.

Later, Mr. Hendrix said he had originally planned to tell the worker to take the rest of the day off without pay. But he didn't take this action when he learned during the hearing that the union official and the superintendent were friends of Rick's father, who also works in the plant. Then, too, Mr. Hendrix said, layoffs deprive the foreman of a trained worker; and because of the physically taxing nature of Rick's work—involving climbing in and out of cars—'it would take three days to train a man for the job and even then he wouldn't be real good."

Mr. Hendrix says his zone also suffers from contract abuses. For example, under the contract he isn't allowed to refuse any worker permission to go to the plant medical clinic; however, he says that some workers take advantage of this provision to shirk their jobs. But on their part, some of Mr. Hendrix's workers claim that he is paranoid on the subject of contract abuses. "He thinks everyone is out to screw him," one worker says. "He dreams some of it up. He wouldn't talk to one girl after she took a medical leave even though they used to talk and buy each other coffee."

In any case, Ed Hendrix feels that his workers might do well to follow his own example. During the past year, he says, he missed only one day—when there were two feet of snow on the ground. He adds that he would have been fetched at home by plant guards in a four-wheel drive truck if other workers hadn't been absent in such numbers that the plant eventually had to close down. But a foreman's life being what it is, Mr. Hendrix says that he was later called on the carpet for being absent.

—LAURENCE G. O'DONNELL

Union Committeeman

The woman on the assembly line at the big Ford Motor Co. plant in Wixom, Mich. was upset. The spray gun she was using was leaking all over her work apron, and the sealant solution squirting out of the nozzle was too thin and runny. She had complained to her foreman, but nothing had been done.

Then Charlie Bragg came strolling down the line, and things began to happen. After Mr. Bragg was apprised of the woman's problem, he had a conference with the foreman. Then he called the department responsible for fixing tools. In short order, the woman had a new nozzle and a new barrel of sealant.

Problems brought to Charlie Bragg's attention aren't always dispatched quite so expeditiously. Nevertheless, few fault him for lack of initiative. He might be called, in fact, "the fixer"—the man to whom workers can turn in times of trouble. For Mr. Bragg is the union committeeman in the plant's Thunderbird trim department, and he comes to the people on the line because they can't come to him.

Officially, the 37-year-old Mr. Bragg is a "district committeeman," a local official of the United Auto Workers Union, elected by the 287 people in his department at the Wixom assembly plant to serve as the full-time representative with management. (The company pays his salary). But unofficially, Mr. Bragg *is* the union to his people. He is the first and often the only union representative they deal with, and he is every bit as important to them as is Leonard Woodcock, the UAW president.

As one of the several thousand district committeemen in the nation's 44 auto assembly plants, Charlie Bragg is by no means unique. Neither is he typical, since union representatives' work often varies, even at the same location.

To some extent, the content of Mr. Bragg's work on a typical day is deceptive. While his fellow workers spend their time monotonously piecing together over 300 cars, their union representative seems to spend much of his time roaming around, slapping people on the back, chit-chatting and poking his head into unfinished cars to check things out. But it's all done for a purpose: finding problems.

"The main function of a committeeman is to settle problems right on the floor," Mr. Bragg says. "I'm a mediator, a foot-soldier out here. Without the committeemen, Ford couldn't run this plant."

Ford might dispute this assertion, but there is no denying that Mr. Bragg's meanderings uncover problems— or that he is the man on the spot. For while Mr. Woodcock and other union leaders are making speeches on such lofty topics as "dignity in the work place" or "shared decision-making," it is Charlie Bragg and the men like him who are fighting disciplinary actions, getting supply-racks fixed, arranging days off, getting bathrooms cleaned and drinking fountains unclogged. On an average day, Mr. Bragg handles about 20 individual problems.

In the course of attacking such problems, Mr. Bragg avoids threats and confrontations. His prime goal, he says, is keeping his constituents happy. But he also must remain on working terms with their supervisors, who, he feels, must regard him as tough, but flexible. Indeed, he uses his ultimate weapon—the formal, written grievance—sparingly; and he says he tries hardest to avert, rather than win, disciplinary cases.

"A grievance can just lie around for weeks," he says. "Meanwhile, the problem might be corrected anyway. What I want to do is take care of the problem—and do it quickly."

Take the case of the open ceiling vent that was blowing a draft of cool air on some workers. When informed of the problem, Mr. Bragg relayed it to the foreman whose "zone" was affected. Hours later, when he returned to the zone to find the vent still open, Mr. Bragg didn't yell. Nor did he write a health-and-safety grievance. Instead, he simply picked up the foreman's phone—in the foreman's presence—and called the necessary people. The vent was soon closed.

"You can get more by trying to find ways to get things done than by screaming," Mr. Bragg says.

Health and safety disputes—such as the vent problem—are serious business at Ford. Not only have they historically been a key factor in local strikes, but now, under new federal laws, they are subject to intervention by government inspectors. In fact, so anxious is the company to resolve them quickly that it issues a weekly list at Wixom of unresolved grievances in this area and meets weekly with the union to clear them up.

But crucial or not, health and safety problems must be sandwiched in among a wide variety of other activities in Charlie Bragg's day. Recently, for example, within the span of a few hours, he got a man's pay adjusted upwards, arranged for the reinstatement of a fired worker and saw that new tools were issued to two other workers. Then, later in the same day, he managed to get a planned disciplinary action against a worker dropped by convincing the man's supervisors that discipline would accomplish nothing. (The worker had stamped 19 cars with wrong serial numbers; the error, Mr. Bragg maintained, was inadvertent).

Then there is the problem of "standards" grievances. According to Mr. Bragg, these complaints—centered on the detailed definition of jobs on the line—supersede even health and safety problems as the toughest issue he must face. "Standards men are running our plant, and it's killing us," Mr. Bragg asserts. "In the old days, you had time to go to the bathroom if you wanted. Now, you need a relief man for that. You can't even breathe, these standards experts went to school, but they don't take the human factor into account."

Mr. Bragg maintains that Ford is constantly trying to

slash the allowed time and boost the required work for each job. Ford disputes this claim. Nevertheless, Mr. Bragg and the other committeemen carry stopwatches for the purpose of timing each assembly-line zone in their districts. If the speed is too high, they complain. (Conversely, however, Mr. Bragg kept quiet on one occasion when the line was moving too slowly.)

The committeemen also fight for workers who believe their jobs contain too many steps to fit the available time. Mr. Bragg, for example, recently handled such a complaint from a veteran worker assigned to put trim pieces on car doors. Timing the man, Mr. Bragg found that only 1.2 seconds were allowed for errors and tool changes between cars. Ford disputed the figure but finally agreed to delete a step from the job.

Such standards problems intensify several times a year, when line speeds or model mixtures are altered to conform with market conditions. Complaints soar during these periods, Mr. Bragg says. "Those are the times you wish you didn't have this job," he says. "You wish you could just crawl in a hole and hide."

But the standards problem isn't a headache only for the committeemen, Mr. Bragg insists. Eventually, he feels, it results in the bane of a plant manager's life: worker absenteeism. "These tight standards and the heavy over-time cause a lot of the absenteeism," Mr. Bragg says. "It's like a spider web to people. They're so tired when they get home, they can't even mow the lawn. So they miss the next day."

This isn't to say that Charlie Bragg believes his workers are always right. Indeed, on some occasions, he says, he is forced to make politically unpopular decisions. "I'm not afraid to tell a man when he's wrong," he says. "There's no sense fighting a fruitless battle. It just creates more problems."

That policy can have painful consequences, though, as Mr. Bragg has discovered. His only election opponent for the committeeman's position, he says, ran against him because of just such a case. "He was working a job installing back-window trim," Mr. Bragg recalls. "He said he didn't have enough time to do it, but I timed him, and he did. When I told him, he accused me of not doing my job."

Mr. Bragg generally tries to avoid such a contretemps by compromise. But in some cases, when this seems impossible between the principals involved, he tries other tactics—one of these being the ploy of playing one manager against another. For example, on one occasion he went all the way to the plant management level to get an unpaid leave for a man who wanted to go to Italy to get married.

"Most of my job is just common sense," Charlie Bragg says. But common sense doesn't always triumph, and Charlie Bragg doesn't always get his way. Recently, in fact, he lost two discipline cases in a row, both concerning absenteeism. Although he had tried to refute company records and had argued against tough penalties for the men, their records were poor. The most he could accomplish was to get their penalties reduced to probation—a temporary solution at best.

Another disappointment came when a carefully arranged compromise in a tough case dissolved because the worker involved decided to take things into his own hands. The man, a chronic absentee case, had suddenly been switched out of a choice job to one that was clearly less desirable. His foreman contended the move resulted from the man's attendance record; but the worker called Mr. Bragg to complain that the switch was really a retaliation because he had left early one day to take his wife home from the hospital.

Mr. Bragg carefully arranged a face-saving compromise in which the man would have been switched back to his old job on the understanding that he, Mr. Bragg, would counsel the worker and persuade him to mend his ways. But the arrangement was wrecked when the worker, before he learned of management's reversal, staged a one-man strike on his new job. Mr. Bragg, furious, berated the worker, but the issue was dead and the man returned to the less desired post.

Problems such as these, Mr. Bragg feels, wouldn't arise in the first place if there weren't bad foremen. "A bad foreman," he says, "is a guy who doesn't care about his people. All he cares about is just trying to get that dollar, and he lets his bosses or his employes run his area. He's inconsistent. He lets things run rampant for a while then tries to crack down all at once without being fair. Nobody respects him."

The real mark of a bad foreman, Mr. Bragg says, is to shunt work onto the shoulders of committeemen. In a case not long ago, he says, a foreman insisted that it was the committeeman's job to intervene in a feud between two workers—a job, Mr. Bragg asserts, that is properly that of the foreman. Nevertheless, he says, "the committeeman is finding himself more and more doing a foreman's work, because they say they're too busy, and they know we'll do it for the people."

On the other hand, Mr. Bragg admits, there are bad committeemen—men who write grievances simply to get workers off their backs or who wait until six months before an election to clear up long-overdue problems. To avoid these pitfalls, Mr. Bragg says that he makes it a point to follow up all requests as soon as possible and to be constantly available. "The natural thing," Mr. Bragg says, "is for a people to wonder, 'What's that son of a gun doing for me?' I try to make sure they see me every day so they know."

Mr. Bragg's vote-getting appeal—he won the last election by a six-to-one margin—indicates that his workers believe he is doing something for them. "He's an outstanding committeeman," says one. "He comes around and talks to you, and when he's paged, he'll make it there as quick as he can . . . He'll win some for you and he'll lose some, but the losses are always close." (The Wixom foremen also seem to respect Mr. Bragg—although their praise isn't always unqualified. "He's one of the better committeemen," says one, Ed Hendrix, "even though he and I don't get along." Mr. Hendrix adds: "He's on his side of the fence, and I'm on mine.")

If Mr. Bragg is the model of the confident committee-man these days, it wasn't always that way. In late 1970, when the president of his local union asked Mr. Bragg, then a repair worker and alternate committeeman, to step into a vacated post of a department committeeman, he wasn't sure he could do the job. "But everybody helped me," he recalls, "and I picked it up pretty fast."

For his efforts as a committeeman, Mr. Bragg earns about $14,000 a year (the same as he would be earning as a repairman); and during his 16 years at Wixom he and his wife (who used to work) have been able to save enough to afford a three-bedroom house, a swimming pool, a pickup-truck camper, and three Honda motorcycles—one for Mr. Bragg himself and one each for the Braggs' two sons, aged 17 and 15. In addition, the family has a red 1969 Pontiac Catalina which Mr. Bragg drives to work at Ford. (Why doesn't he drive a Ford car? "I like Pontiacs," he says.)

Mr. Bragg spends some time as a volunteer fireman and an active member of the Masons. He used to coach Little League baseball and play golf weekly, but he has had to give up those activities because of the time and presure of his union post. This time and pressure worries his wife, Sally, the high school sweetheart whom he married after graduation in 1955. "She's proud of my being a committee-man," Mr. Bragg says, "but she also says it's too time-demanding. She says it's wearing on me. I don't see it, but she does." He says that he isn't tempted by offers he has had to become a foreman. "I just don't feel comfortable in a white shirt and tie," he says.

—WALTER MOSSBERG

The Troubleshooter

It's a scene straight out of grade-B television drama.

The workmen are installing a huge, 40-foot-high stamping press that can exert up to 1,000 tons of pressure to shape metal. The work is hard, and tempers are short. A burly, irascible ironworker has increasingly shown his dislike for the forman's manner. Finally, reacting to one order, the ironworker explodes with a torrent of four-letter words. It looks like a fight.

Enter 46-year-old Whitey Lanham, a cigar-puffing model of calmness. He is a baldish, heavyset, muscular man, 5 feet 10 inches tall and weighing about 195 pounds. His hair is whitish gray, with thin sweeping sideburns. He wears a gray smock over his street clothes. A short steel ruler and a couple of cigars just out from its pockets. He somewhat resembles "Archie Bunker."

Acting as though unaware that two men are on the verge of slugging it out, Whitey takes a tack that has often worked for him. He turns his full attention to the job at hand, suggesting that if the crew were to lower one big part in a slightly different way, the task might be easier. Moments later, everyone is back at work. End of crisis.

For Whitey Lanham, machinist extraordinary, the role of unobtrusive peacemaker is just part of the job. He has come to Detroit to supervise the installation of the big press, a $250,000 item. His employer, USI Clearing division of U.S. Industries Inc. in Chicago, has sold it to Davis Tool & Engineering Co., a Detroit supplier of parts to auto makers and it is up to Whitey to see that the press is installed properly and works right.

The job requires all kinds of talents. Whitey functions not only as a peacemaker but also as a skilled field engineer, as a machine-design man, as a sales representative and even as a public-relations agent for his employer.

"That's the great thing about my job," Whitey says. "I never know what's coming next. One day it's one thing, and the next day it's something entirely different. Maybe one afternoon I'll be up to my elbows in dirt and grease, and that night I'll be having dinner with the president of the company that's buying the press."

While Whitey Lanham works for a machine-tool company, he has counterparts all over industrial America. These "roadmen," often called field service representatives, perform tasks as diverse as installing a computer, investigating a knotty service problem with a new jetliner engine or servicing a pump for an oil company. Basically, they install new machinery or equipment, make sure it begins operating properly and return later to troubleshoot if problems develop.

Because their jobs tend to be more complex than many, the Whitey Lanhams of the world are more than mere cogs in the industrial machine. Called roadmen because they spend so much time on the job away from home, such men rarely think there's anything special about what they're doing. But as a supplier's man dealing directly with major customers and their problems, the roadman is crucial to his company's reputation and its continued well-being.

Says George Pope, president of USI Clearing: "Whitey is our man on the spot to guarantee the integrity of the product. If he doesn't do the job right, we've lost the sale and will never sell the customer another press." James Inglis, chief engineer at Davis Tool, says Mr. Pope's appraisal is entirely correct. "If Whitey didn't do it right," he says, "we'd never buy another machine from Clearing."

At the outset, this job looks as if it will be routine. After arriving at the Davis Tool plant, in an industrial area west of downtown Detroit, Whitey makes a cautious prediction. "This machine should be pretty well assembled inside of a week," he says, "but it's difficult to know how long any job will take because I'm working with different men every week."

As it turns out, partly because of the men he is working with, the job takes more than two weeks.

The press weighs more than 140 tons. It has been assembled and was briefly operated before it left Clearing's plant in Chicago, but because of its size it was disassembled and shipped in parts to Davis Tool.

The actual installation is done by a local contractor hired by Davis. Usually such contractors get their workers from union hiring halls. Whitey hasn't any direct control over the contractor's men, but if their work doesn't satisfy him, the warranty on the press can be invalidated by Clearing.

Problems inherent in this modus operandi quickly become apparent. Says Whitey as he watches a half-dozen men already at work on initial assembly: "You can tell they're not millwrights by the way they handle tools. See, they're using pipe wrenches on finished metal." In fact, one of the men Whitey is referring to turns out to be a truck driver by trade.

If the men using the pipe wrenches were damaging important parts, Whitey would take the matter up with the contractor's foreman. But they aren't, so he diplomatically says nothing.

Tact is a large part of Whitey's job. Shortly after the flare-up between the ironworker and the foreman, Whitey finds himself sitting at the same lunch table with the ironworker at the boisterous L'Amour Lounge, a few blocks from Davis Tool. After gulping two big hamburgers, washed down by two boilermakers (whiskey chased by beer), the ironworker begin denouncing the foreman. Whitey listens politely but doesn't take sides. Almost imperceptibly he shifts the conversation to another subject.

(While Whitey is the model of decorum on the job and seems to be universally liked by both laborers and executives, his sharp tongue frequently gets him in trouble after work. When he made an insulting comment to a regular patron of a bar in a Holiday Inn in Detroit, the bartender asked him to leave immediately, calling his remark "extremely offensive.")

Whitey has always been called Whitey because of the color of his hair. Appropriately, in view of his muscular build, his given name is Hercules. He's tough, but not always as tough as he thinks. Over the years, he says, he has spent $5,000 getting his teeth fixed after barroom confrontations, quite an outlay for a man who, considering his responsibilities, gets a modest salary. Whitey, a member of the International Association of Machinists, makes $12,000 to $17,000 a year, depending on the amount of overtime.

Whitey estimates he spend 85% to 90% of his time away from home. If the job is a particularly long one, like the 26-month stay in Lordstown, Ohio, where he supervised installation of more than 100 Clearing presses at new General Motors plants in 1969-71, he often rents a small apartment.

His wife, Frances, sometimes visits him, and sometimes Whitey flies to their mobile home in Worth, Ill., a suburb southwest of Chicago, for the weekend. Other times, Whitey likes to fish ("My wife doesn't care what I do as long as I take her fishing," he says) and hunt (he mentions with pride that he bagged an eight-point buck on a hunting trip in the fall of 1972 in Illinois). He also likes to shoot pool, but he says he is so skilled at it that he has trouble finding a worthy opponent. Among other things, Whitey is not modest.

Like most traveling men, Whitey knows the liveliest bars in his territory, but his real passion in life is finding good restaurants. His prize discovery so far, he says, is an Italian restaurant called Colombo's in Parkersburg, W. Va. But wherever he is, he eats whatever strikes his fancy, regardless of price, although his expense account allows just $11.50 a day for meals and, except in unusual circumstances, makes no provision for entertainment.

"You shouldn't let price interfere with pleasure," he says.

Nor does he let pleasure interfere with work. At Davis

Tool, Whitey works long and hard, frequently consulting blueprints from his home office to be sure the massive parts are being put together correctly. Among other things, he explains, the bed of the press has to be perfectly level, and the parts must fit together with tolerances of no more than a few thousandths of an inch.

Supervising this kind of activity, Whitey frequently must be a machine-designed expert. After a huge upright is lowered through an opening in the roof, for instance, Whitey is busy checking its surface for nicks and other irregularities. In this case, he spots some nicks that would affect the machine's operation, and he insists that they be filed away before the upright is lowered into its final position.

When the foreman asks for advice on how to fit one of the large pieces, Whitey freely gives the advice, then watches in silence as the foreman proceeds to do it his own way. After a while, with the foreman getting nowhere, Whitey, in a friendly way, repeats his suggestions. This time the foreman follows them, and the job goes smoothly. Says James Demetral, vice president of manufacturing at Clearing:

"Whitey has to be a diplomat and not call them a bunch of dingbats. He has to lead them by showing them he knows what he's doing."

There is little question that he knows precisely what he's doing. He has been supervising the installation and repair of big presses for more than a dozen years, and during that time he has run into just about every problem imaginable. In fact, Mr. Demetral says Whitey's skill is so valued by some customers that they insist Clearing hold up shipment of their new presses until Whitey is free to supervise installation. Other customers, however, prefer one of the 15 other Clearing roadmen.

Often Whitey must operate as a field engineer. During the installation at Davis Tool, when an air accumulator wouldn't fit into the allotted space in the deep concrete pit where the press rests, it was Whitey's job to come up with a solution.

After discussing the problem with Davis Tool's engineering department and then outlining his proposed solution by telephone to Clearing's engineering department, Whitey got the go-ahead to alter the air accumulator so that it would operate in the space provided for it. The alternative would have been to order a new air accumulator, of different dimensions, and wait for its arrival.

Almost as often as he irons out technical problems, Whitey acts as an unofficial sales representative and public-relations man for Clearing. During the Davis Tool installation, he had lunch a number of times with members of the Davis family. Conversation centered on the job, but a good deal more was at stake, says Richard L. Davis, president.

"You tend to rate a supplier by what kind of man they send to supervise the installation and how knowledgeable they are," Mr. Davis says. "And that has a bearing on who you buy from the next time around."

Whitey says he has been offered a supervisor job in plant maintenance for an auto company, a job paying about $10,000 more a year than he makes. He turned it down, he says, because "your life isn't your own when you work for a big auto company; a lot of times, you're working every weekend."

"Money," Whitey says, "doesn't mean that much to me."

—WILLIAM S. HIERONYMOUS JR.

Part Four

PRACTICING THEIR SKILLS

Skills can be learned in college, such as those of astronomy, or they can be learned through years of experience, such as running a big paper-making machine or guiding a big ship into harbor. Either way, these skills are honed and are kept sharp through constant practice. More often than not, these skills are multifaceted; the men in charge of building the world's tallest skyscraper or drilling for oil in the high seas are required to be captains of their ships—literally and figuratively—as well as masters of their specialties.

The Stargazer

"My work," Jim Houck says, "is as useful as a piece of wilderness or a work of art. It's not going to dig a ditch for anyone. It's probably not even going to run someone's car, though there's always the chance that we might find something that will do that. But it's something that mankind can point to as an accomplishment."

It is also work that is painfully slow, frequently frustrating and, from time to time, fraught with mystery and intrigue. For James Houck is an astronomer, a ground-based outer-space explorer who spends most of his waking hours studying planets, stars, meteors and other heavenly bodies in an attempt to unravel the mysteries of the solar system. And as such, while the skyborne men of NASA go on to fame, if not fortune, the 32-year-old Mr. Houck, his feet rooted firmly on earth, will probably continue to labor in the comparative obscurity accorded all but a few of the world's astronomical community.

"I'm not in it for riches or public recognition," the young astronomer says. "If I were interested in that, I'd try to learn to play football, or something."

But in place of accolades are challenges and, some astronomers say, the excitement of discovery. Indeed, not since the age of Galileo (1564-1642) has there been such a period of rapid development in astronomy, the most ancient of the sciences and one that has excited man's imagination since human beings first took note of the heavens. And largely because of such advances, the oldest science in recent days has been attracting a flood of the world's youngest, most talented scientists, many of whom are helping to shed considerable new light on the nature of the universe and are consequently changing age-old conceptions.

"Every new discovery is a surprise," one astronomer

says. "Every new object found has embarrassed the hell out of everyone in the field, because they didn't imagine it as anything like that."

The surprises and the embarrassments have been particularly plentiful in recent years, when conceptions that held sway from the time of the ancient Greeks have been shown to be erroneous. Through the centuries, for example, the universe was viewed as an unchanging cosmos of fixed stars. Then, during the first few decades of the 20th Century, discoveries indicated that the galaxies of the universe were undergoing steady expansion and that each galaxy comprised a slowly rotating collection of stars interspersed with dust and gases. It was only during the last decade that the universe was shown to be much more violent than had ever been imagined—with exploding galaxies and quasars, high-energy particles almost everywhere, and magnetic fields.

The particular interest of Jim Houck is infrared astronomy; one of the newest, and some say the most exciting, areas in the field. Despite the fact that infrared radiation from the sun was discovered more than 170 years ago, only in the past decade did technology advance to the point that sensitive infrared detectors could be produced. And today only 30 of the country's 2,000 professional astronomers are infrared-radiation specialists.

In preparation for his specialized career, Mr. Houck majored in physics at Pittsburgh's Carnegie Tech, graduating with a bachelor-of-science degree, and then spent four and a half years at Cornell getting his doctorate. He joined Cornell's faculty as an assistant professor in 1968; and since that time he has pursued the answers to extraterrestrial questions on almost a full-time basis, usually rising about 7 a.m. and concluding his work late in the evening, often seven days a week.

Within his specialty, Mr. Houck's particular interest is the earliest stages of a star's birth. And in going about his work, contrary to what might be thought, he doesn't spend 12 hours a day peering through a telescope into outer space.

Rather, on a typical day he is found seated in his small, cluttered office pouring over data gathered by telescope-bearing rockers, airplanes or balloons—a necessary way of working in infrared radiation frequently doesn't penetrate the earth's opaque atmosphere, and penetration is particularly hampered by the high water-vapor content of East Coast air.

Much of Mr. Houck's office work involves setting up so-called models, or groups of assumptions about a particular stellar system. He has often spent weeks and months—sometimes even years—in tedious blackboard and computer calculations to explore the logical consequences of the assumptions underlying a particular model. The assumptions themselves are often borrowed from the work of other astronomers, and the calculations involve all the known laws of physics, chemistry and other sciences. In any case, the results can occasionally be frustrating.

"Science is a case of making a lot of false starts," Mr. Houck says. "Sometimes they pan out; often they don't. So you keep plugging away."

Most of Mr. Houck's research thus far has been collected by a helium-cooled infrared telescope, about six inches wide by three feet long, that was launched in a rocket from the White Sands (N.M.) Missile Site. However, the rocket, which was fired to a height of about 100 miles an hour on six occasions, crashed in July 1972. "She got creamed on the sixth flight," Mr. Houck says, pointing to a color photograph picturing a heap of what appears to be scrap metal lying in a grassy area. "The parachute never opened, so she just went kabloom."

The unfortunate equipment had been built over the better part of a year by Mr. Houck and other members of Cornell's astronomy department; it is being rebuilt, largely with new materials. But over and above this activity, Mr. Houck is director of the Cornell Observatory, something of a problem in itself since the bright lights from new dormitories and the almost constant nocturnal cloud cover in the Ithaca area have made night viewing almost impossible. ("We probably had a clear night at one time," Mr. Houck says. "But I don't remember just when.") For this reason, a new observatory is being built, under Mr. Houck's supervision, in a more secluded area.

Research, however, is Jim Houck's raison d'etre, and the framework of his studies is the so-called classical theory of how stars are born. To wit: Initially, there is a large cloud of gas and dust that first contracts and then fragments into separate entities; these "blobs" of matter continue to contract and eventually become either stars or planets. This theory, however, is simply a framework and lacks numerous details and explanations—gaps that Mr. Houck is hoping to help fill. "There are little bits of information each astronomer gathers in the hopes that the jigsaw puzzle will fit together," he says.

Mr. Houck has focused his telescopes on the dust clouds (scientifically designated H-II regions) that surround the stars in our galaxy rather than studying the stars themselves. The reason, he says, is that by collecting readings on the infrared radiation emitted by the dust clouds, he is able to draw conclusions about the properties of the stars they surround. Thus far, his research indicates that infrared radiation from very distant sources is much stronger than had been thought and that, consequently, the sources are considerably larger than had been expected.

While much of his research is based on data amassed by photometers and spectrometers attached to rocket-borne telescopes, Mr. Houck also from time to time assumes the classic pose of the astronomer and positions himself in front of a telescope in a ground-based observatory. But, he says, even when he is looking through a telescope, he really isn't seeing anything; rather he is merely focusing the equipment on sources from which he hopes to obtain infrared readings. In line with this part of his work, he spends a week about once every four months at the Mount Lemmon Observatory near Tucson, Ariz., where the atmosphere is more suitable for telescopic viewing than Ithaca.

Use of the Mount Lemmon telescope is free, but the Arizona excusions cost Mr. Houck and the graduate student who accompanies him about $1,000 in travel expenses for each trip—a fact that keeps his traveling limited. In 1972, he received $90,000 worth of federal and private funding, and counted on landing $100,000 in 1973. He adds, however, that the competition for contracts is getting keener every year and that red tape often means delays of up to nine months between the time funding is approved and the actual arrival of the money.

Out of Mr. Houck's research funds must come not only his traveling expenses but also the costs of materials for his telescopes, the costs of publishing the four or five papers he writes a year, the salaries of the technicians and graduate students who work with him, and half of his own salary. (He puts his total salary at "something like" $15,000 a year; the other half is picked up by Cornell.) "It's paying salaries for people," Mr. Houck says of the money being spent on astronomy. "It's not just being put in a hole and buried."

That may be, but federal funding for astronomy has stayed fairly constant in recent years, despite increased numbers of astronomers, and future slashes aren't ruled out. Indeed, more and more citizens are criticizing the advisability of spending money on space exploration of any kind at a time when dollars are urgently needed to combat earthly ills such as crime and poverty. And despite certain practical application of astronomical research—helium, for example, was first discovered on the sun and today plays a major role in industry—it is argued that, for the most part, astronomers merely compile data to satisfy human curiosity.

If the practical applications of astronomy often appear elusive, if not nonexistent, some astronomers take it all in stride. "I certainly can't claim we're the most relevant group of people," concedes Jesse Greenstein, professor of astrophysics at the California Institute of Technology. "But I must admit that if some astronomer received signals from outer space and warned everyone that the space people are coming with their three purple heads and their supersonic guns, we'd suddenly seem very relevant."

For Jim Houck, this type of relevance seems almost unimaginable. True, he says he is convinced that life exists on other planets; but he scoffs at the continuing flow of flying-saucer reports. "We're just not worth the attention" of extraterrestrial beings, he says. "We're just a mundane, junky planet. It's just not worth visiting."

This isn't to say, however, the Mr. Houck is unconcerned with the world around him. He believes, for example, that "too little money is being spent on domestic problems. For instance, I think more money should be spent on (fighting) pollution." And he further believes that such money could be made available without denting the nation's astronomy budget.

"There are a lot of pockets it can come from before you get to astronomy's pocket," he says. "The cost of a 200-inch telescope is less than the cost of a cloverleaf on an interstate highway. Yet there's only one 200-inch telescope. How many cloverleafs do you think there are?"

What's more, Mr. Houck believes that some of the money lavished on the U.S. manned space program could have been better spent on other research. "Too much time and money has been spent on it (in order) to make it seem glamorous," he says. "That's why people are bored with outer space. They see these four- or six-day spectaculars on television which nothing comes of. There's never any effort to explain to people the significance of this giant fireworks show."

Whether the end of the manned space program will divert funds to ground-based space observation remains to be seen. A study by the Astronomy Survey Committee of the National Academy of Sciences recommends that funding for basic astronomical research be increased by 5½% a year from the $270 million in fiscal 1973 to an average of $335 million a year over the next decade. Without increased funding, the report says, important progress in astronomy will be stalled at the threshold of success.

Even now, astronomical researchers say that schools have been having increasing problems bearing the costs of taking on young, up-and-coming astronomers. Cornell, for example, employs about 30 graduate students in the astronomy field, but the school expects the number to drop for monetary reasons. "The brightest people are being attracted to this field, but we can't accept them because of insufficient funding," says Martin Harwit, chairman of Cornell's astronomy department. "We now have to turn away students," Mr. Harwit adds, "where we never had to in the past. And we probably won't be able to retain as many as we do now."

Jim Houck's future at Cornell, however, seems assured. (He's excellent, Mr. Harwit says.) And unless astronomy's dollars dry up altogether, he will continue, as he puts it, to plug away. "I work about 80% of weekends," he says, "and I haven't had a vacation in five years." He adds that he wishes "there were more hours in a day" to afford greater time with his wife and two young sons.

If Mr. Houck plugs away long enough, he says, he thinks he'll make "an average contribution" to his field. He adds: "I might hit it lucky. I might make a significant contribution. But I won't be unhappy if I don't."

—N.R. KLEINFIELD

The Fossil Finder

With a red-handled ice pick, Jim Jensen chisels the outline of a bone from the Colorado mountainside, wisking aside with a small brush the flecks of grey dust that cover the purple-black fossil.

"Just look at that," he whispers, as the side of the 10-inch-long bone (which he identifies as belonging to the rib structure of a plant-eating dinosaur) takes shape in the mountain. "That's the first time light has shined on that bone in 140 million years."

Shedding light on old bones is James A. Jensen's job. The 55-year-old Mr. Jensen, curator of the Earth Science Museum at Utah's Brigham Young University, is a vertebrate paleontologist—a fossil and bone man—and his passion is discovering, preparing and reassembling the bones of dinosaurs, those fearsome reptiles of long ago whose numbers included the largest land animals ever to inhabit earth.

The last dinosaurs vanished, for reasons still unknown, some 70 million years ago. Yet public interest in them is very much alive. "People have always been interested in giants," says Edwin H. Colbert, curator emeritus of New York's American Museum of Natural History and a dinosaur authority, "and the dinosaurs are completely different from anything we have nowadays—they're records of a past which is completely gone."

Recovering that past is a tricky assignment, but one that fascinates Jim Jensen (who never graduated from high school, but holds an honorary doctorate of science from Brigham Young). Mr. Jensen is "a crackerjack man in the field," says John H. Ostrom, a professor at Yale and curator of vertebrate paleontology at its Peabody Museum of Natural History. "He's one of the best," he continues.

"He has a real nose for finding things, and he has gotten some beautiful specimens."

Most of Mr. Jensen's best finds have come from remote, windy Dry Mesa Quarry, perched on the shelf of a tree-studded plateau, high above the Escalante Valley on the rugged western slope of the Rocky Mountains. Here, a small team headed by Mr. Jensen has uncovered evidence of what may be at least seven new species of dinosaur, which would have roamed the land towards the end of the Jurassic period, more than 140 million years ago. That was before the birth of the Rockies, at a time when stream waters rushed over today's dusty mountainside and entombed the remains of many of the creatures of that age.

One of those creatures, which Mr. Jensen discovered, is the largest sauropod ever found, he says. (The sauropods were the four-footed, long-necked plant eaters, such as brontosaurus, that were the largest of the dinosaurs.) The "new" animal's shoulder blades were each eight feet long. The shortest of its neck vertebrae discovered stretched three feet, and the longest was almost five feet long.

Another find in the quarry was a huge meat eater that apparently was capable of killing the giant sauropods. The carnivore grew to a size unexpected for that point in earth history. It apparently was nearly as big as Tyrannosaurus rex—the last and largest known meat eater (which was about 18 feet tall, 50 feet long and may have weighed eight tons)—but the rock formation in which it was found indicates the animal lived some 40 million years before Tyrannosaurus rex.

To Mr. Jensen, such discoveries are the thrill of the hunt. "After all the bones I've dug up," he says, his eyes sparkling, "I still get excited when I see a new one."

The affable Mr. Jensen figures he has dug up the fossilized remains of more than 30 types of previously undiscovered, extinct animals over his career, and that includes "about a dozen" new dinosaurs. In the process, he adds, he has spent about 3 years sleeping in tents ("I'm sick of them," says Mr. Jensen, who now hauls along a trailer when possible). But given the effort, his success in finding new animal remains isn't all that surprising: The bones are there if one knows where and how to dig.

There's evidence that during their more than 100 million years on earth, dinosaurs thrived in most parts of the world, yet man's knowledge of them remains spotty. In some countries, such as the Soviet Union, dinosaur collecting currently is an active and well-supported field of scientific endeavor. But in the United States—which went through a frenzied period of dinosaur hunting in the late 19th and early 20th centuries—getting backing for such projects these days isn't easily done.

Dinosaur digs can be expensive, their logistics are staggering, and the bones they yield often are bigger than many institutions care to store or are equipped to reconstruct. To many funding sources, paleontology lacks the appeal of some of the more modern and practical sciences. "The museums like to have dinosaurs because they attract a lot of public support," says Mr. Colbert, who, since retiring from his post in New York, is a curator at the Museum of Northern Arizona, at Flaggstaff. "But the work on the big dinosaurs is fairly restricted now, mainly because of economics."

Mr. Jensen has resigned himself, for now, to hunting dinosaurs on a shoestring. When he first opened this quarry in 1972, he stretched a $20,000 budget (provided by Brigham Young and Sierra Club) over four and a half months; but in 1973 he wasn't able to raise the money for a return dig. In 1974, with a budget of about $10,000 mainly from Brigham Young, he has restricted himself to a month-long dig. Despite the financial headaches, new notes, "we've succeeded in finding new things and dragging home new bones."

Perhaps the most interesting bones that Mr. Jensen has dragged home recently have been those of the new carnivore, for now dubbed "the sauropod killer." They're being collected here, in the Uncompahgre National Forest, with the blessings of the Forest Service and the Smithsonian

Institution, which must approve digs on federal property. It was purely by chance that the giant animal's existence became known.

On Memorial Day 1971, Vivian and Eddie Jones, long-time rock hounds and friends of Mr. Jensen, sighted an unusual, fossilized bone while prospecting on a slope of the Uncompahgre Plateau, several hours' drive from their home in Delta, Colo. The Joneses previously had discovered three nearby dinosaur bone deposits (one of which yielded a seven-foot-long humerus, or upper arm, that's now on display at the Smithsonian), but they couldn't identify the new, pestle-shaped bone.

The reason soon became clear: The bone was unlike anything that ever had been found in these parts. Mr. Jensen examined the fossil while visiting the Joneses later that year, and identified it as the toe bone of an enormous carnivore—an animal larger than any meat eater known to have existed that far back in time. He quickly laid plans to see what other bones there might be in the area.

In the summer of 1972, Mr. Jensen and a small team from Brigham Young opened the quarry on the mountainside here, and throughout the summer they scoured the rock for fragments of dinosaur bone. The quarry was closed and filled in at season's end (to guard against scavengers), and it was left untouched until spring 1974, when a bulldozer reopened it.

The 1974 camp is pitched amid weathered pinon trees and knots of scrub oak. By 7:30 every morning, except Sundays, the crew—awakened by the clanging of a cowbell—is in the "bone hole" to start the long and tedious work day that doesn't end until 4:30.

Mr. Jensen has been aided by his field assistant and preparator, Ken Stadtman, and two college students. One is Kevin Maley, who is from New Jersey's Pomona State College and had expected desert instead of mountains; the other is Brooks Britt, a cheery 18-year-old from Brigham Young who runs five to 10 miles after work most days.

The four spread out over the quarry, which has been

dug about 20 feet into the mountainside and is about 25 feet long (the 1972 quarry, on whose site this year's dig is taking place, was about 300 feet long). With noisy pneumatic chisels, they dig into the soft clay of the Morrison rock formation in search of the bones. The quarry—which commands a magnificent view of the wild valley below—is hot and dusty, and the work is hard and sometimes frustrating (Kevin Maley was here a week before he found his first bone). No dogs are allowed.

When a bone is spotted, the worker carefully whittles away the clay and rock around it with a trowel or ice pick, cleaning off loose fragments with a whisk broom or brush. A coat of shellac is applied to harden the fossil, and the bone is tentatively identified, if possible.

Smaller bones, if they're well positioned, often can be carved out of the quarry completely and held together by shellac, surrounding rock or Elmer's glue. Larger bones, however, usually are wrapped in a protective plaster cast for removal and transporting by truck to Mr. Jensen's "bone barn" or to his laboratory, which is on campus in Provo, Utah.

In the lab, bones are cleaned, reassembled and identified, and the better specimens may be readied for display. (The scale of things is indicated by the lab equipment, which includes a block and tackle for moving bones, which can weigh tons.; The huge dinosaur skeletons that one sees in many museums usually are crafted over a framework of pipe, and Mr. Jensen prides himself on his skill in concealing the framework in his skeletons. Missing bones are filled in with plaster replicas.

Dinosaurs have been Jim Jensen's love since boyhood, when he began to collect and identify fossils in the mountains surrounding his Utah home. But it wasn't until 1956 that he got into paleontology full-time. That year—after a string of colorful jobs, ranging from longshoreman to dress designer, and membership in four unions—Mr. Jensen joined the staff of Harvard's Museum of Comparative Zoology. In 1961, he returned to Utah at the invitation of Brigham Young University to launch a program of vertebrate paleontology there.

In a 1969 National Science Foundation-backed trek to Antarctica, Mr. Jensen—as a member of a research team—collected a fossilized tooth that has been taken to indicate that Antarctica, Africa and South America once were linked as a land mass.

(That same year, Mr. Jensen published a controversial scientific tract holding that ostriches aren't birds at all, but are "feathered reptiles." Likewise the emu, the rhea, the cassowary and the apteryx, he said.)

Mr. Jensen makes it clear that, for him, the thrill of his quest is in uncovering the past. "When your eyes are the first eyes to set sight on anything, it's exciting," he explains. "When Balboa first saw the Pacific, it had always been there—but it still was exciting to discover it for the first time."

—ERIC MORGENTHALER

A Tall Order

Wearing a hardhat, suit and tie and mud-spattered loafers, burly Ray Worley hurried to the nearest phone on the 92nd floor of the unfinished skyscraper. Hands thrust into his pants pockets, he cradled the receiver on his shoulder, seemingly unaware of the bone-chilling winds whipping across the open floor.

"What d'ya mean that's not your work," he screamed, after a few seconds of conversation. "Don't tell me what's in your contract. My building is falling behind schedule, and you give me nothing but excuses." Without waiting for a reply, he slammed down the phone and charged off to check on another aspect of "his" building.

The target of the verbal assault was one of the more than 60 subcontractors building the 110-story Sears Tower just west of the "Loop" in Chicago. When it was completed in 1974, it became the headquarters for Sears, Roebuck & Co., the world's largest merchandiser. The 1,450-foot structure is the world's tallest building, topping New York's World Trade Center towers by 100 feet, and the world's largest private office building.

As general superintendent for the building's general contractor, Diesel Construction, a division of Carl A. Morse Inc. of New York, 42-year-old Ray Worley was responsible for coordinating more than 1,600 construction workers and hundreds of truckloads of materials that arrived each day at the cluttered two-block site. In brief, his job was to see to it that the building got built right and on time.

"If you think of the building as a ship, Worley is the captain," says Richard Halpern, Diesel senior vice president who had over all responsibility for the project. "My office staff has to furnish the ship and keep it supplied. Ray's field staff takes the raw materials and makes sure they all fit together so that everything goes smoothly."

Ray Worley is one of an elite breed of construction men who are part executive, part hardhat. Every major construction company has one "general super," and the bigger ones have several. Diesel, for instance, has two, each responsible for buildings in a section of the country. Ray's territory extends from Ohio to the Rocky Mountains.

Seeing that things turned out right at the Sears building site was no mean task. The building contains 74,000 tons of steel, four million pounds of aluminum, 145,000 light fixtures, 1,500 miles of electrical wiring, 80 miles of elevator cable, 25 miles of plumbing pipe and the equivalent of 28 acres of outside aluminum wall or "skin." Its 101 acres of concrete floor could pave 78 football fields; its 17,000-ton refrigeration system is enough to air-condition more than 6,000 average six-room homes. Its power center would serve a city larger than Rockford, Ill., the state's second largest city.

All this arrived at the site by truck, and because there was little space for storage it had to be used almost immediately to avoid a monumental foulup. Added to these logistical problems were those posed by labor unions, subcontractors, safety inspectors and the whims of the owners. "I'm a pusher—a screamer and a yeller," says Ray, who stands six feet tall and weighs 290 pounds but never seems to slow down or to be out of breath. "If I didn't operate this way, men would be getting in each other's way, jobs wouldn't be getting done and this building would never get built."

Says Carl A. Morse, chairman of the company that bears his name: "As the general contractor our prime objective is to save our clients time and money through efficient management. The fact that Ray Worley is on the Sears job says a lot about his ability to accomplish these goals."

Few men in the industry work as hard as Ray Worley. He usually left his four-bedroom suburban home in Buffalo Grove, Ill., around 5:45 a.m. and, with light traffic on the expressways, arrived at his office across from the

Sears site about 6:30. He didn't stay in the office long. He "walked" the job at least twice a day—once in the morning and once in the afternoon. In addition, he sometimes was required to attend one or two meetings during the week with Sears executives—hence the coat and tie. He rarely got home before 8 p.m., and he worked a full eight hours on Saturday.

"The Sears job isn't really any different than others Ray has worked on," says his wife, Joan. "Ray has always worked long hours. In fact, if there aren't projects to work on he starts to get antsy." When Joan was delivering the older of their two daughters, Ray left the hospital to report to a job site. "I'm not a doctor," he says. "I can't deliver a baby, but I was the only man who knew" certain things about a job, "and they needed me."

When Ray walks through the building, he doesn't check every floor, only those at a critical stage of construction. Even with 1,600 men on the job, some floors may have only one or two men working, while others are buzzing with men and equipment. A quick walk around the floor, a few words to a foreman and Ray has made mental notes of things that need checking and follow-up calls that have to be made.

On the 73rd floor, where a crew of men one day were spraying a synthetic fire-proofing material on steel beams and concrete forms, Ray noticed that the residue from the spraying wasn't swept up in one area. He called both his foreman and the subcontractor's foreman over. "That's your work," Ray told the subcontractor. After the foreman balked, Ray told him in no uncertain terms: "Clean up the mess or I turn off the heat up here. It's up to you." After the job was completed, he explained, "Work progresses much better on a clean floor."

A superintendent needs a thorough knowledge of the subcontractors' contracts and of union rules. "The super's role has changed a great deal," says Diesel's steel super Al Belda, who worked on the antennas atop the Empire State Building in the late 1930s and has worked on many major high-rise office buildings since then. "If a man wasn't working, you could fire him on the spot and there would be 10 men ready to take his place. Now, you have unions and work rules, and if you're not knowledgeable enough they'll take advantage of you."

Ray says philosophically, "You can't control all the men on a job—where they go for lunch, how many beers they have. About 50% of the men take pride in their work and the fact they're on the Sears Tower, but to the rest it's just another job."

Ray seldom passes a man without some greeting. He knows many of the workers by name. "Buildings are built by a lot of people doing their thing and you have to understand them," he says. "Construction people don't like to punch timeclocks, and they work under hazardous conditions. If you're going to holler at these guys, you have to turn around and take them out for a drink now and then."

Ray Worley was born and raised in St. Louis. His father was a structural ironworker and, Ray says, "one of the best riggers in the country, but just about as nutty as ironworkers are today." Ray says his father "boomed" all over the country, living in apartments near the job, while the family stayed in St. Louis. After graduating from high school, Ray got some work through the Ironworkers local union when it needed extra help. "My father would fire me whenever he came into town, because he didn't want me to be an ironworker, but I always knew I wanted to go into construction," he recalls.

At 18, Ray enlisted in the Army and ended up at Ft. Hood, Texas, playing football while ostensibly in the artillery. After the service, he returned to St. Louis, married and worked during the day as a surveyor for a large contractor. He went to college three nights a week and attended Army Reserve meetings one night a week. The construction firm transferred him to New Jersey after several months. "They thought I would make a great cost engineer," says Ray, "But I drove the accountants nuts."

After a stint with another large general contractor and several more years of night school, Ray joined Diesel in 1957 with a civil engineering degree and seven years of experience in the industry. By the time he was 28, he was the superintendent on a 19-story building. Since then, he has worked on nearly a dozen high-rise buildings.

"The company has asked me to move to the office, but I'd rather stay in the field," says Ray. "Halpern gets his kicks from negotiating a contract, I get mine from coordinating it until there's a finished product. I enjoy being on a building where you have some goofy problems and can feel some sense of accomplishment." Even in the field, Ray makes a lot of money. Mr. Halpern, his boss, says Ray was "in the $40,000 class last year (1972) and will make more than $50,000 this year (1973)."

Ray's biggest problem on the Sears Tower was the weather. The building originally was scheduled to be topped out and all concrete poured by late in 1972, but a 17-week strike of elevator installers in the summer of 1972 halted work on the project and forced critical steel work on the upper stories into another Chicago winter. Between September and the end of December 1972, U.S. Steel Corp.'s American Bridge Division, which fabricated and erected the steel, lost more than 40 workdays on the site because of bad weather. Ironworkers can't work when it rains or snows, when it is too windy or when the temperature falls below 10 degrees; it's simply too dangerous.

In good weather, "Bridge" can put up two floors a week but because of an unusually long stretch of bad weather early in 1973, steel work was bogged down on the 92nd floor. If the steel isn't up, it delays laying the concrete floors. If the concrete can't be poured, the fire-proofing can't be sprayed, the curtain-wall men can't put up the aluminum skin and hundreds of tradesmen needed to finish the interior can't work.

"You expect bad weather, but not this bad," Ray moaned. "We've nearly caught up on everything. I had to send about 200 men home for two days recently. In Chicago, you get used to getting up, calling the weather bureau and crying every morning."

Despite the strikes and bad weather, William A. Toombs, Sears' man in charge of the project, said that "Construction costs are within 1% of our original budget." Officially, the retailer says its headquarters cost "in excess of $150 million." A Sears officer initially put the figure at "more than $100 million," but one source close to the project says, "Someone realized that would only take us up to the 50th floor."

Sears kept track of the costs required to make all the material, deliver it to the site and arrange it in the building. It used a computer program called the "Critical Path Methods" of job scheduling. A master plan was issued, and each subcontractor was interviewed every two to four weeks to update the printout. While Sears thought the method is "important" to its monitoring the project, Ray tended to downplay it. "The Critical Path Method works well in everything but sex and construction," Ray said. "I don't need a computer to tell me when the job is slipping."

If Ray can cut down on construction time, he saves everyone money. "If I can get the subs out of here ahead of schedule, I'm saving them overhead and increasing their profit and they cry all the way to the bank," he said. "Also, the sooner we get Sears moved in and the building finished, the sooner Sears can start collecting rent." Sears occupies about two million square feet with 1.7 million available for outside tenants.

But Ray is more than a pusher. The subs look to him for advice, and he often was called upon to solve problems that occur daily on a project of this size. "If there's a frozen water pipe or some materials don't get to the site on time, they come after me and I have to decide whether to lay some men off or find something else for them to do," Ray said. "In the meantime, 40 men, each making over $10 an hour, are standing around. You can't hold up the job, but if you make the wrong decision it can be multiplied by 110 floors."

Ray's an innovator, too. He designed a system for removing trash from the building, using specially designed carts that fit on the front of lifting machines. One of his ideas on the Sears building even resulted in a patent. Normally, electric and telephone lines are installed in floor channels or conduits, but access points to these lines are covered over when interior walls are later erected. To reach these points, the electrician or telphone installer had to punch holes in the walls, but Ray invented an inexpensive, metal box-like device to plug the access points, allowing easy entry without damage to the walls.

Safety, too, must be considered. "You hope you can make it through a project without a serious accident," Ray says. One ironworker was killed when he fell off a beam and landed on his head two floors below. Normally, there are nets to catch anyone who might fall, but they had been taken down that day to allow movement of a derrick.

"The government has just started issuing citations to the subs after an inspection last summer," he says. "There were only 61 minor violations and one major one. That's not many for a job this size. Some were rather small and nit-picky, which indicates to us that we have a safe job." The wail of an ambulance siren on the street below sent Ray running to the window. "Keep goin' you S.O.B.," he mutters.

That night, only a few miles out on the Kennedy Expressway on his way home, Ray picked up the mobile telephone in his 1972 Chevy station wagon and called the night superintendent in the Sears Tower, reminding him of several things that were to be done before the midnight shift reported to work. Finally home, he ate dinner alone and "relaxed" by working on remodeling his basement until two in the morning.

"The building begins to live and breathe after a while, and it's hard not to bring the problems home with you," Ray acknowledged. "But when I work around the house I don't plan ahead and I let my wife make the decisions about what kind of wallpaper to hang in the john." Just then, a shifting wind rattled a nearby window and Ray said, "I hope it's a dry, clear day tomorrow."

—TERRY P. BROWN

Offshore Oilman

Visibly tired and cold, Joe Fry enters the fourth hour of a frustrating vigil at the drilling controls of the Sedco J, a giant three-legged steel spider floating in 300 feet of choppy Canadian Atlantic some 180 miles off Halifax, Nova Scotia.

From a platform above a windswept deck larger than a football field, a muddy drill pipe rotates downward several feet, grinds away at an obstruction two miles beneath the ocean floor and then rotates back up again amidst the scream of winch and cable. The monotonous process, controlled by Mr. Fry through the maze of levers and knobs around him, is repeated over and over. It seems to get nowhere.

Then without warning, the rhythmic pattern is broken. Instead of rotating back out of the hole in the drill floor, the pipe plunges further downward, shuddering as it goes. Mr. Fry's face breaks into a grin, his first real smile in two days. "We've done it," he exclaims. "We've gone all the way through."

Tackling a difficult problem—in this case, obstructions in an exploratory well that had threatened lengthy drilling delays—and solving it through perseverance and know-how is what Joe Fry is paid more than $20,000 a year to do. He is a tool pusher, which is oil-field jargon for drilling-rig superintendent. For 30 years, Mr. Fry has helped drill oil and gas wells from south Texas to Indonesia.

Oil and gas exploration is pushing further offshore and into increasingly remote areas of the globe to slake the energy thirst of bustling nations. Mr. Fry, age 49, like his tool-pusher counterparts in the tropics of the Far East or the treacherous North Sea, is facing some of the toughest challenges of his career.

For one thing, both the waters and the weather in this area of the Atlantic are among the most unpredictable in the world. Overnight, calm seas and light winds can turn into 50-foot swells and 80-mile-an-hour gales. Floating ice poses a serious threat to navigation; in 1973, crewmen hastily weighed anchor and towed the Sedco J from a location off Newfoundland when ice packs that could trap and crush the 10,000-ton rig swept into the area. Spring fogs, replacing winter snows, chop visibility to a few feet from a few miles in a matter of hours. Anyone unlucky enough to fall into the 34-degree seas must be rescued within about 15 minutes or perish.

In this rugged marine environment, oil and gas companies have drilled more than 70 exploratory wells since 1969. Some of these wells have turned up oil and gas. However, none is producing because oilmen don't believe enough reserves have been found yet to justify the heavy expense of production and storage facilities.

Thus the search, which itself is not cheap, continues. Mobil Oil Canada Ltd., the Canadian arm of Mobil Oil Corp., and its partners are laying out more than $45,000 a day to keep the Sedco J drilling. About half that amount goes for keeping a supply ship nearby, services such as deep-sea divers, and purchases of the pipe, cement and chemicals needed to drill. The remainder is the fee paid to Sedco Inc., a Dallas-based international drilling-contracting firm that owns the rig and employs Mr. Fry and other members of his crew.

For one week out of every two, Mr. Fry labors to make sure Mobil gets it money's worth from the Sedco J, shouldering responsibility both for the $20 million rig and for the safety and discipline of its 60 workers.

The schedule might appear less demanding than the one imposed on most other crew members, who stay on the rig two weeks out of every three, working 12-hour shifts each day they are aboard. However, during his week, Mr. Fry is on call 24 hours a day, meaning that when problems arise sleep becomes a luxury. In the course of one particularly busy day, Mr. Fry didn't get to bed until nearly 2 a.m. Only three hours later, he was up, dressed and, with a cup of hot coffee in hand, back on the job again.

Clearly a man happy in his work, Mr. Fry says the job has been getting "more exciting" since he first began working offshore in 1963. "My big worry now is getting too old too fast," he explains. "I don't want to miss out on the things this industry will be doing in the next several years."

At the beginning of one stint, Mr. Fry arrives at a hangar near the Halifax airport nearly three hours early to await the chartered helicopter that makes daily runs— weather permitting—to the rig. Dressed in street shoes, slacks, sport shirt and cardigan sweater, the burly (six feet tall, 195 pounds) Texan, with his suitcase and tinted glasses, looks more like a tourist than the boss of an oil rig. Only the missing ring finger on his left hand—lost in a 1951 drilling accident—hints that his occupation isn't ordinary.

The 90-minute flight is uneventful, and most of the other passengers—all wearing bright orange water-survival suits over their clothing—gaze idly at the white-capped Atlantic below. Mr. Fry, however, is already on the job, using the time to confer with a Mobil foreman who is coming to oversee the rig's progress.

Landing at the Sedco J, Mr. Fry immediately hands over the packet of mail for the crew he has brought from shore. In an aside to a visitor, he explains the "three ethics of the oil field—you don't fool with a man's mail, his paycheck or his wife." Next he confers briefly with the tool pusher he is relieving, and then radio his status report back to shore. Changing into work clothes, boots, a well-worn jacket and hard hat, Mr. Fry prepares for an inspection tour.

The first stop is the drilling area itself. To reach it, Mr. Fry must cross about 40 feet of open deck and then climb 24 metal stairs. He does so easily, tilting his body into the 45-mile-an-hour wind to keep balance. Only when a newcomer tries it does the simple task become difficult. The stinging wind, with its subzero-degree chill factor, produces instant tears, making vision bleary at best. The deck is spotted with patches of ice, and even thought the 28-foot waves pitch the rig only three or four degrees, the combined effect is a lot of slipping and sliding. A nearby crewman, amused by the spectacle, calls out, "Just like Florida, eh?"

Despite the weather, the drilling floor is bustling with activity. In an operation, known as "tripping," pipe is rapidly being pulled up from the bottom of the well hole in order to change a drilling tool. As each 90-foot interval of pipe appears above deck, four men, their faces splattered with mud, wrap it with chains and attach huge metal tongs to it. Backs bent and muscles straining, they then work to unscrew the section. Once that is completed, the unhooked pipe section, still suspended by a cable from the derrick above, is shoved and pulled over to a rack for temporary storage. As the next interval is brought up to the floor, the grueling process is repeated.

Men work this hard on drilling rigs on land, but seldom under these conditions. Drilling operations here are suspended only when winds exceed 60 miles an hour and waves run above the 45-foot level. "We operate in weather which would shut down most other kinds of offshore rigs," Mr. Fry says.

Salaries of the Sedco J's crew members—almost all of them Canadians—range from $13,000 a year for maintenance men—the lowest category in a crew and the rank at which most begin their oil-field careers—up to $20,000 a year for the experienced men who operate the drilling controls. The rewards can be even greater for those promoted to tool-pusher supervisors. "It's one of the few jobs left where a man with an eighth-grade education can end up making $25,000 to $30,000 a year," says A.R. Kelley, who heads all Sedco operations off eastern Canada.

Living conditions aboard the Sedco J aren't bad either. Four hot meals a day are served by a catering service in the galley. (Sample fare: chowder, halibut steak, vegetables, french fries, assorted pies and ice cream.) Movies are shown in the recreation room at night. The drill crews don't even have to make their own beds; that's done daily by the caterers, who also clean each of the four-man, nine-by-16-foot sleeping quarters. These amenities are provided the crew free of charge.

There are rules to be obeyed. Among them: no liquor, no drugs and no horseplay. And while no one disputes oil-field workers' reputation for playing hard while they work, Mr. Fry encounters few violations. "After 12 hours on the drill floor, a man doesn't want to do much except take a shower and go to bed," he points out.

Nor are these men subjected to the brusk, sometimes high-handed "do it or go to town" treatment often accorded oil-field workers in Mr. Fry's younger days. Although he does "a little ass-chewing" when a mistake is made, and will fire a man who errs too often, the soft-spoken tool pusher prefers to use diplomacy to get things done. "You just can't demand that somebody do something," he exlains, "when it's easier to go through the back door, plant the seed of an idea and let them believe that they thought of it first."

Unlike his counterparts on land, Mr. Fry has responsibilities stretching far beyond supervising drilling operations. Aboard the Sedco J, he is also master of a vessel that stays afloat by using the same technique that raises and lowers a submarine. Three caissons at each point of the triangular deck extend down below the water line to submerged pontoons. If the rig needs to be raised further above sea level, water ballast is pumped from each pontoon, increasing buoyancy. When under tow, the Sedco J is controlled from a bridge like one that might be found on any large, oceangoing vessel.

These nautical aspects of the Sedco J's operation are more fun than work for Mr. Fry, who admits to a boyhood desire to go to sea. But if anything goes seriously awry out here, the consequences could be severe indeed.

For instance, oil spills are closely guarded against—neither Mobil nor any other oil company wants a repeat of the adverse public reaction that followed the 1969 spill in

California's Santa Barbara channel. But if one does occur? "Let's just say that a tool pusher with a spill on his record won't have much of a career left," Mr. Fry says.

If a well goes wild and catches fire, the crew can hardly run away on foot. So the Sedco J is equipped with two saucer-shaped survival "capsules" that are each capable of sustaining 28 men for five days on the water, two similarly equipped enclosed lifeboats, four inflatable life rafts and an assortment of life jackets and life rings. As an added precaution, a supply ship stands nearby around the clock.

Mr. Fry, who drills the crew once a week in escape procedures, professes not to worry too much about a catastrophe. "We've got back-up systems that back up the back-up systems," he says.

During his week off, with his wife, Desley, and two children at their comfortable, three-bedroom home in Dartmouth, Nova Scotia, the tool pusher claims he doesn't worry much about the rig at all. "I've learned to turn it off," he says. In those seven days, Joe and Desley, an Australian he met and married while drilling offshore of Queensland nearly seven years ago, occupy their time much as any suburban, middle-class couple here would. They occasionally attend curling matches—a shuffleboard-type game played on ice—or meet with friends for a quiet evening.

But he has thought about the unthinkable. His wife confides, "Joe doesn't talk about it much but I know that if something did go wrong out there he wouldn't leave that rig until he knew all the other men were off."

—DANFORTH W. AUSTIN

Man of the World

Pan Am pilot Douglas M. Moody, waiting for takeoff clearance, glances out the jumbo jet's cockpit 30 feet above ground and spots a small executive plane approaching his left wing.

"He's getting too close," mutters Captain Moody. "Too close. Damn, we're going to blow him right out of here if he doesn't watch out."

It's a moderately busy morning at Heathrow Airport's Runway 28-left near London, where Capt. Moody's Pan American World Airways Boeing 747 and seven other planes are milling about. To an experienced pilot, like Capt. Moody, the straying executive plane is only a minor hazard. Nevertheless, the incident contributes its bit to the cumulative pressures that are attendant to piloting an airliner these days—pressures induced by worrying about late takeoffs, malfunctioning radios, sudden bad weather or, more and more in recent years, the possible presence of hijackers and hidden bombs.

Fatal crashes involving scheduled airlines have risen sharply of late. In 1972, such accidents soared to 41 from 33 a year before, the death toll climbing to 1,285 from 967. As usual, "pilot error" was blamed for the majority of crashes. The pilots involved, of course, rarely survived to defend themselves. But other pilots say they're increasingly fatigued by trips of 10 hours or more in cramped cockpits, their bodies strained by shifting time zones and inadequate rest between flights.

Capt. Moody is paid about $60,000 for flying 900 hours a year. To some, his life seems glamorous; certainly, it is much-traveled. But a few days with Capt. Moody reveal that, glamor and travel aside, a senior pilot for a world-wide carrier is faced with strenuous demands—not the least of which is being entrusted with the lives of hundreds of passengers while subject to heavy physical and mental fatigue.

This particular week in Doug Moody's work life begins on a slightly sour note. After a two-hour drive from his home in Darien, Conn., he arrives at New York's Kennedy Airport to find Pan Am Flight 602, destination London, delayed 17 minutes by a late cargo of baby chicks. To the dismay of some ground staff, the pilot insists the exact departure time be recorded. (A 14-minute delay wouldn't have counted officially as late.) "It's for their own good to have the right time put down," he says. "Might as well correct whatever delayed us for next time." But aided by strong tail winds, the flight arrives five minutes early in London anyway. The time in England is 6:35 a.m.

In Pan Am's operations room, where he drops off the flight log, Capt. Moody bumps into a fellow pilot who good-naturedly accuses him of being a golf hustler. Capt. Moody, tan, tall, slim and everyone's handsome ideal of a pilot, breaks into a smile that makes him look younger than his 55 years. His tan was partially acquired the previous week in Bermuda, where he won a golf trophy.

"Watch out for those Arabs," Capt. Moody needles his colleague, who'll pilot the same jumbo jet to Istanbul and Beirut that morning.

Then he hurries to the bus waiting to ferry him and other Flight 002 crew members to the nearby Skyline Motel. "Can't keep the girls waiting any longer," he says. Apologizing to the dozen stewardesses, he climbs aboard. They sit glumly, accustomed to waiting for the cockpit crew.

After an all-night flight, Capt. Moody must make an important decision. Although it's 7:30 a.m. in London, it's still the middle of the night for his New York-attuned body and he could easily sleep for seven hours. In that case, however, he might have trouble sleeping that night and wouldn't be rested the next morning, when he's scheduled to pilot Flight 101, Pan Am's 11 a.m. plane from London to New York. He decides to skip breakfast and retires for a nap until noon, when he'll lunch and, he hopes, make a quick transition to his present surroundings.

Other pilots seek different solutions to the rest problem. "There's no right answer," according to James Waugh, a pilot in charge of Pan Am's flight standards. "Some pilots skip the daytime nap entirely. Others need a longer one to catch up. We think it's up to the individual to decide for himself."

A pilot's circadian rhythm, his 24-hour biological inner clock, is constantly disrupted in this way. Dr. Kenneth G. Bergin, a British specialist in medical problems relating to aviation, says flying through time zones contributes to the stress and fatigue a pilot undergoes. What's more, pilots don't become accustomed to sleep deprivation. Dr. Bergin once accurately forecast the time and place of a fatal aircraft accident, which came "at a difficult airport after an all-night flight from a place where pilots couldn't rest adequately before takeoff." Dr. Bergin has no doubt that "there is a very real relationship between the fatigue, pilot error and accident rates.

Doug Moody's fatigue following his New York-to-London hop seems to be gone after his nap. In slacks and a natty sports jacket, he leaves the motel at 12:30 and strides off for lunch at a pub that he claims is a 10-minute-stroll away. The "stroll" develops into a half-hour hike. "After all that time on my rear, I enjoy walking," he says. In addition to golf, he rides a bike and exercises by standing on his head for a few minutes daily. "That could be dangerous," he admits. "One Pan Am pilot had a heart attack doing that and broke his neck."

(The strict medical standards imposed on would-be aviators mean that pilots as a class enjoy better than average health. The Federal Aviation Agency requires two stiff physical exams a year, and Pan Am has its own annual checkup.)

After an unhurried pub lunch, Doug walks back to the Skyline for an afternoon of gossip with other airmen. He dips into a book called "The Only Way to Cross'—a testimonial not to the marvels of flights but to the by-gone era of ocean travel. The one-day London layover doesn't tempt him into the 40-minute trip to town. A couple of drinks, a roast beef dinner and he retires before 10 p.m. "All that stuff about air crews partying up is nonsense. Most crews like their sleep," Doug says—which is perhaps just as well, since pilots are prohibited from drinking eight hours before a flight and are strongly discouraged from drinking heavily right up to the eight hour deadline.

Doug breakfasts at 8:30 the next morning, declaring himself well-rested. Leafing through the International Herald-Tribune, he is particularly interested in the newspaper's weather outlook for New York. "The forecast is probably as good as the charts I'll get here," he says.

Because of the plane's late arrival, Flight 101 will take off 30 minutes late, at 11:30. Doug picks up a six-page weather chart and other flight sheets. Conferring with the dispatcher, he decides on a flight path he hopes will minimize the stiff winds that make westbound trips an hour longer than eastbound. He requisitions 224,000 pounds of fuel—enough for 9 hours and 37 minutes of flying, or a good two hours extra for alternate airports or circling time if needed.

Doug looks over Heathrow's takeoff noise-abatement regulations and then flicks through the day's flight bulletings. There's an item, for instance, that "all flights planned to overfly Bulgarian airspace must contact Bulgaria/Sofia control at least 10 minutes prior to entry."

"Hope we can ignore that one today," he says. Airmen know that all sorts of unexpected events disrupt flights. A Pan Am bulletin relates that a South American flight carrying a heavy fish cargo has been delayed a full day. One engine was severely damaged when a pelican flew into it.

Having filled out his forms, Doug wanders to the plane. Instead of the conspicuous black "brain box" customarily used by crews to carry the heavy flight manuals, Doug totes his books in a blue Pan Am bag. In the cockpit, flight engineer Dock Lee is running a host of checks on the engines, electrical circuits, hydraulic system and on scores of instruments and warning systems.

As Doug squeezes into the pilot's left-hand seat, First Officer Clair Miller beside him punches the selected flight plan into a device that looks like an electronic calculator. This is the Inertial Navigation System, or INS, a computer that comes close to enabling the 747 to fly itself. The INS, with three keyboards and electronic read-out displays, stores an incredible amount of navigational information and is integrated with the plane's automatic pilot, thereby guiding the aircraft within time limits through its pre-selected flight pattern and, ultimately to its destination.

A stewardess enters for soft drink orders. "Hi, I'm Doug, he's Dock, that's Rusty," says the captain, indicating copilot Miller and immediately putting the girl at ease.

Without encountering any problems, the crew finishes the preflight checklist; the cargo and passengers are loaded on time; the four engines roar to life. Dock tapes a piece of paper over an inoperative switch, informing Doug about the fault. And the aircraft heads for its 3,730th takeoff.

For Doug, it will be yet a few more hours of flying time to add to the more than 24,000 he has accumulated since joining Pan Am in 1941. This experience places him in the airline's top seniority bracket and gives him preference under Pan Am's complicated system enabling pilots to bid for flights on a seniority basis.

Doug tries to squeeze the maximum 80 hours a month of air time into two weekly light schedules, thereby giving himself two weeks' free time. Other pilots space flights evenly throughout the month or seek out short hops that enable them to work a Monday-to-Friday routine similar to suburban commuters. One veteran finds flying strenuous enough without undergoing time-zone changes and sticks to north-south routes. "If God had wanted us to fly east and west," he says, "He'd have made the equator run north and south."

On the drive to the runway, Doug manages to just pass in front of a BOAC jumbo, also heading for New York. A few more minutes are spent anxiously watching out for that too-close executive jet, then the tower clears a National DC8 for its Miami flight. Over the radio, Doug listens in as a Lufthansa 737's German pilot twice misunderstands instructions and is firmly told by the tower to just stay put. Then the Pan Am 747 is cleared for takeoff.

Capt. Moody taxies forward, turns right and within seconds the jumbo is lumbering smoothly down the runway. The flight engineer slides forward in his motorized chair to help with the throttles. The co-pilot calls out the increasing ground speed, past takeoff abandonment, past minimum liftoff and, at exactly 11:48 a.m., the 736,000-pound aircraft rises very slowly (too slowly for some passengers) but easily into the crowded air corridors of southern England.

To cover the 3,041 ground miles between Heathrow and Kennedy, the jumbo will travel at least 3,430 miles. Unable to emulate the crow's flight, the plane makes the trans-Atlantic journey by flying over 17 prescribed checkpoints within a carefully regulated timetable. Soon it soars over such alien (except to airmen) English landmarks as Breacon and Strumble. Then it passes the south coast of Ireland and heads over the ocean at its normal cruising height of 35,000 feet and a speed of 479 miles an hour.

With the INS computer and autopilot flying the plane, Rusty and Doug punch updated data into the system to compensate for drift and to comply with the controller's instructions. The stick with its familiar semi-circle steering wheel moves eerily by itself as the aviators scan the horizon, the instrument panel or charts on their laps. Meantime, Dock Lee is monitoring a baffling array of instruments that seem to be measuring everything but the amount of coffee, tea or milk consumed by passengers. He slides forward often to adjust the controls; in fact, the crew's hands are so well integrated as they cross overhead or in front of one another that it appears one person with three heads and six hands is flying the plane.

"Flying the 747 is a matter of good management and

teamwork," says Doug. "We're constantly checking one another, checking each set of instruments against the other's. Checking the speed, the compass heading. At seven miles a minute, you don't have to go very long in the wrong direction to get awfully lost."

"The name of the game," Rusty says, "is staying ahead of the plane."

Over the radio, the Shannon controller is heard telling the National flight that it is drifting slightly off-course and advising the BOAC that was passed on the runway to maintain its interval. When aircraft fly the same "track," or flight course, they must adhere to 15-minute minimum intervals.

Doug, listening to another radio channel, lets out a famous dirty word. "After all that garbage I gave out on the intercom about how good the New York weather is," he says, "now they say it's raining there. Damn, the people will think we're idiots. I knew I should have stuck to the Trib's report."

Except for an occasional trip to the toilet, the crew members are pretty much confined to the surprisingly tight cockpit, located above the first-class passenger compartment. The cockpit, with two extra seats for auxiliary crew, is smaller than those in some other jets. There's a lot of noise and vibration, which most pilots find fatiguing. The sun's rays are strong, helping to produce the traditional squint lines around a pilot's eyes. Toward the end of a flight, the warm cockpit can induce a pleasant sense of drowsiness that pilots must constantly combat.

One way a pilot immediately will be aroused to a state of full alert is to hear the gong, cricket, siren, honk or any of other warning sounds that indicate a serious malfunction in instruments or controls. The startling sound of the warnings themselves, according to a British pilot, isn't "conducive to cool thinking and action" and might well petrify a pilot or cause a heart attack. Others think that the limit has been reached on the number of warning sounds, each requiring a different reaction.

Doug says the most important emergency rule to follow after any warning sound or signal is, do nothing before you do anything. "Panic probably caused more accidents than anything else," he says. "The first thing to check is make sure it's not a false alarm."

The most dreaded sound is the fire bell. "A fire way out here over the ocean," says Rusty, "leaves us no place to go if we can't put it out." The 43-year-old co-pilot once experienced such an emergency, an engine fire that the crew luckily was able to extinguish. "Do you know the classic definition of flying?" he asks. "Several hours of boredom—followed by a few seconds of stark terror."

In 32 years with Pan Am, Doug claims, he has never experienced an engine fire or any other heart-stopping emergency. When pressed, he recalls landing in Turkey during an airport shoot-out. "I've had a fairly colorless operating career," he says, adding: "I'd just as soon keep it that way for the next five years or so."

The clouds below, as predicted, have thickened. In a while, the plane passes St. John's, Newfoundland, the first North American checkpoint, and starts the two-hour flight down the Eastern seaboard, past Halifax, Yarmouth and Nantucket. With Kennedy airport 30 minutes away, Doug says he'd like to try an instrument landing. He also learns the New York weather has changed again—this time for the better—and conforms to his original forecast.

The automated, instrument landing requires corresponding instrumentation at the airport's runway. Some pilots, cozily at home with manual landings, aren't keen on instrumental landings and shy away from them. Although Pan Am requires pilots to be familiar with the instrument landing, those who are reluctant aren't forced to practice the maneuver unnecessarily. "We always hope our guys recognize their limitations and try to stay within them," says Mr. Waugh, the pilot supervisor.

"Some pilots fly out of love," says another pilot, "some are strictly for the money. And some are afraid."

Approaching the runway, the big jet is buffeted slightly

off-course by strong cross-winds but still manages a fairly smooth touchdown. Immediately, warning lights flash and alarms go off. It's an ordinary occurrence, however, alerting the crew to disengage the various instruments and return to manual controls. The engines are reversed, the brakes engaged, the tires squeal comfortingly.

For most of the plane's 199 passengers, a bit weary after the seven-hour-47-minute flight, the landing marks the end of a journey. For Capt. Doug Moody, however, New York is just the halfway point in the day's travels. In a few hours, he will be hitching a ride back across the Atlantic on Pan Am's Flight 002 to London. Later in the day of arrival in England, he will fly on to Frankfurt as a check pilot. (According to FAA regulations, all pilots must be checked annually on their flight technique; the task is normally left to senior pilots like Doug.)

And so it will go. But despite the considerable wear and tear, Capt. Doug Moody has few complaints. "It's a good life," he says. "For all their bitching, I've never heard of a pilot quitting."

—FELIX KESSLER

Hard Driver

A crowd of close to 200 watches silently at the 10th green of the Pasadena Golf Club here as the perfectly coiffed woman leans over a putt. Kathy Whitworth, who has earned more than a half-million dollars as a professional golfer, taps the ball 25 feet downhill and into the cup for a birdie. The crowd cheers.

Across the fairway, only four spectators gather at a tee as Jan Ferraris, a pro from San Francisco, blasts a drive 260 yards. Two of the onlookers are so engrossed in a conversation about a roast-beef dinner that they ignore the shot. "Imagine that," says a man in pastel Bermuda shorts, "for only $3.75 they let you go back for seconds at no extra charge."

The lack of attention from her tiny gallery doesn't bother Miss Ferraris. At the Orange Blossom Classic in St. Petersburg, Fla., as at most big tournaments, the crowds gravitate toward stars and big money-makers such as Kathy Whitworth, Jane Blalock and Laura Baugh.

Jan Ferraris is neither a star nor a big winner on the Ladies Professional Golf Association (LPGA) tour. In 1974, the 28-year-old pro's U.S. winnings totaled only $10,000 (she finished 40th on the official money list). In nine years on the circuit, she has never wound up higher than 16th. She has won only three tournaments and faces the prospect that, after hundreds of rounds of tournament golf, she may never be rich or famous.

But for Miss Ferraris, as for many others on the LPGA tour, being a woman professional athlete is bringing increasing satisfaction. Golf is starting to benefit from the public's interest in women's sports, and many women who couldn't have survived playing golf in the past now are making a modest but adequate living.

Although golf hasn't made the dramatic advances of

women's tennis, it has come a long way. Betsy Rawls, a top pro, recalls how 25 years ago 15 women traveled from tournament to tournament by car caravan, competing for a total of season's purse of about $25,000. In 1974, the LPGA tour swelled to 112 members who jetted around the country to split a $1.8 million total purse.

"In those days, you didn't do it for the money," Miss Rawls recalls. "You had to love it." Today, it's hard to imagine anyone loving the life—a constant grind of tournaments and practice—but the rewards are far more tangible.

Miss Ferraris, for example, grossed $25,000 in 1974. That included her $10,000 LPGA money, $10,000 from a Japanese tournament and $5,000 from a television dishwashing-liquid commercial. Her expenses, including caddies, motels, car rentals, air fare and food, came to about $12,000. While on tour, she cuts expenses by sharing a room with a young Australian golfer, Penny Pulz.

Her income has enabled her to build up some savings, to a point that she complains about the problems of investing. "Wherever you go, people have a hot deal for you. It's hard to know who to trust with your money," she says. She keeps $10,000 cash readily available "to grab hold of whenever I want to." She has doubled her money on a land investment near a Cape Cod golf course. She also owns part of a Palm Springs, Calif., condominium and is pondering how to invest some funds tied up in bankers' acceptances.

Sometimes Miss Ferraris, a solidly built woman with a pixieish manner, thinks about quitting the tour and teaching golf. (She dropped out of college after her freshman year so her career choices are somewhat limited.) But the lure of the pro circuit is strong. "How many other ways are there for a women to clear $13,000 by actually working 30 weeks a year?" she asks.

Actually, the 30 weeks of tournament play are spread over about 10 months, and Miss Ferraris is on the road most of that time. She also makes several trips to Japan and Australia each year to compete in tournaments. "The traveling is getting to me," she admits. "I don't enjoy packing and unpacking. I don't enjoy going to the laundry to wash clothes. And I don't enjoy eating hotel food. Being Italian, I like eggs fried in olive oil. I can't get that, so I've given up eating breakfast, even before a tournament."

The tedium of traveling between one golf course and another is apparent as Miss Ferraris talks to a reporter in her motel in St. Petersburg. Reaching for another beer and lighting a cigaret, she says, "When you first start on the tour, you do a lot of sightseeing. But after you've seen the Alamo five times, what do you do?" Most often, she says, she collapses in front of the television set in her motel room at night and watches "cop things" like "Kojak" or "Columbo."

Following the sun on the pro tour does little for one's social life, she adds. She avoids casual dates. "One-time-going-out-to-dinner really gets boring, and I would just as soon watch TV as tell my whole life story all over again," she says.

She prefers to date men who are athletes. "When he (her athlete-date) is talking about mental pressures before and game and the letdowns after one, I know what he's talking about," she says.

To break the routine, Miss Ferraris occasionally skis. "It's really good to look down and see white," she says. "You get tired of seeing grass all the time." But the diversion isn't entirely relaxing, "because you have to worry about hurting yourself," she adds. "One cut on the hand can mean having to change your whole (golf) grip."

Although Miss Ferraris is glad to be earning a living at pro golf, she criticizes the LPGA for not trying harder to promote players. And she chides her sister golfers for failing to demand more promotion.

"Look at the St. Petersburg tournament," she says. "Men wouldn't play for $35,000 total prize money. We don't have anyone to market the LPGA. Publicity is how you get the purses up, which increases outside interest and creates more ways (such as product endorsements) to earn money."

Betsy Rawls disagrees. "There's no God-given right to make a living at golf," she says. "I don't think we should be playing for $100,000 a week like men do, because they are more spectacular and that's a different kind of show. You can't create publicity out of thin air."

Despite her frustrations, Miss Ferraris enjoys the competitive life. She took up golf at age 10 when her father, an orchestra leader at a well-known San Francisco hotel, would take her to the golf course to keep him company. At 13, she entered her first tournament.

Those who watched her compete in those days say Mr. Ferraris pushed his daughter hard. "I remember one tournament when she was doing badly," one observer recalls. "Instead of playing through, he pulled her out so they could rush over to enter another tournament."

The pressure continued in high school, when Miss Ferraris remembers having to juggle activities around to please her father. She ran through nine holes after school in order to get back to campus in time to watch a basketball game or play on the volleyball team. "Back then," she recalls, "women athletes were regarded as weirdos. You had to go overboard to show everyone you weren't." These days, she and her father don't discuss golf at all.

As an adult, she finds that winning is a constant preoccupation. "You really have to be blood and guts to succeed out here," Miss Ferraris says. "You can't let too many things interfere with what you have to do. The biggest challenge is to play better. I feel my potential lies in the top 10 and that's frustrating. You play with people and you know in your heart you're better than they are, yet they beat you every week."

Blood and guts notwithstanding, friends praise her for being a helpful critic. On the practice day before the tournament in St. Petersburg, she looked across the green at roommate Penny Pulz, a 23-year-old newcomer to the tour, and yelled, "You're getting the idea, but you're not driving enough with your legs. Not so much body."

On the second hole of the practice round, it started to rain, and Miss Ferraris, who had a cold, tried to continue. Drenched by the time she reached the third hole, she gave up, heading for the clubhouse. The rain let up and her threesome started to play again, but one hole later, the practice day was rained out for good.

Her cold wasn't much better at the start of the tournament the next day, but Miss Ferraris showed up at the practice tee; she wore blue-checkered pants and a blue shirt. A local photographer asked for a picture. She complained, "I don't know why they have to do this today when they could have done it yesterday." But when the photographer gave the cue, she leaned on the golf bag and smiled for the camera.

Her nerves began to show almost immediatley. On the first tee, she hit what looked like a beautiful shot, but the wind took over, sending the ball into a water hazard. She also had trouble putting. By the sixth hole, three putts had circled the cup but missed.

Difficulty with putting was a common malady at the tournament. On another green, Hollis Stacy of Savannah, Ga., was in trouble too. At one point, her exasperated 13-year-old sister Martha, a golf enthusiast, pulled Miss Stacy aside. "Look," Martha is overheard demanding, "would you just relax on the putts?"

On the last hole, Miss Ferraris hit the ball into the water again, taking a two-stroke penalty and winding up three over par. The rest of the tournament went much the same way, but there were bright spots. "Wow," said a man shaking his head at her five-foot-four-inch frame, "That little body, and she hit that ball 225 yards. I wish I could do that."

But Miss Ferraris failed to pick up momentum. By the third and final day, thousands of spectators had gathered, most watching two separate rounds featuring Amy Alcott, a freckle-faced 18-year-old from Santa Monica, Calif., who had a one-stroke lead over veteran Sandra going into the final hole. It was Miss Alcott's first tournament as a pro.

Sandra Post arrived at the final hole first, sinking a long putt to finish one under par and tie the tournament. Miss Ferraris sat on the grass drinking a beer, watching as Miss Alcott, wearing a red ribbon in her hair, sank a spectacular 15-foot putt to win the tournament by one stroke. The crowd went wild.

A poised Amy Alcostt accepted the $5,000 prize and was bombarded by reporters and photographers. No one gathered around Jan Ferraris, a former rookie of the year, who in 1972 won this very tournament. This time, three years later, she won $140 for finishing eight over par.

"Well," she said philosophically, heading for her car, "$140 is better than a kick in the fanny."

—JOAN LIBMAN

The Paper Maker

Lee Warren lights a hand-rolled cigaret and lounges on a bench in one of the sweltering paper mill's rare cool spots. As his voice competes with the roar of seven huge paper-making machines, his eyes keep darting back to his own machine 40 yards away.

"If I wore earplugs, I'd be lost," he shouts. "I can tell as much by the sound as I can by looking at that machine." Then, by way of explanation, he helps a visitor pick out a barely identifiable whine emerging from the overall din. To Mr. Warren, the pitch of the whine means that everything is running right—not too fast, not too slow—along the 100-yard-long heap of machinery known as No. 7.

James LeRoy Warren is a papermaker. He works at the big Erie, Pa., mill of Hammermill Paper Co. His is a craft that, at first glance, would seem to have been industrialized to the point of blotting out individualism, making people just interchangeable cogs in an assembly-line process. Even Mr. Warren's job title—machine tender—makes him sound like a servant of his monster machine.

But in fact it is the machine that is the servant. Mr. Warren's is a highly skilled trade, and No. 7 is simply the tool he needs to ply that trade. Only after a 19-year apprenticeship—the industry average is 20 years—did Mr. Warren become a full-fledged machine tender. Now, at age 60 a veteran of 40 years in the business, he is described by Hammermill's plant superintendent, Horton Girdler, as "a papermaker's papermaker."

Americans, who use about 630 pounds of paper per person per year, rarely stop to consider how it's made, or who makes it. Most everybody knows that wood is somehow involved, but that may be all they know. Even a Hammermill foreman confides that when he started at the mill he thought "they sliced the paper like cheese" from some giant wood block.

There are, of course, many kinds of paper products—from stationery to cardboard boxes to toilet tissue. Each requires a different type of paper, and the skills required to make the various types can vary. There are 1,800 paper-making machines in the U.S. and 7,200 or so people who operate them. Lee Warren's speciality is the making of what the industry calls "fine" paper, used for writing bond and photocopy stock.

Despite the development of modern technology and computer controls, the basic papermaking process has changed little since the early 1800s when two English brothers, Henry and Sealy Fourdrinier, patented the first machine to produce paper in a continuous process. Indeed, Lee Warren's No. 7 is still known as a "Fourdrinier" machine, though it was built in 1947 and has since been updated with computer controls. It's the Erie plant's largest and most sophisticated machine, but by industry standards it's only middle-sized. (Hammermill is the nation's 10th largest maker of fine papers.)

To operate such a machine requires five people—a machine tender like Mr. Warren and four assistants.

Standing near the "head box" at the "wet end" of the machine, Lee Warren watches as a special blend of chemically treated hardwood chips is diluted from the consistency of oatmeal to a smooth-flowing, fibery slurry that's 99.5% water. The slurry pours onto a large mesh conveyor belt, or "wire," where vacuum devices begin to suck out the water. The forward movement of the belt causes the wood fibers to align parallel to the machine, while side-to-side shaking locks the fibers into a tear-resistant web.

Twenty-five years ahead, the paper solution, still four-fifths water, leaves the wire in a continuous stream and begins a journey through the machine's "Dry end," an intricate series of felt-lined presses and dryers. The heat from huge revolving drying cylinders needed to evaporate the water raises the temperature around the machine to about 120 degrees.

At the start of the drying trip, the "Hammermill Bond" watermark is embossed across the 165-inch-wide sheet by another cylinder, while the dry paper at the far end is polished by a large smooth roller to provide its finish. Every 25 minutes a finished roll, containing 7,500 feet of paper, is removed and taken elsewhere in the plant to be cut and boxed.

Overseeing this process requires fantastic skill, no matter what type of paper is being produced. But fine writing paper's exacting "formation"—the way the tiny fibers join together—is among the most difficult and subjective specifications required for any paper.

Today, things are going smoothly on the machine. Because of the noise, crew members communicate that fact to Mr. Warren through an elaborate series of hand signals. Still, he takes a leisurely 200-yard stroll to the end of his machine and back—he makes the rounds about 25 times on his shift—surveying the operation first hand and talking things over with the crew. They seem to be taking it easy, too. It's a paradox perhaps peculiar to the paper business, says C. Edwin Brandon, chairman of the paper technology department of Miami University in Oxford, Ohio, that "the more the crew is sitting around loafing, the happier management is. Then they know the machine is running along fine, and they're making money."

All too frequently the fragile paper tears—or "breaks," in papermaking jargon—due either to irregularities in the pulp stock or problems with the machinery. Suddenly, a shrill siren pierces the normal cacophany and transforms the inactivity into an urgency resembling that inspired by a "battle stations" cry on a warship.

Indeed, to a papermaker concerned with his production totals, a break is an emergency. And while the flaw—perhaps a clot of paper lodged in a roller—is being meticulously scraped off by hand, billows of "broke," or a continuing stream of torn paper, are likely to be mounting elsewhere on the machine.

Even on a day without breaks, however, it's far from accurate to characterize the machine tender's inactive periods as "loafing." Automation has reduced drastically the manual work load over the years. But Mr. Warren's routine still includes constant surveillance of dozens of gauges, searches for such flaws as overheated bearings, and painstaking attempts to improve the roll of paper emerging from the polishing roller. In addition, a call for a change in the variety of paper requires a complete readjustment of the complex machine, during which the computer plays only a small part.

In all adjustments, of course, Lee Warren's margin of error is quite literally paper-thin.

"If the man at the wet end doesn't know what he's doing," Mr. Warren says, "you don't have anything left at the other end. That's called making hay." (Hay is another word for broke.) That's why Mr. Warren handles the wet end himself. The most exquisitely sensitive area under his control is the first "draw," where the paper leaves the wire and passes into the dryers. At that point the still wet, weak stock is unsupported. And if it hasn't formed just right through the draining and vacuuming process, there's plenty of hay.

Surprisingly, all the automation installed on paper machines so far hasn't reduced crew sizes at all. One reason: When a break occurs there's no device yet invented to clean up the mess. The people who do that are the machine's crew, consisting of a "back tender," who is second in command and handles the "dry end," and at least a third, fourth and fifth hand. It is as a fifth hand, the lowest ranking crew member (at least on a machine the size of No. 7), that most papermakers start out—serving as an errand boy and a "broke hustler."

Nor have various new electrical devices seriously threatened the colorful—and often profane—paper mill sign language that has evolved over the years. If the paper is too dry, for example, a two-handed gagging, parched-throat gesture tells the tender. The indication of a paper break, however, has been largely replaced by the siren, set off by electric eyes in the machine. (In sign language, a break would be indicated by bringing the little fingers of both hands to the mouth, as if whistling.)

Does Mr. Warren resent the intrusion of cold mechanical and electronic devices in his work? "No, indeed," he answers. "Whenever they add a new gauge, it makes something else to watch, but it's much easier for me. It gives me more time to spend making sure the paper meets specifications."

It's also safer, since it reduces the need for crewmen to stick their hands in the machine to make changes. Still, papermaking is a dangerous job. The talk of the Hammermill plant this day is of an accident during the prior night shift, when a new employe caught his hand in a roller, breaking three fingers and spraining his wrist.

"It used to be you could tell a papermaker by his missing fingers. But it isn't that way so much any more," says Mr. Girdler, the mill superintendent.

Automation, of course, has resulted in a more consistent paper quality. With computers to monitor production, Mr. Warren says, there haven't been any recurrences of the day in the mid-1950s when he was bawled out for making his paper too good. That transgression occurred once when the then-new machine tender, starting with a satisfactory roll of bond, made a few adjustments to see how close to perfection he could come. "That day, at that particular time, everything was right—the stock, the machine—and the paper came out like glass," he recalls. The foreman, though, wasn't quite as enthusiastic. Mr. Warren remembers being told harshly that the company "couldn't make paper like that on any other machine. He said that when the customer saw that, he wasn't going to want anything else." The "perfect" paper was rejected and the old adjustments reset.

Mr. Warren joined Hammermill during the Depression as a fourth hand, managing to skip the fifth-hand spot because the company was adding on help as it shrank the workday to eight hours. From the start, Mr. Warren's goal was to be a machine tender. "I was shooting for the job from the first day," he says.

Today, he is widely respected within the plant. Fellow employes note that most of the foremen and the other machine tenders in the mill have worked under Mr. Warren at one time or another and received the benefit of his experience.

All this responsibility brings him about $14,000 a year including overtime, he says. That includes a small premium paid to the man who runs the more-sophisticated No. 7.

Because papermaking is a continuous operation, mills employ a three-shift schedule for workers, who come in for seven straight days before getting days off. When their workweek is up, the crew members get from one day to 4½ days off in a rotation system. That way the four crews assigned to each machine stay together and serve on all the shifts equally.

Mr. Warren, for one, thrives on the schedule, enjoying hobbies that allow him to use the mornings when he's pulling the 3 p.m.-to-11 p.m. work turn, his favorite. "I'll go hunting for four hours, come back at noon and still be in good shape to go to work," he says.

He also spends a lot of time maintaining a 14-acre trailer park he owns near an interstate highway. The park doesn't provide any income yet, he says, because he's putting as much into it as he's getting out. But he expects it to help support him after he retires.

Sipping some homemade white wines with a visitor, members of the Warren family make it clear that retirement is a point of discussion these days. Mr. Warren concedes that he'd like to spend more time hunting, fishing bowling, and keeping up his park. "But when you retire, then it seems in some ways your life is over," he adds.

That's especially true when you've spend a career working up to and then holding the most challenging job in the paper mill, as Mr. Warren's supervisors say he has. ("That's nothing. All of life is a challenge," Mr. Warren responds to such praise.)

His wife, Lois, says she'll "lay odds Daddy won't retire till he's 65. He's too active." And their 39-year-old son, Kenneth, an Air Force jet mechanic, jokes about retiring before his father does. The Warrens also have two daughters, Janet and Anita.

A current topic in papermaking circles is just how far automation will go on the Fourdrinier, and what might be the impact on the tender's job.

"Up until about 50 years ago the paper industry was almost exclusively an art requiring the skill of the papermaker, and there was little science about it," says Miami University's Prof. Brandon. But now more and more functions of the machine tender are being studied in an attempt to find new computer applications. Still, "the human brain and human skill have just never been totally replaced," Prof. Brandon says.

Jerome P. Brezinski, an official of the Institute of Paper Chemistry in Appleton, Wis., agrees that the machine tender is assured of keeping his position. But, he adds, "he is getting closer and closer to the day when his job is to try and develop balance between information that sensors are providing for him."

Norman Spencer, manager of Mead Corp.'s Kingsport, Tenn., paper mill, suggests that one day the paper-machine tender may have to be a full-fledged engineer rather than a 20-year veteran of the machines.

No one wants to predict, however, when a paper mill might start relying on less-experienced men to conduct the complex process. And people in the industry acknowledge that because of the great capital expenditure needed for mills, older lines become obsolete very slowly, thus insuring crews jobs for years to come. Hammermill's No. 1 machine at Erie, for instance, was built in 1899 and is still churning away.

A more relevant question, therefore, may be whether

paper mills can continue to find young people who are willing to go through 20-year-apprenticeships in order to have a crack at Lee Warren's job. Norman Spencer, the Mead Corp. manager in Tennessee, isn't too worried. "Problems are evident when you first get young people working on a machine," he says. "But as the years go by they get to be dedicated."

—ROY J. HARRIS JR.

Steering Clear

Wind whipping against his wiry frame, George Young gingerly steps over the side of the wildly pitching tugboat and onto the gangway of the container ship cruising in upper New York Bay. It is a brilliantly clear day, but there is a brisk breeze blowing, and the weather is considerably colder in the middle of the bay than it is on the shore. Sheets of water clap together between the tug and the ship as Capt. Young nimbly climbs up the steps of the gangway.

"You know, I don't like jumping from one boat to another in this kind of weather," Capt. Young says glancing down at the waves. "The wind is horrible. It's worth your life."

But Capt. Young has been out in the bay in far worse conditons, including dense fog, hurricanes, hailstorms and blizzards. And through it all, day in and day out, from before the rest of the city awakens until long after it has gone to sleep, the captain performs his job: He is a harbor pilot, one of the small and relatively unsung group of men who maneuver giant ships in and out of the world's great ports.

"There's no underestimating this business," says Capt. Young, whose area of operations is New York Harbor. "Maybe nobody knows about us steering a ship out there in the dense fog, but we're mighty important. That cargo isn't going to get in without us. I don't like to brag, but I've probably put the suit on your back."

Perhaps so, though not without some assistance. For there are actually two sorts of harbor pilots. One is the bar pilot, who usually belongs to a pilots' association and who brings a ship up the channels that lead from the sea, through the harbor and up to a few miles away from the pier. There, he is relieved by the second sort, the docking pilot, who normally is employed by a towing company and who, guiding one or more tugboats from the ship's bridge, brings her into dock. When it's time for the ship to leave, the dock pilot moves her from the dock and out into the open water of the harbor, where a bar pilot takes over for the harbor trip's final leg back out to sea.

Capt. Young is one of about 300 docking pilots in the country, about 70 of whom work in New York Harbor, the country's busiest port. Bar pilots are more numerous—about 1,000 in the U.S., with about 135 working in New York. The use of bar pilots, in fact, is compulsory in most of the world's large ports and waterways, including New York Harbor. Under New York state law, all ships in foreign trade or under a foreign flag must carry a bar pilot when entering and leaving New York Harbor and while moving between points within the harbor. Coasting vessels—small ships plying coastal waters—are exempted if an officer on board has a federal license to navigate in these waters. While no regulations stipulate that a ship carry a docking pilot, tugs would refuse to service ships without one, and thus because of the dangers involved it would be extremely difficult, if not impossible, for the ship to dock.

There are probably few—if any—docking pilots better than Capt. Young. According to McAllister Brothers Inc., the towing company that employs him, Capt. Young is not only the finest of the 21 pilots it has but also is the "premier pilot in the continental United States."

"You name the ship, and I've docked her," says Capt. Young, who, at age 59 in 1973, is lean and balding with a somewhat grizzled face and a gravel voice. Indeed, in his 27 years as a full-fledged pilot, he figures he has docked and undocked more than 30,000 ships, including those bearing such legendary seafaring names as the Queen Mary, the Queen Elizabeth, the Constitution, the United States and the nuclear ship Savannah.

In fact, Capt. Young has docked practically every kind of vessel venturing into New York Harbor in recent years. Destroyers, aircraft carriers, submarines—all have been maneuvered to safe and secure berths under his expert guidance. And when the most recent version of the movie "Mutiny on the Bounty" opened in New York several years ago, it was George Young who docked the replica of the Bounty that sailed into the city for a promotional visit.

Over the last several decades, however, Capt. Young's working life has gradually changed. With the airplane all but doing away with the ocean liner, the docking pilot's life is rarely enlivened by confrontations with traveling movie stars and celebrities. Today, the captain mostly concerns himself with tankers and container vessels.

But more is gone than the glitter. In 1972, 18,600 ships passed through New York Harbor, compared with 25,500 in 1966. Not so very long ago the harbor held a thicket of ships and the waterfront was a constant hustle and bustle, but the dominance of the airplanes, among other factors, has left the city's waterways lined with unused piers, rotting sheds, abandoned warehouses and empty lots. Bridges have reduced the 40-odd ferry routes that once crisscrossed the harbor to only the Staten Island and Governors Island ferries, and whereas a dozen towing companies once serviced the harbor's shipping trade, now there are a mere two.

"The whole harbor is dying," Capt. Young says. "Someday there aren't going to be any piers left." Which means, of course, that there won't be any harbor pilots left, either. (Though the number of docking and bar pilots has held constant nationwide, there were 25 fewer working New York Harbor in 1973 than there were five years earlier.)

Such a pessimistic state of affairs was all but unthinkable in the early years of Capt. Young's career, although the promise of a bright future wasn't what prompted him to become a harbor pilot in the first place. In fact, although his father was a harbor pilot on Long Island Sound, George Young was initially set on a law career. Toward that end, he entered Notre Dame University in 1932; but after six months he was forced to quit and find work to help his family through the Depression. He first became a deckhand, then slowly worked his way up to the job of pilot, getting his first license in 1935. It was another 10 years of grueling experience, plus a five-day-long Coast Guard examination, before he earned an unlimited license that qualified him to pilot any type of vessel.

Capt. Young won't disclose the pay for his risky job, but other sources put it at about $35,000; his wages are determined by the number of ships he handles, using a scale based on the length of the ship and the distance he pilots her.

A good example of the toughness of his work is provided by his docking of the Sea-Land McLean in Port Elizabeth, N.J. Longer than three football fields, the Sea-Land McLean is the biggest and fastest container vessel in the world—not exactly every pilot's dream. Capt. Young, however, relishes challenging assignments, and most of the 15 or so ships he docks a week are the biggest ones that enter the harbor. "It's nothing to me to dock some pint-sized boat," he says. "My Aunt Tillie could do that. It's the big monsters I like. They're what I call fun."

Fun with a ship like the McLean, though, means sometimes floating along with less than a foot between the ship and bottom of the harbor. And it means that if a boat turns up ahead of her, it is impossible to stop the ship, and almost impossible to turn her out of the way. If the McLean, for instance, came up the harbor at full speed and backed her engines down, her momentum would carry her forward another couple of miles at a fair clip.

In the event of a collision, there is a pilotage clause in the contract between a towing company and a ship owner that frees a pilot from any responsibility for damage. But while a ship owner can't sue a pilot or towing company for negligence, another vessel involved in a collision, or the owner of a pier that is damaged, can. Generally, however, only the ship owner is sued for damages, though suits have been won against pilots.

On this particular job, Capt. Young is picked up by a McAllister tug at 12:30 in the afternoon at the Hoboken dock, where he parked his car after driving down from his home in Old Tappan, N.J. Though he normally goes out into the harbor four or five days a week, he may be asked to report for work at any hour of any day. Often, although a ship is supposed to report its estimated arrival a day in advance, it is an hour and day that he's not expecting to be called. In this case, the McLean has arrived a full day ahead of time.

Being always on call imposes restrictions on Capt. Young's life. When he's expecting a ship, he says, he hesitates to even go around the corner for cigars. Whenever he leaves his house, he usually phones in a number where he can be reached, and he has been called away while in the middle of bridge games, while dining in a restaurant and while playing golf. "Once, I was losing bad at golf, and I was glad to be called away," he recalls. His wife gets a bit more annoyed, but he says "she's always hated ships. Once, I took her on a cruise and she got seasick at the pier."

Aboard the tug, Capt. Young shows no signs of nervousness. He lounges with his feet up on the window sill, scanning the newspaper and puffing on a pipe. For all anyone would know, he was going to bring in a canoe rather than the world's largest container ship.

Enroute to near Stapleton, Staten Island, where Capt. Young is due to board the McLean, the tug receives a call from the company to help dock a tanker in the Battery. Capt. Young and the tug pilot are visibly annoyed, afraid they'll be late to meet the McLean. By 1:30, however, the tanker is docked, and the tug heads once more for Stapleton.

Enroute Capt. Young checks the tide tables and finds that low water was at 11:08. He already has been informed that the wind is westerly at 25 knots. The captain must have an intimate knowledge of what weather conditions do to the harbor, since he docks rain or shine, snow or sleet, whether he can see or not. He must also know the location of every shoal, every sizable deposit of debris and every other shipping hazard in the cluttered harbor. In effect, he must have in his mind a topographical map of the bottom of the harbor and of the harbor's adjacent rivers, creeks and inlets.

There are many instances, Capt. Young says, when he hasn't a chance to think at all. Instead, he must rely on instinct to produce split-second decisions that could mean the difference between a disastrous collision and a smooth docking. "I've done things I couldn't have figured out how to do if I were sitting with a computer in front of me," he says. "You've got to use your experience. And you've got to have old Lady Luck with you."

It is 2 p.m. when the McAllister tug pulls up alongside the McLean. The ship has just passed under the Verrazano-Narrows Bridge and is about eight miles from Port Elizabeth. Up close, the ship looks about the size of Topeka, Kans., and the tug seems life a raft. Capt. Young checks markings on the hull to determine how much of the ship is below water—in this case about 34 feet, which means he must avoid all shallower portions of the harbor. He also notes that the ship "needs a good coat of paint."

A steel gangway is lowered from the McLean, and Capt. Young carefully mounts the steps. He then takes an elevator another 85 feet or so up to the bridge from which he will work.

Capt. Young doesn't physically steer the ship in the sense that he turns the wheel. Rather, he gives directions by radio to a quartermaster in the wheelhouse, while, at the same time, guiding the tugboats that assist with the docking. In this instance, there are four tugboats. Normally, the captain uses a walkie-talkie for the tugs and an intercom for the quartermaster. But the McLean's intercom isn't functioning, so he must rely on a walkie-talkie for both.

The ship is cruising at about 10 knots, a relatively slow speed but one that seems a lot faster up on the bridge with a biting wind whipping in your face. Capt. Young is constantly barking orders to the quartermaster: "Right 15." "Left 30," "Slow ahead port." "Slow ahead starboard." "Midship." (The numbers stand for degrees to turn the ship's rudders.) It isn't long before it becomes clear why there's a need for an intercom rather than a walkie-talkie to the quartermaster. Now and then, Capt. Young will command something like "right 15," and soon after someone else talking to some other vessel will be picked up ordering "left 30." "It can scare the hell out of you," Capt. Young says.

Things go smoothly as the big ship glides by an endless stream of tugs, dredges, barges, excursion boats, ships and pleasure crafts. Suddenly, the McLean comes upon a tug pushing a garbage barge that is heading smack for the ship. The tug has the right of way, but Capt. Young radios for it to clear away. The tug pilot first puts up a fuss but finally surrenders and chooses to move rather than face a likelihood of being smothered by a 40,000-ton ship.

Only once was Capt. Young involved in a collision, and that was a minor scrape when a cargo ship he was piloting nudged a small tanker. But he says it is possible, especially in foggy conditions, to come so near another ship that you can reach out and shake hands with the men on the other bridge.

A more common peril for the captain has been fire, which he has fought on 10 occasions. In fact, he was aboard one of the first tugs to reach the famed French liner Normandie when she caught fire during the Second World War. "When a ship burns, you feel like it's a person who has passed away," he says. "Everyone who works in the harbor regards a ship as almost a human being." Capt. Young also brought in the Israeli passenger liner Shalom after she collided with a Norwegian tanker in heavy fog and rain off the New Jersey coast in 1964, splitting the tanker in half.

As the McLean nears her berth, the harbor begins to narrow considerably, and Capt. Young orders the engines slowed to guard against the tremendous wash from the ship tearing the shore apart. It is almost 3 p.m. when the ship arrives at Port Elizabeth. After passing through a raised railroad bridge, she has to be backed down to avoid plowing into water that is only 14 feet deep. Because of the ship's great weight, she has to be eased into the pier as gently as possible, and, in this case, it takes the four tugs a half-hour to shove the McLean into the pier. Capt. Young laments that the tugs aren't more powerful.

His work finished, Capt. Young reports to the officer's messroom for some coffee and pastry. Shortly afterward, a crewman lumbers into the messroom, and Capt. Young asks when he expects the ship to be leaving. "Oh, about midnight, I guess," the crewman says. Capt. Young frowns. "Great" he says. "That means I'll be up all night again. Nothing new."

—N.R. KLEINFIELD

The Tour Escort

The bus glides by sleepy Pennsylvania towns and green hills as J. Walter Odermatt talks through a microphone about life in rural America. Suddenly, turning to his seatmate, he pauses to whisper: "Did I already say it in German?"

The 42 passengers, who come from Germany, Italy, France, Belgium and Switzerland, forgive Mr. Odermatt such occasional lapses of memory. They know that as a tour escort for American Express Co., he often must repeat everything he says for weeks on end in two, three, even four languages. "He's bound to forget now and then," says Aldo Rinaldi, Mr. Odermatt's boss.

That's just one of the hazards of life as a multilingual tour escort. On the road seven days a week for months at a time shepherding Europeans across the U.S., 41-year-old Walter Odermatt has no permanent home; he goes from hotel room to hotel room. His possessions—principally the string ties with silver-dollar medallions, hand-crafted leather belts and richly decorated shirts that make up the flashier part of his wardrobe—fit for the most part into three red suitcases that go with him everywhere.

"I tried to get married three times, but it didn't work out," Mr. Odermatt says. "After I told them what kind of job I had, they said, 'Let me think about it.' And I never saw them again."

Yet despite it all, Walter Odermatt says he wouldn't trade jobs with anyone. And the travel industry needs people like him because foreigners, enticed by favorable monetary exchange rates, are swarming to the U.S. on vacations. Some 3.8 million were expected in 1974, 9% more than in 1973 and triple the number a decade earlier, according to the U.S. Travel Service of the Commerce Department. But not enough are coming to allow tour operators to segregate every tour into groups by language, so the operators still have to hire escorts who speak several languages well.

Mr. Odermatt is fluent in French, German, Italian, English and Spanish, and nearly fluent in Portuguese. Some American Express escorts know more languages, but Mr. Odermatt is the company's only full-time escort, largely because qualified people willing to tolerate an escort's irregular life are hard to find. (Escorts are fairly well paid: Mr. Odermatt makes around $14,000 a year, plus allowances for meals, hotel rooms and laundry; he also gets tips that range upward from about $150 a tour). American Express, the biggest operator of U.S. tours for foreigners, has 10 to 15 escorts who lead enough tours to be considered professionals. It engages between 20 and 35 freelance escorts as needed.

A typical day for Mr. Odermatt on a two-week swing through the East Coast begins at 6:30 a.m. in Niagara Falls, Ont. This is a "free morning" for the tourists, meaning they can do anything they want, but Mr. Odermatt arises early to make sure breakfast comes off smoothly. It doesn't, and Mr. Odermatt has to threaten to take the group elsewhere before things are straightened out. After that, he stands in the hotel lobby and answers questions.

Most of the tourists already know something about the falls. Mr. Odermatt talked about them the day before en route from Pittsburgh. He tries to tell the group as much as he can in advance. "When things start to go by, you don't have time to go into detail in all those languages," he notes.

After ten years of leading tours, Mr. Odermatt no longer has to bone up much on the points of interest. For example, it was in 1972 that he had last taken a "Rainbow Trails Tour," as American Express calls this swing through New York, Pennsylvania Dutch country, Washington, D.C., the Shenandoah Valley, Pittsburgh, Niagara Falls, Toronto, Montreal, Quebec and Boston.

Yet the spot he is least familiar with—Pittsburgh—he

has visited 10 times before. And although Pittsburgh is primarily an overnight stop on the journey, Mr. Odermatt, from a tour of several of the city's steel mills he took a few years ago while chaperoning some Russian executives, was able to serve up a few tidbits on the importance of Pittsburgh to America's economy, how steel is made and how a typical steelworker works and lives. "That's what they really want to know," Mr. Odermatt says. "How we live."

Mr. Odermatt and other tour escorts agree that the hardest part of their job isn't speaking several languages or remembering obscure facts; it's coping with the often improbable behavior of the tourists themselves. "I've even been offered money for the front seat on the bus," Mr. Odermatt says with amazement. Adds Yehuda Evan-Zohar, an American Express escort who's working on a doctorate on the psychology of travel: "Tourists are like little children."

Mr. Odermatt's approach ranges from diplomat to drill sergeant, depending on circumstances. When he isn't delivering his monologue, he mingles with the tourists, trading small talk and trying to detect and resolve complaints before they get out of hand. "He's great at putting people at ease," says Antonio Sismondo, the bus driver during this tour.

But Mr. Odermatt also tries to establish control at the outset. Almost invariably, one or more of his charges show up late for the first day's excursion, generally a bus tour of Manhattan. And equally invariably, Mr. Odermatt departs on time, leaving stragglers behind to fend for themselves. The point isn't lost on the group. "You've got to let them know who's boss," Mr. Odermatt says.

At 11:40 a.m. on the day at Niagara Falls, Mr. Odermatt's mastery seems in doubt. His group of 42 tourists is scattered hither and yon, and their 50 suitcases haven't been loaded on the bus. The Skytop Restaurant, where the group is to have lunch, has warned him to arrive no later than noon "or forget it," and the restaurant is a mile away in heavy midday traffic.

"We'll leave in exactly five minutes," Mr. Odermatt says, looking at his watch.

"Wanna bet your life on that?" shoots back Tony Sismondo, the bus driver.

Five minutes later, having pressed the bus driver and a reporter into service as baggage loaders, Mr. Odermatt counts to 42 and the bus rolls out the driveway. "You're still living," Mr. Sismondo concedes.

When addressing the group, Mr. Odermatt strikes a conversational tone, describing people and places informally and in generalities. "It's like in Europe," he comments during a monologue on rural America. "The boys didn't want to work on the farms any more so they went to the cities to work in factories." Summing up the economic importance of the Great Lakes in a minute and a half, he mentions how industrial cities dependent on cheap water transportation grew up around the lakes and how the Welland Canal and the St. Lawrence Seaway link the lakes to each other and to the outside world.

He avoids all but the most essential dates and statistics. People don't remember them anyway, and "If I say this is a very old town, founded in seventeen-hundred-and-something, the Italians will laugh because their history goes back hundreds of years before Jesus Christ." Of all the questions he is asked, by far the most frequent concerns salaries: How much does a plumber (or laborer, or lawyer, or executive) make in America?

The tourists seem to like Mr. Odermatt's approach, and they're especially happy, in the words of Mechthild Fischer, a young German schoolteacher, that "he isn't the type who cracks jokes all the time. I've been on too many tours where the guide thinks he's the end as a comic and I never think they are."

Born in Stans, Switzerland, near Lucerne, Mr. Odermatt grew up speaking a dialect of German. His father, a meat importer, traveled frequently on business, and Walter caught the travel bug early. As he traveled, he began to pick up other languages. "Speaking a language is the only way to learn it," Mr. Odermatt maintains. "I am constantly meeting Americans who majored in German in school but couldn't order a beer in Berlin."

At age 20 Mr. Odermatt came to the U.S. and worked on a ranch in California for a year, learning English and developing a fondness for the American West that's still with him as a naturalized U.S. citizen. After traveling for several years, trying his hand at a meat-importing business of his own (and losing $7,000), and working for a while as a management trainee for Bank of America, he began leading American Express tours in the mid-1960s. He's done it ever since.

"I don't think I'll live to be 71 like my father did," Mr. Odermatt says. "I live much too fast. I smoke absolutely too much. I get up early in the morning, and I often go to bed late. I always know what date it is, but sometimes I forget the day. To me, every day is like Sunday."

—URBAN C. LEHNER

Part Five

EXPRESSING THEIR TALENTS

Talent is one of those elusive qualities that is hard to define. Does a concert pianist have it while a honky-tonk piano player doesn't? Maybe, but then a lot of it is in the eyes of the beholder. Or ears, as the case may be. Anyhow, it is clear that some people's work rests largely on innate abilities or capabilities that aren't readily transferrable to others. Whatever it is they have to offer springs from within themselves, and sometimes their talents demand a lifetime of devotion whether or not there is money enough in it to support themselves.

The Novelist

To Michael Avallone, time is something to be raced. He eats fast. He talks fast. He walks fast and reads fast. As if he has been told he is down to his last day on earth, he continually checks his wristwatch, almost as if he is calculating how best to squeeze the most activity into the least amount of hours, minutes, even seconds.

"I just hate to waste time," Michael Avallone says. And lest anyone believe that Mr. Avallone is merely mouthing a cliche, consider the following: In the last 26 years, he has so well used his waking hours that he has found time to write 146 published novels, 250 short stories, 600 articles and the scripts for five children's records—not to mention thousands upon thousands of letters.

Michael Avallone, age 50 in 1974, is part of that species of author that critics disdain as hacks, that publishers adore as men of iron and that the general public reads voraciously with little or no idea as to the writer's identity. With machine-like persistence, such authors annually crank out a half-dozen or more books, year after year, practically all of them so-called paperback originals (books that appear strictly in soft cover). And with paperback sales burgeoning—they reached a record $252.8 million in 1973—Mr. Avallone and the small number of other rapid-fire writers able to keep up with him are finding their skills in greater demand than ever.

And according to Michael Avallone, such skills aren't really all that difficult. "You start with some implausible idea and then work it to its logical conclusion," he says of his novel-writing method. "In the first chapter, you create the problem. I've started with a room blowing up, a corpse jumping out of a coffin and a guy putting on his clothes backwards while he's dying. Then, as you write it, it works itself out. There's no magic to it."

Maybe there isn't, but Michael Avallone has certainly proven himself to be one of the most successful practitioners of quick writing. Under his own name and 14 pseudonyms (including Vance Stanton, Troy Conway and Jean-Anne de Pres), he writes detective books, gothic novels, sex novels and novelizations of television and movie scripts. He has been known to polish off a 60,000-word book in as little as two days, though his book output is about a dozen a year. (In 1967, however, his total novel output was a staggering 27.) Ten Avallone works have sold in the millions, the most successful, with sales of three million copies, being a novel based on the characters of television's "The Partridge Family."

Mr. Avallone's Herculean output brings him about $50,000 a year. (Although he writes occasionally for a flat fee, he typically receives a $2,000 to $3,000 advance and 4% royalties for a book.) And it is because of this comfortable income and because of his prodigious output, Mr. Avallone believes, that the publications and critics that make books sell and authors famous ignore him. "There's this tremendous prejudice against anything that's done fast," he reasons. "People like the picture of the author in rags up in the attic scraping away and living on cheese and apples and putting his blood into his book."

Well-dressed and well-nourished, the stockily built Mr. Avallone does his work in a smallish room on the ground floor of his pleasant, split-level house in East Brunswick, N.J. And if his comfort shouldn't be held against him, the author says, neither should his speed. "It's not as if my books are just hacked out, like lettuce on a chopping block," he says defensively, insisting that every book he writes is the best he can do and that if he devoted the rest of his days to a novel that occupied only 48 hours of his time, that novel would be no better. He adds: "I believe in spontaneity."

Michael Avallone's spontaneous creations emanate from a battered, ink-splotched Olympia typewriter. Typing with two fingers, he works at a 50-word-a-minute pace and almost always maintains that pace regardless of how many hours a day he puts in (sometimes as many as 10). Each page is mailed to his publisher almost exactly as it leaves the typewriter.

Mr. Avallone's ideas spring from an idle thought or a personal experience, and sometimes he begins a book with just a title in mind. He keeps a clipboard on which he posts potential titles, such as "Die Avenue" (the name came off a matchbook cover) and "Mad Avenue" (an abbreviation of Madison Avenue). "Die Avenue could be a street where everybody dies," he explains. "Mad Avenue could be a place where everybody's screwy, or where there's an infamous insane asylum located."

Whatever the genesis of their titles, most of Mr. Avallone's books are heavily autobiographical, and this is particularly true of the 23 novels he has written concerning the adventures of Ed Noon, a fictional private detective. This isn't to say that Messrs. Avallone and Noon are one and the same; but many details of the detectives life parallel those of the author's, and, more important, Ed Noon leads a life that Michael Avallone envies. Why? Because every Ed Noon book is characterized by fantastic heroic deeds and happy endings—and Michael Avallone worships heroes and longs for happy endings, both of which he knows are rare commodities outside of novels.

"In my books, there is always the hero who hits a home run in the ninth," he says. "Of course, in real life it doesn't happen that way. . . . But in my books, I quit after everything comes out happily ever after. Six months later, maybe the hero dies of cancer, and the heroine dies in childbirth. I'm not interested in that. My beat is sunshine."

The sunshine beat is perhaps all the more attractive because it is so far removed from the Bronx street corners where the young Michael Avallone sold paper bags to help his family get by. Born in October 1924, Mr. Avallone was hurled into a world of chaos and poverty that seemed to get worse every day. His father, a sculptor and stone mason, sired 17 children, and death was commonplace in the

Avallone household. Before he was 10 years old, the author recalls, he had been excused from school five times for family funerals of brothers and sisters. (This part of Mr. Avallone's life is also reflected in his books; for despite the heroics and happy endings, his fictional landscapes are scattered with a supporting cast of life's losers: Nymphomaniacs, freaks, and others whose mental and physical malformations are touched on with sympathy—although unlike the heroes and heroines, they rarely achieve happy endings.)

To escape the rigors of his home life, Mr. Avallone found refuge and solace in local movie theaters. He would sit enthralled by movies involving heroics, he recalls, and he particularly enjoyed "The Plainsman," starring Gary Cooper in the role of Kit Carson, which he saw at the age of 12. In fact, "The Plainsman" so appealed to Mr. Avallone's heroic bent that he wrote down what he remembered of the film when he got home. Then and there, he decided he would write for a living.

After graduation from high school in 1942, Mr. Avallone continued to live at home and worked as a shipping clerk in a stationery store for $17.50 a week, all the while spending the better part of many nights writing in the family bathroom. A year later, he enlisted in the Army and was sent to war in Europe, where he became further acquainted with suffering, loss and death.

At the end of the war, Mr. Avallone returned to the stationery store and the part-time life of a yet unpublished author. Then, after a year of intermittent writing, he completed a novel about an artist who goes blind. No publisher wanted it. (The book, "Take Me by the Hand," would be sold 14 years later.) Two other Avallone novels completed in 1948 fared no better.

Frustrated, Michael Avallone tried his hand at a baseball anthology and then a poetry collection. Again, no one was interested (both are still unsold). Having married a clerk at the store, and in rather precarious financial straits, Mr. Avallone turned in desperation to another genre: the fast-paced suspense novel. In 10 writing sessions, he dashed off an Ed Noon mystery. His loser's life was over.

The first Ed Noon book was published in 1953 and was Mr. Avallone's first book in print. Heady with literary success, he quit the stationery store to edit, and write for, a group of 28 men's magazines. Then his marriage broke up, and he says he spent several years leading a rather aimless life. In 1960, he remarried, and his life, he says, began to take direction. Two years later, he quit magazines to write books full-time.

It wasn't long before Michael Avallone found his niche as a writer and discovered that his chief appeal lay with a broad audience impatient with complex, time-consuming books. Consequently, he says, his books are geared for quick reading (the typical reading time of one of his novels, he says, is an hour and a half). "My reader is the man on the street," Mr. Avallone says. "He's people. My books aren't designed for the ivory-tower, English-lit type."

But catering to such people, however uncomplicated their tastes, isn't without its mental pressures; and as a release, the author spends weekday mornings at a neighborhood candy store playing pinball. Not only is he addicted to the game, but he is also fascinated by the endless chatter of the store's customers, many of whom inadvertently supply him with material for his books.

Michael Avallone's ceaseless search for material is only equaled by his quest for another—and, thus far, more elusive—goal: fame. His money, his nice home, his wife, his three children are all important, Mr. Avallone says; but over and above all these blessings, he would still like to be famous. Consequently, as long as the country's book reviewers don't deign to mention an Avallone book, much less its author, Mr. Avallone has taken it upon himself to promote celebrity by scattering calling cards, bearing his name and the titles of some of his books, around the world. Bus drivers, cabbies, airline stewardesses have all been recipients of Avallone cards; he also leaves them in homes, museums, subways, hotel and motel rooms, monuments—

indeed, everywhere he goes. "It's sort of like leaving your mark on the world," he says. "It's like creating a time capsule."

The ultimate impact of the cards remains to be seen, leaving Michael Avallone in the meantime to ponder what brings about public acclaim. "Just think of what I've done," he says. "It's remarkable. I've written 146 books, and yet I'm like a prophet without honor in his own country. My dream is that I can walk down the street and somebody on the other side will look across and say, 'Hey, that's Michael Avallone. He's the writer."

—N.R. KLEINFIELD

The Silversmith

Bill de Matteo strides down sun-splashed Duke of Gloucester Street in Williamsburg, Va., grinning his boyish grin and looking like Milton Berle's brother.

He is talking about his work, and with the kind of enthusiasm most men lavish upon their hobbies. For Bill de Matteo is doing exactly what he wants with his life—working with his hands to hammer out beautiful objects from silver, which he considers quite simply the most beautiful, most challenging material there is.

"What is silversmithing?" he asks. "It's a combination of engineering and art. There is always something you're trying to say, and the challenge is to care enough to say it well. I started silversmithing with my father. And I've never, ever made a piece I'm satisfied with, really."

This admission might surprise anyone familiar with Bill de Matteo's most successful works as master silversmith in Colonial Williamsburg's living museum of 18th-Century American life—with, for example, the matched silver riding crops he made for Queen Elizabeth and Prince Phillip, or the hand-wrought replicas of Paul Revere's lanterns for President Kennedy. But William de Matteo is a perfectionist, and silver is an especially tantalizing material for a perfectionist to confront.

It is, after gold, the most plastic of all the metals. Cold and gleaming dully in its unworked state, silver shows little of the allure that has drawn men to it for centuries. But beneath the blows of the craftsman's hammer it becomes alive and almost infinitely responsive. There is almost no form it cannot be coaxed into. And thus it is a medium that allows no excuse for failure: If the craftsman's actual product falls short of the promise of his design, he has no one to blame but himself.

A mere handful of men accept this challenge in

industrialized, 20th-Century America. During America's colonial years, some 300 silversmiths worked in Boston, Philadelphia and New York alone, and the most famous of them all was Paul Revere. Today almost all silver articles are made by machine, and there are probably fewer than 50 silversmiths who execute their own designs by hand in the traditional manner.

The decision to become one of them seems to have flowed naturally from the personality and philosophy of Mr. de Matteo, a warm, somewhat shy man of 49 with a special feeling for tradition and harmony. "If we ever lose this feeling for the esthetic, this feeling of doing things with our hands for other people, I think we'll have lost something from our way of life," he says. "Something human.

"I hate unpleasant things," he continues. "I hate billboards. I hate for people to fight. Being a silversmith is just a delightful, lovely way to go through life."

But it can also be a tense, demanding way. It is no accident that over Mr. de Matteo's workbench is pinned a single New Yorker cartoon. It depicts a dog-tired executive trudging up his front walk. His wife is warily extending him a martini on 20-foot tongs. Bill de Matteo likes martinis himself, and he says there are days when he trudges home in great need of one.

"A lot of people tell me, 'Oh, I envy you,'" he says. "I don't think they realize how emotional the work is. When I'm working on a piece, I guess I'm pretty hard to live with. I sit at the bench, and I really don't see or hear anybody else. I get annoyed when somebody calls. There's an anxiety. I know what I want to do, but I'm not sure whether it will come off."

Much of Mr. de Matteo's work is almost routine, working himself or overseeing the work of others in on the silver, brass and pewter reproductions sold in Williamsburg. But about a half-dozen times a year he is asked to design and execute a piece for some special occasion. These are the projects that test his creativity and craftsmanship to the fullest.

Early in 1973, before the Watergate scandal had fully blossomed, for example, the White House Correspondents Association asked Mr. de Matteo to come up with something special for presentation to President Nixon at the association's annual dinner. He decided upon an adaptation of an 18th-Century inkwell in the form of a globe. It would take him about 200 hours and perhaps a hundred thousand hammer blows.

The hammer is to the silversmith what the paintbrush is to the artist, the primary tool for creating order out of chaos. It becomes almost an extension of his arm, and a favorite hammer is an intensely personal tool with a balance and a feel uniquely its own. There are only three basic types of silversmithing hammers, but Mr. de Matteo has hundreds of variations of them. He says it is almost impossible to buy a really good hammer today, so when he needs another one he usually forges it of steel himself. Some of his best hammers, though, are almost 250 years old. He purchased them when a venerable London silversmithing firm went out of business.

Mr. de Matteo began his inkwell project with a sheet of rolled silver, only somewhat more handsome than a sheet of tin at this point, and gradually hammered it into a hemisphere. This formed the bottom half of the globe. The top half was made of two quarterspheres that, at the touch of a button, would separate and swing down around the bottom hemisphere, exposing compartments for presidential paper clips and the like. The quarterspheres had to be both perfectly spherical and slightly greater in circumference than the bottom hemisphere—something so hard to do by hand that only one 18th-Century craftsman ever bothered making such globes.

"Now we know why," says Phil Thorp, who came to Mr. de Matteo as an apprentice 17 years ago and is now an accomplished silversmith who often assists his former teacher. Mr. de Matteo finishes his thought for him: "Because he was crazy," he says with a grin.

Mr. de Matteo was on hand in April 1973 to help present the globe to Mr. Nixon, the third President he has made gifts for since 1961. That was the year he made, on nine days' notice, the silver reproductions of Paul Revere's lanterns for President Kennedy, a project he still regards as the "most fun" of all.

Only one of Paul Revere's original lanterns survives today, and to even see it, Mr. de Matteo had to convince a suspicious officer of the Concord Antiquarian Society that he could be trusted not to steal it. Then had had to shovel his way into the snowbound headquarters of the society. Still taking no chances, the society escorted him and the lantern to the boardroom of a bank—and locked him inside while he sketched and photographed it.

Back in Williamsburg, he and Mr. Thorp worked 18-to-20-hour days hammering up the reproductions. They finished at 4 a.m. the morning of the presentation, too tired to drink the champagne that Mr. Thorp had purchased for the occasion.

President Kennedy, who was having his troubles with congressional Republicans at the time, accepted the lanterns in high good humor. He would, he announced, hang "one if by Dirksen and two if by Halleck."

For President Johnson, Mr. de Matteo once made a pair of bookends with silver reproductions of Sam Houston's spurs. And once, for Winston Churchill, he made a town crier's bell hand-forged from a single piece of silver by a method seldom used since the 18th Century. "Its silver tone is gentle," Sir Winston said. "I shall ring it whenever I feel there is duty to be done."

Recently, in honor of the 15th anniversary on the job of Colonial Williamsburg's president, Carlisle H. Humelsine, Mr. de Matteo hammered up a perfectly smooth and graceful model of the hull of Mr. Humelsine's sailboat. "It was like drawing a caricature," he says. "I left out an awful lot of detail, but I think I got the feeling of a boat. What I ended up with really, was a piece of sculpture, symbolizing his boat and what it means to him."

Mr. de Matteo holds a degree in sculpture from Columbia University, and the sailboat reflects an increasing tendency in his work in recent months. He is breaking away from the reproduction and adaptation of 18th-Century forms to experiment more and more with abstract designs.

For the moment, though, Mr. de Matteo is adamant that most of his work is not art. It is a position he has held now for some 26 years of running debate with his wife, Jayne. Mrs. de Matteo, a commercial artist, argues that if her husband takes, say a coffee pot and lifts it "above the ordinary" through sheer elegance and craftsmanship, he has produced art. He is producing art now and has been for a long time, she thinks, but she says he's too stubborn to admit it.

Mr. de Matteo disagrees. There was a time when he told people that the only difference between him and a plumber was in the material they used. He has mellowed now, and he doesn't say that anymore. But his basic argument is unchanged.

"I think an artist is someone who expresses himself in an abstract way," he says. "He isn't bound by function. I don't see how when you make something functional it can even be called a work of art. Now, it can be pretty. But when you make a coffeepot, it also has to hold liquid. You're immediately bound by function.

"Is a Rolls-Royce a work of art? It's beautiful. It's mechanically perfect. But it's not a work of art."

These sentiments would draw no argument from many other craftsmen in Colonial Williamsburg's large and growing program. They are proud to be craftsmen, making functional objects. Some would be downright offended to be called artists.

A case in point is George Pettengell, Williamsburg's master cooper. For at least five generations, Mr. Pettengell's ancestors had plied this ancient craft of making kegs and barrels from wood. Then the London brewery where

Mr. Pettengell himself worked switched to metal kegs. Moved by an almost religious sense of duty to preserve his father's craft, Mr. Pettengell came to Williamsburg.

"George just goes bananas when somebody comes into his shop and says, 'Oh, honey, isn't that barrel just beautiful,'" says a Colonial Williamsburg spokesman. To such well-meaning comments, he has been known to reply icily: "And it also works."

Colonial Williamsburg's crafts now encompasses more than 20 skills—everything from weaving and basketmaking to gunsmithing and harnessmaking—and goes well beyond providing entertainment for tourists, says Peter A.G. Brown, a Colonial Williamsburg vice president and director of museum operations. On a deeper level the craftsmen are an integral part of the Colonial Williamsburg motto: "That the future may learn from the past."

"I think the world needs to remember that the industrial revolution didn't solve everything," Mr. Brown says. "Through craftsmen we can gain a sense of excellence, a greater respect for materials and the satisfaction that we can make, with our own hands, things of great utility and beauty."

The craftsmanship program is probably the most extensive on the continent, and its financial mainstay is Bill de Matteo's silversmithing operation. The entire program now costs roughly $1.5 million a year to operate, of which about $1 million is recouped through the sale of handicrafts. (The foundation subsidizes the rest.) Annual sales of silver articles alone bring in around $750,000.

For Bill de Matteo himself, this is a mixed blessing. When he began work in Williamsburg 20 years ago, his was a one-man operation. Today he oversees some 40 people, including three apprentices and Williamsburg's artisans in other metals. This yields him an annual income he describes as roughly similar to that of a university professor of similar experience, enough to support a comfortable life in a contemporary brick house outside the historic district.

But is exacts a price as well: Dreary staff meetings are consuming more and more of his time.

Even so, most days still find him spending at least some time in the small workshop overlooking a boxwood-lined garden. He was there one day in 1973, alternating listening to classical music and the Watergate hearings on FM radio, and hammering out a small but special project. It was a bracelet for his daughter, Deane.

Its design reflected Mr. de Matteo's increasing preoccupation with abstract, sculptural forms. The face of the bracelet was divided into two parallel bands, one flat and straight, the other twisted into languid curves. The drama of the design lay in the juxtaposition of these two forms—the curved line playing off the linear one, complexity playing off simplicity.

Under repeated hammer blows, the silver had become work-hardened and unresponsive. So Mr. de Matteo began this day's work by heating it with a blowtorch-like flame. This process, called annealing, removes the internal stresses that build up during hammering, making the silver pliable once again.

Under the flame the silver changed color rapidly, from blue-gray to yellow to yellow splotched with red. "That's about 900 degrees now," Mr. de Matteo commented. A few seconds later it glowed cherry red, having reached the annealing temperature of 1,100 degrees.

Unlike steel, which must be hammered when red-hot, silver can be worked at room temperature. So after the bracelet had cooled, Mr. de Matteo began the most important step in the project, coaxing the twisted band into a more graceful curve.

Holding the bracelet firmly against an anvil-like device with his left hand, he struck the curved band repeatedly with a narrow-headed hammer. The blows were not heavy, but there was nothing tentative about them. Actually, though, the left hand was doing the really important work, holding the bracelet steady and in correct positon.

Each blow perceptively smoothed out the curve and

coaxed the metal into more fluid lines. Still, there seemed something awkward about the total effect, and Mr. de Matteo was dissatisfied. He seemed on the verge of abandoning the project as he had a twisted strip of metal inside his workbench drawer, the unsuccessful result of an earlier experiment. But he pushed the two bands together with his fingers, decided he liked the effect better and returned to his hammering.

"Well," he said presently, "it's not the most successful bracelet in the world, but it's not the most unsuccessful either. The lines are at least pleasant." He handed the finished bracelet to a polisher. The polisher promptly declared it a "weirdo."

Later, when the bracelet had returned from its final polishing with rouge (grit-free iron oxide) it shone with a high brilliance unmatched even by gold. It was that rarity in an industrialized, technological society: an object made by hand, individualized by hundreds of tiny indentations that told the story of its molding. To Bill de Matteo, there is still a place for such objects and a need for the time-honored crafts that fashion thelm.

"Society as a whole, as we know it, doesn't need craftsmen, any more than it needs beachcombers," he said. "But I think it would be dreadful for us if we were ever to live in a society without beachcombers. They don't mean a thing, except that they give those who care something to think about."

He stood in his shop, surrounded by his hammers and the bright gleam of silver, searching for a summation. "I'm not satisfied with the silver I make," he said finally. "But I'm very satisfied with the life I lead."

—DENNIS FARNEY

Ars Gratia Artis

"I'm sure there is no afterlife, no recovery, no saving grace," says Jon Anderson, who is a poet. "That's the worst thing in the world you can say, and it makes me as uncomfortable as anyone else, but I still have to confront my life in those terms. I suppose I'd do it anyway, even if I weren't a poet, so why not turn it into art?"

Mr. Anderson, a pleasant, expressive, slightly built man, relaxes shoeless in the livingroom of the small rural cabin he shares with his wife, Barbara, and their two large dogs and two cats. He also teaches creative writing at Ohio University in Athens, and one of his students, who has two dogs of his own, has moved in temporarily, geometrically increasing the confusion.

"Actually, it isn't all that grim," he continues. "I'm pleased if I write something well, and being a poet excuses my eccentricities. People don't think it's strange if they find me reading a comic book in my office at school."

As poets go, Jon Anderson must be counted as a success. At age 32, he already had two collections of his works published in book form, and his poems have appeared in anthologies, The New Yorker, Poetry magazine and numerous smaller periodicals. Reviews of his books have made The New York Times Sunday book section, and the critics, in their own peculiar language, apparently think he is very good. ("Mr. Anderson . . . is a quick-change artist whose constructions lie somewhere between sustained, evolving metaphor and surrealistic fiction—something quite different and quite his own," wrote the Times' reviewer of Mr. Anderson's first book, "Looking for Jonathan," which came out in 1968.) His second book, "Death & Friends," was nominated for a National Book Award in 1971.

For all that, though, Mr. Anderson has made precious

little money for his poetic efforts. In a dozen years as a published poet his total direct income from his art has amounted to barely $2,000. About $1,000 of that has come as royalties from his books and $212 more resulted from the publication of a single poem in The New Yorker several years ago. He earns his living by teaching and giving an occasional poetry reading at $100 or $200 a crack; the latter is one of the few ways he has benefited financially from the attention his work has received. "The problem of selling out doesn't seem to exist in poetry," he says with a smile. "There's no one to sell out to."

This is a condition he shares with just about everyone in his field. "Serious" poetry—that which seeks to confront honestly the basic emotional conditions of human life—exists in this country and most other places largely as a form of literary charity, with its practitioners left to fare as best they can. Most poets who are without independent means support themselves by teaching, doing other kinds of writing or following more mundane occupations. It has long been so: Longfellow taught, Whitman and Poe were journalists, Wallace Stevens was a lawyer and insurance executive.

This is not to say that a good deal of poetry doesn't get published in the U.S. Between 500 and 700 books of poems come out each year, and many small "reviews" and "quarterlies" are devoted exclusively to the form. All are inundated by submissions from real or would-be poets. Swallow Press, a small Chicago firm that publishes a half-dozen books of poems a year, says it gets about 3,000 manuscripts from which to choose annually, for instance.

This also is not to say that some contemporary poets don't cash in. The six books of poems by Rod McKuen, a songwriter, singer, record company owner and former bit-part actor, have registered hard-cover sales of about eight million copies, believed to be more than any poet since Shakespeare. Mr. McKuen's verses are generally considered too sentimental to be "serious," however.

Otherwise, pickings are decidedly slim. Aside from The New Yorker, magazines that carry poems typically pay little or not at all, and many depend on subsidies to survive. This category includes Poetry magazine, the largest (circulation 10,000) and most prestigious in its field. Its contributors, be they well-known or obscure, are uniformly rewarded at the rate of $1 a line.

As for books, "We, like other large publishers, put out a few volumes of poems a year because we feel we have an obligation to give poets a voice," says Richard McAdoo, editor-in-chief at Houghton Mifflin & Co. in Boston. "We certainly don't do it for the money. It takes sales of about 5,000 copies for us to break even on a book, and very few books of poems do that well. A poetry title that sells 10,000 copies over a period of years is considered a great success. Some novels sell that well in a month."

There's no special mystery why "serious" poetry doesn't command a larger audience. Its language tends to be allusive, its structure individual and often jarring to the uninitiated and its meaning unclear, at least on the first reading. As such, it requires far more effort from the reader than he is otherwise asked to put forth. Its dominant theme—how man (or, a man) faces the inevitability of death—is one that most people would rather not dwell on.

Thus, the poet takes up his work with the knowledge that his form almost certainly cuts him off from a large part of the reading public. Jon Anderson accepts this without regret. "My prime motive for writing is self-confrontation, and I find poems the best way to employ language to do this," he says. "My poetry isn't for everyone. It's for people like myself who want to contend with themselves. I think of my poems as intimate conversations with close friends, to whom I'm not afraid to reveal my vulnerability and loneliness. It might sound exclusive, but that's the way it is. There are other writers to take care of other audiences."

Mr Anderson was born and raised in Boston. His parents were divorced when he was young, and his mother, who raised him, later remarried. His step-father is a bank teller; he doesn't recall his natural father. As far as he knows, he has no literary forebears. "My mother wrote poems at one period of her life, but not seriously," he says. "A lot of people do this as a kind of journal-keeping. All it takes is a pencil and paper, you know."

He came upon poetry as a teen-ager. "I had a lot of time on my hands one summer, so I read a book of poems by T.S. Eliot. I thought I understood them, and it gave me a great feeling of intellectual superiority. I already thought I had the sort of deep, rich inner life that poets were supposed to have, and I like to play with words, so I tried a few. It was very heavy, symbolic stuff. Every word had at least three meanings. It was the kind of thing I hate to see my students do."

The young Mr. Anderson started sending batches of poetry off to magazines, often including letters explaining that he was only 17 years old and asking for comments and criticism. "I was hoping to be discovered as a prodigy," he says. It didn't work. He didn't even begin receiving rejection slips until someone told him that he should include stamped, self-addressed envelopes with his submissions.

He first broke into print as a student as Northeastern University in Boston. Metronome, a now-defunct magazine devoted to jazz, paid him $10 for a poem on Billie Holiday, the singer, which he titled "Lady Blue." "I still have it, but I won't show it to you," he says. "It's awful."

Mr. Anderson kept writing poems and sending them to magazines, but had little further luck getting published until he enrolled as a graduate student in the University of Iowa's highly regarded writer's program. "At Iowa, I got some decent criticism for the first time, and it helped me immensely," he says.

He was at Iowa in 1966 when he first cracked Poetry magazine. "I'd sent them about 20 batches of my work over a period of a half-dozen years before they finally bought one," he notes. "I guess they admired my perseverence." Shortly afterward, The New Yorker, which he also had subjected to a lengthy siege, published his 50-line poem "The Parachutist." He says the payment he received for that poem gave him "visions of financial comfort." But alas, no more were to follow despite repeated attempts.

Getting first books of poetry published can be extraordinarily difficult, and Mr. Anderson says he was lucky here. He submitted a collection of his work to a contest conducted by the University of Pittsburgh Press, and it was selected from some 600 entries as one of three that the concern would publish the next year. Its title, "Looking for Jonathan," represented something of a compromise with the standards of honesty he set for his work, he admits. "My real name is Jon, not Jonathan, but I figured that 'Looking for Jon' would sound like I was trying to find the men's room."

His next book, "Death & Friends," was also published by the University of Pittsburgh Press. It came out two years later. "I wanted very badly to get a second book into print," he says. "So many poets dry up after their first books; I had to feel I could do it again if I wanted to. Now, I feel no sense of crisis about being published. I have a book-length collection ready, but I'm not satisfied with about a third of the poems in it. I'll work on it for another year or so, I think."

Jon Anderson does his writing in a tiny office in his rented home, which is situated at the foot of a wooded hill several miles from a main road. He generally sits down to write around midnight and keeps at it until 6 or 8 a.m. He has managed to schedule his classes at Ohio University for the late afternoon and evening to accommodate his nocturnal work habits.

"A common misconception about poems is that they begin with an idea, which the poet then tries to decorate with words," he says. "That's not true for me. I almost always begin with a phrase that appeals to me, that looks like it might lead somewhere. If things go right, the phrase evokes more phrases and *then* the content appears. It's a kind of magical process—a form of self-hypnosis. Most of the time I don't fully realize what a poem means, or if it means anything, until after I've written it.

"It usually takes me three nights to write a poem, once I've screwed myself up to sit down in front of a typewriter," he goes on. "The first night, I put down a phrase or two and stare at them. The second night I write something that sounds like a poem, but it's usually just an imitation of one. By the third night I've exhausted myself to the point where I can speak honestly."

Mr. Anderson does no research and doesn't seek out experiences about which to write. "My material comes from inside my head, from my thoughts, or fantasies or dreams," he says. "An event might set these off, but not until much later. It isn't a logical process. It's more of a kind of free association."

By way of illustration, he turns to his poem, "A Song for Children," that appeared in "Death & Friends":

Where are the tired adults
we must court & entertain?
We are helpless, like history,
we do not want to begin.

Now to be bathed, now to be kissed,
now to be put to sleep.
We are soft dolls, or cups,
the silences they keep.

"My ex-wife Linda and I were driving in Portland, Ore., where we lived," he says. "It was about 4 a.m. and it was raining, and we were very tired. All of a sudden we saw a car up against a bridge abutment. We stopped; it was her idea. There was a guy in the car, pressed between the steering wheel and the seat. He looked like he was in bad shape.

"We went to get help, but people wouldn't let us in. They must have thought we looked like a couple of crazy hippies. Finally, someone let us make a phone call. By the time we got back to the scene, the police had arrived. I don't know why, but I went from cop to cop telling them my name, as if it were somehow important that they know it.

"Later, I had this strange feeling that since we'd saved this guy we were responsible for him. I imagined us bringing him to our home, paralyzed, and that I would sit with him in the dark talking to him, and he would have to listen because he couldn't move or speak. I tried a poem about this, but it didn't come off—it was too surreal. A couple of weeks later, it occurred to me that very young children were in the same condition I'd imagined this man to be in. They must sit silently while their parents pour out their emotions to them. 'The silences they keep' is the key line, I think. The poem is about helplessness and the fact that life is pushed on us. Now that I reread it, I guess it's about privacy, too."

Mr. Anderson says that his poems reflect his feelings about his personal situation when he writes them, and these have changed over the years. "The poems that went into 'Looking for Jonathan' were written mainly for the music in them. I was young, and free of most responsibilities."

His later collection had a quite different tone. "Anderson's world is one in which the human condition is scarcely bearable, and separation is the strongest reality," wrote a reviewer of "Death & Friends" in the Hudson Review. "It is a world that cannot accept the dual nature of humanity: the flesh and the soul simultaneously there, each mocking the reality of the other . . . (we have) the figure of the saint, who escapes but only by deliberate pain, from the condition of the body . . . (he quotes) 'The saint flagellates himself; it seems/to be another man. Not pain,/but the aesthetic of pain is learned./He knows there is no reward for being hurt./Slowly he strips his skin.'"

"I was going through a bad time then," the poet acknowledges. "I was in a new teaching job at Portland University, and I had few friends. My marriage (which was to end in divorce) was breaking up, I felt very much lonely and alienated."

Now, he says, "I've come to terms with a lot of things. I've got a good marriage and a feeling of home. I like teaching here. I'm looking around myself more, and I'm more involved with other people. I feel that I'm more alike other people than I'm different from them. Everyday human things seem more important to me. I think I said that in my last poem in 'Death & Friends.'" ("Because of death, they are valuable./A man waters his lawn.")

He ruffles through a notebook and pulls out a poem titled "Years," which is to be included in the new book he is preparing.

Sometimes in weariness I stop.
Because I've been lucky
I think the future must be plain.

My friends talk quietly
& we have all come to the same things.
Now if I die, I will
inherit awhile their similar bodies.
Now if I listen
someone is telling a story.
The characters met;
they enchanted each other by speech.

Though the stories they lived
were not the same
many were distracted into love,
slept, & woke alone, awhile serene.

"It's about life in proximity to others," he says. "It says that there are consolations. The important word, though, is 'awhile.'"

—FREDERICK C. KLEIN

Making Music

George Crumb sits on a revolving stool between two pianos in the den of his split-level home in Media, Pa., and explains why he turned down an offer to write the musical score for the popular movie, "The Exorcist":

"I thought it would be a disturbing thing for my work," he says. "Sure, I have respect for the guys who do that kind of thing, but that's just not my line of work."

George Crumb's line of work is composing what is usually referred to in the business as "serious" or "new" music. Exactly which works constitute serious music is subject to varying opinions, although it might be said as a rough sementic guide that so-called serious compositions exclude the fields of jazz, rock and pop and are most often heard in concert halls rather than, say, over the jukeboxes of cocktail lounges. In any case, the compositions of the 45-year-old Mr. Crumb are taken seriously enough that he won the Pulitzer Prize for Music in 1968 (for "Echoes of Time and the River") and that Teresa Sterne, president of Nonesuch Records, describes him as "our own modern Beethoven."

Two of Mr. Crumb's most widely played compositions are "Night of the Four Moons," in which the main instruments are a banjo, an alto flute and an electric cello, and "Voice of the Whale," a 15-minute piece based on the "singing" of the humpbacked whale (and sounding, according to one reviewer, like a "transcendental kazoo"). Thomas Frost, director of artists and repertoire for the Columbia Records Masterworks Series, says a recording containing both these pieces was issued in April 1974 and is already a best seller for serious music. "I think we'll be programming more Crumb in the future," Mr. Frost says.

If true, this is encouraging news for Mr. Crumb—particularly since his field is small and isn't especially lucrative. Indeed, he earns only half as much from composing as he does from teaching composition at the University of Pennsylvania where he is a full professor and composer in residence. (He declines to reveal his salary at Penn, but full professors at the university earn about $30,000 a year.) His income from recordings was expected to total a mere $500 in 1974.

"America is a country of jazz and pop," says Rudolph Nissim, head of the serious-music department of the American Society of Authors, Composers and Publishers, better known as ASCAP. "Serious music is second-class."

This isn't to say, of course, that serious music is disregarded by Americans. But the nation's 28 major symphony orchestras mainly program the tried and true classics of yesterday's giants—Beethoven, Mozart, Schubert—and leave the works of current composers such as Mr. Crumb to university symphonies and chamber groups. According to one music publisher, there are about 2,000 composers of serious contemporary music in the U.S. currently vying for a musical platform.

George Crumb might well be considered to be prominent among the 2,000. Certainly, he is no starving artist. He lives comfortably with his wife and children in Media, a Philadelphia suburb, and his tenured status at Penn has given him almost complete financial security. He also receives "a couple of thousand commission offers a month" to execute musical works for fees ranging from $1,000 to $10,000. And if he isn't rich and if his name isn't a household work, it's quite possibly because he turns most such offers down.

Mr. Crumb deliberately limits his output to one or two pieces a year, he says, both because he finds it impossible to compose music just for the sake of composition. "I can only write things I believe in," he says. In mid-1974 he was working on a piece for two pianos that he tentatively called "Music for a Summer Evening." He wrote five movements of the work in March and April, but in the months following he wrote nothing because he couldn't decide whether he needs a sixth movement.

"The question is whether the work stands as it is," the composer says. "I can't put my finger on what's wrong. In a way, it needs that extra movement, and I hope I come to see decision fairly soon because it's been driving me nuts for five months."

But five months in Mr. Crumb's musical scheme of things isn't really very long, especially when it's considered that he has been composing on and off for some 36 years. Born in Charleston, W.Va., on the day of the great 1929 stock-market crash (a birth date, he suggests, that "may have something to do with the melancholy quality of my work"), he soon came under the musical influence of his parents. His late father was a clarinet player who performed with local bands and taught music. His mother was a state employe during his childhood years and played the piano for recreation.

"It was the Depression era, so we were too poor to buy records and things like that," he reminisces. So the family made its own music. Mr. Crumb says he taught himself to play the piano by ear, and by the time he was nine years old he was composing music he describes as "little pieces in the style of Mozart." He did perform on his high-school track team, but his extracurricular activities were largely—indeed, almost exclusively—centered on song.

"The teachers used to yell at George because he wore his hair long, was a terrible dresser and composed music in English class," recalls George Crumb's wife, Elizabeth, whom he met in a high-school harmony class and married two years after graduation. Mrs. Crumb has been playing the piano since high school, but she confesses that she's unable to play her husband's piano works because of their complexity.

Complex as it may be in the making, the Crumb sound is perhaps best described as lean. But it is also often dreamlike and, compared with other contemporary music, surprisingly emotional. Any given Crumb piece is full of a variety of sounds: A chorus sings across the strings of a piano; an oboe player picks up a harmonica and blows a little tune; a piano player attacks the keyboard with his knuckles; a violin is made to sound like a mandolin.

George Crumb usually explains in his titles what a particular piece will sound like. His "Ancient Voices of Children," based on poems by the Spanish poet Garcia Lorca, uses a boy soprano and a toy piano to recall the suffering of children in civil-war Spain. "Black Angels (Thirteen Images from the Dark Land)" evokes superstition and terror; the four string players who perform the piece shout the numbers one through seven in Swahili, Japanese, French, Spanish, Russian, English. Mr. Crumb maintains that he is apolitical; but he says of this piece, written in 1970, "I thought at the time we were living in a dark land."

Most of those who are familiar with Mr. Crumb's music believe he has made his reputation by writing music that sounds new but that the untrained listener can appreciate. "He's one of the avant garde, but he doesn't do what they do," says Donal Henahan, a New York Times critic who has also called Mr. Crumb "one of our best talents."

This accolade wasn't earned without a great deal of hard work, much study and a few detours from composing. After graduating from high school, Mr. Crumb went on to Mason College, a now-defunct musical conservatory in Charleston, and graduated in 1950; from there, he went to the University of Illinois, where he obtained a master's degree, and then to the University of Michigan, where he began studies toward a doctorate.

Before receiving his doctorate, however, he spent a year in Berlin at the Hochschule for Musik. "I was supposed to be there to study composition," he says, "but the experience was disappointing. The director had a number of duties, and I got very few lessons. So I played the piano."

After Mr. Crumb returned to the U.S. in 1955, he returned to Michigan and completed his doctoral studies, receiving his degree in 1959. His first postdoctoral job;

teaching piano to nonmusic students at the University of Colorado. (One faculty member there remembers him as "a rather secondary piano teacher who wasn't too happy at it.") Finally, Mr. Crumb met up with David Burge, a pianist at the university who persuaded him to write some piano pieces. The result was "Five pieces for Piano"; and the work, which was widely performed by Mr. Burge on a concert tour, was favorably reviewed and quickly snapped up by a recording company.

But the budding composer by no means achieved instant fame. According to sources in the music industry, his first publisher was less than enthusiastic about Crumb works; in any case, only one Crumb piece was published in 10 years. Mr. Crumb left the publisher and for two years published his own music, copying scores by hand and doing his own mailing. Finally, he retained a lawyer and signed on with a new publisher, and his works saw light.

"All composers are taken advantage of," says Mr. Crumb's lawyer, Robert Miller, who also happens to be an accomplished concert pianist specializing in Crumb works. "Few of them have anyone looking out for their business affairs."

Among Mr. Crumb's recent business activities were his negotiations with William Friedkin, the director of "The Exorcist." Although Mr. Crumb turned down Mr. Friedkin's offer to write the score for the picture, the director nevertheless did manage to include the Crumb touch by using 30 seconds of "Black Angels" in assembling the final "Exorcist" score. For this, Mr. Crumb was paid $2,000—about 40 times what he has made from sales of "Black Angels" in its full recorded form. (Under a formula basic to the recording industry, a composer receives a meager quarter of a cent for each minute of music on a given recording—multiplied by the number of recordings. However, the industry's two licensing outfits, ASCAP and Broadcast Music Inc., both provide their struggling serious-music people with "multipliers," whereby a composer actually pulls in more money from the licensing agent than he'd earn from the record company.)

Such bonanzas are a welcome addition to a serious composer's revenues, particularly since such a composer rarely receives substantial funds from public performances of his works. The nation's 65-year-old copyright law affords composers royalties only when their music is performed for profit, thereby cutting out potential returns from college campuses and public television. Then, the composer must split all royalties with his publisher, who, under the law, owns the copyright in return for publishing the score.

Congress in 1974 was considering a bill that would revise the old copyright law to provide composers with some performance royalties from nonprofit sources. Meanwhile, about the only serious-music composer who makes substantial amounts of money from his music alone is the 73-year-old Aaron Copland, who brings in more than $100,000 a year. In the 1973-74 season, Mr. Copland's works were played in 396 paying performances in the U.S. compared with 100 for the late French composer Claude Debussy, 139 for Leonard Bernstein and 54 for George Crumb.

According to Mr. Crumb, the process of composition is "an abstract problem" that mainly involves "getting rid of something, trying to get it out the best you can." When he isn't teaching, he rises at 7 a.m. and plays the piano—mainly Mozart, Bach and Haydn—for a couple of hours after breakfast, usually getting to work in his den at 9:30. Unlike many composers, he doesn't work at the piano but sits instead at a long wall desk.

"It's possible to work at the piano or away from it and still not hear what you're playing," Mr. Crumb says. Indeed, if he uses the piano at all, it is often only to poke around inside the instrument, extracting new timbres from the strings. "Sometimes I don't know about the weird sounds that come from that room," muses his wife. "The weirdest one is when George starts singing."

—R.G. FREEMAN

Heeded Words

In 1963, E. Clifton Daniel, then assistant managing editor of The New York Times, called Edward Durrell Stone, the architect, and asked Mr. Stone his opinion of Ada Louise Huxtable, whom the Times was about to hire for the newly created post of architecture critic. "I spoke a kind word about her," Mr. Stone recalls.

Mrs. Huxtable, who shortly thereafter was hired by the Times, hasn't always returned the favor. In the fall of 1971, in a display of the critical ferocity for which she has become famous in architecture circles, she turned on her onetime benefactor and friend with a scathing review of his creation, the John F. Kennedy Center for the Performing Arts in Washington, D.C. Describing Mr. Stone's vast new white marble building, with its red carpeted and crystal-chandeliered interior, as a "superbunker" of which Nazi architect "Albert Speer would have approved," she said that Mr. Stone had opted for "safe and sanitary kitsch" instead of greatness and originality. In a subsequent appearance on the television program "Firing Line," she called the center "the biggest, most-banal building I've ever seen in my life."

It pains Ada Louise Huxtable, or so she says, that she must sometimes attack the work of men, such as Mr. Stone, whom she admires. In fact, after her review ofthe Kennedy Center appeared, she wrote Mr. Stone to say that her critical remarks "hurt me more than you." Be that as it may, Mrs. Huxtable has never flinched from telling her readers exactly what she thinks. "That's professional behavior," she explains.

It's also the kind of behavior that has made Mrs. Huxtable the delight of readers across the nation, an object of some awe in the architecture world, and perhaps the most powerful individual on the Times' roster of critics—including the newspaper's mighty reviewers of drama. For while most plays, at least in the universal scheme of things, can be considered ephemeral, buildings are erected to endure at the very least for a generation. They are quite simply, *there;* we confront them daily; and they often profoundly affect the way we live.

True, Ada Louise Huxtable—whose power is belied by her petite, fragile appearance—can't have a building she dislikes dismantled, as a drama critic's displeasure can, and often does, close down a play. But by creating the magnitude of public awareness about the architecture that has never before existed in this country, Mrs. Huxtable has "made architects and city officials a little more self-conscious about what they're doing," says Harmon Goldstone, chairman of New York City's Landmark Preservation Commission. As a result, Mr. Goldstone says, "New York City is, and will be in the future, a better-looking place."

His opinion is shared by others in the world of architecture. Robert Stern, a leading New York City architect, feels that "serious architects in this city don't like doing things they know she won't approve of." And Jaquelin T. Robertson, director of New York's Office of Midtown Planning and Development and a man with a considerable say about new buildings, urban projects and zoning, says: "I would consciously go out of my way to get her advice on issues."

The chances are excellent that Mr. Robertson might accept Mrs. Huxtable's advice, too. "She has such a keen understanding of the politics, the money and the realities involved in any given situation," he says, "that I can treat her as a peer. In that way, she's alone among all architecture critics."

In view of such accolades, and Mrs. Huxtable's considerable power, it seems surprising that a decade ago she was a virtual nonentity. Born Ada Louise Landman in New York City (she won't specify how many years ago), she received a B.A. from Hunter College and then attended the Institute of Fine Arts of New York University, where she took every course that school offered in architecture. She was hoping to obtain a master's degree as an architecture historian; but she left the institute without getting her degree when her proposal for a thesis on 19th- and 20th-Century Italian architecture was turned down.

From 1946 to 1950, Mrs. Huxtable was an assistant curator at New York's Museum of Modern Art; her areas were architecture and design. She spent the next 13 years as a freelance writer. Her by-line first appeared in the Times in the early 1960s over occasional pieces in the paper's Sunday magazine. (Her first piece in the Times was actually a letter to the editor she wrote protesting the "inadequacies" of a photographic exhibit devoted to Venezuelan architecture.) She came recommended to the Times by the late Aline Saarinen, an old friend and then as assistant Times art critic; Mrs. Saarinen had written occasional architecture pieces for the Times until her marriage to Eero Saarinen, the late architect.

In 1963, the Times asked Mrs. Huxtable to become its first full-time daily architecture critic. "I turned it down," she says. "I was afraid that would be too much. But Clifton (Daniel) said that if I didn't take it, the Times would have to find someone else to do architecture." Rather than be supplanted, Mrs. Huxtable accepted Mr. Daniel's offer. (Mrs. Huxtable's starting salary isn't known, nor will she divulge her current income. According to a source at the Times, however, most of the newspaper's critics have an annual salary of $30,000 to $40,000 a year, and it is believed that Mrs. Huxtable's current pay is toward the upper limit of that range.)

With her columns thenceforth regular, she rocketed almost immediately to fame. Lewis Mumford, the widely respected architecture critic of The New Yorker magazine until his retirement, says "it wasn't until the Times got Huxtable that people really began to pay attention to architecture criticism."

Indeed, in the years following Mrs. Huxtable's appointment, her articles have been credited with a number of developments affecting the looks of cities, towns and villages across the nation. In New York, for example, she succeeded—where planners had failed—in persuading the builders of a row of skyscrapers along the west side of the Avenue of the Americas to build a shopping mall, some three blocks long, behind the new buildings to replace those shops destroyed in the process of renewal.

"I explained," Mrs. Huxtable says of this effort, "that what (the builders) were doing was no way to develop a good corporate image." (The success of her persuasive abilities brought a "Dear Ada Louise" thank-you letter from Mayor John Lindsay—one of many similar tributes from the former mayor. "I've had so many," Mrs. Huxtable says, "I've started writing back 'Dear John.'")

Another Huxtable article persuaded the city fathers of Windsor, Vt., to forgo the planned demolition of the elegant old Windsor House; a drive-in bank was to have been constructed on the site of the historic residence. A similar plea stopped construction of a road that would have cut through a lovely Japanese garden attached to the Peabody Museum in Salem, Mass.

Important as it is, Mrs. Huxtable's by-line isn't always necessary for her to achieve action. An unsigned Times editorial that she wrote in 1972 is credited with having called attention in the House of Representatives to covert language in a Senate bill that would have provided funds for an extension of the west front of the Capitol—an addition that she and other groups opposed. (While she is hopeful the extension will never be approved, Mrs. Huxtable isn't taking the House's veto for granted. "Nothing is ever dead," she says.)

But Ada Louise Huxtable doesn't always get her way. Despite her printed pleas, the city of Manchester, N.H., went ahead with plans to tear down the century-old Amoskeag mill complex flanking the banks of the Merrimack River for more than a mile. In Mrs. Huxtable's opinion, Manchester's decision was tragic, in that "an acknowledged monument of American industrial history and urban design" was being razed for "a researched, consultant-approved and officially adopted urban-renewal scheme, consisting almost totally of parking lots, that mocks the quality of vision and design now being ruthlessly effaced."

For her attempts in New Hampshire, Mrs. Huxtable says, she received a threat from William Loeb, publisher of the arch-conservative Manchester Union Leader, "to send me a rat." From other quarters came cries that Mrs. Huxtable was solely interested in antique preservation rather than contemporary creation—a charge that she denies. Rather than having tunnel vision solely focused on the past, Mrs. Huxtable says, she is against "blind mutilation in the name of urban renewal." She adds: "Our heritage is too precious to see it go down the drain without a struggle."

Few deny this observation, but some architects and others complain that Mrs. Huxtable has no clear vision of what she would actually like to see in the way of urban development. "She doesn't help remold architecture so much as she contents herself to follow the trends and comment on them," says James Rossant, the designer of a planned community at Reston, Va., outside the nation's capital.

(Mrs. Huxtable's appraisals of Reston have been mixed. When the community opened several years ago, she praised Mr. Rossant's effort as "an attempt to create amenity planning (with) good ambiance." However, she pointed out in a subsequent article that although Reston had achieved "great success as a suburban community," this end result didn't live up to the broader vision of the town as initially conceived.)

Another detractor is Vincent Scully, professor of the history of art at Yale, who said in a letter to the Times, "It has never been possible to value Mrs. Huxtable's writing for critical acumen or command of history. Its most positive quality has seemed to be a kind of hectic candor, but that, too, must be called into question now." Mr. Scully was complaining about a Huxtable review of the Scully book, "American Architecture and Urbanism."

Despite such skirmishes, Ada Louis Huxtable remains hugely popular among the nation's intelligentsia. Her writings have brought her no less than 10 honorary doctors' degrees. And in 1970 she became the first person ever to win a Pulitzer Prize in the award's creative category for criticism.

Welcome as the Pulitzer was, it did create some problems for Mrs. Huxtable with her peer group at the paper. On the day the prizes were announced, she says, John Canaday, the Times' art critic—and, later, a Pulitzer candidate himself—confronted her and, much to her surprise, "flung a four-letter word at me." Mrs. Huxtable attributes his behavior at that time to the "incredible sense of jealousy" that exists among so many Times reporters, and she immediately adds: "John's been beside himself ever since" because of his behavior that day.

What he actually said, says Mr. Canaday, was: "I congratulate the critic. I deplore the person." Mr. Canaday, who also recommended Mrs. Huxtable for her job as the Times' regular architecture critic, says that after she got the job, "she engaged in a series of undercuttings, which included an insistence that I not cover architecture at Osaka (during that city's Expo '70). Her health wouldn't permit her to go at the time, and I'd taken a year of Japanese lessons. What she told me was: "I know you'd write charming stories, but I'd write important ones.'"

Mr. Canaday, who concedes that "I chose the wrong time to let off steam" in attacking Mrs. Huxtable, says he still considers her "the finest architecture critic alive."

Admirers of her work are also found in the ranks of architects themselves. For example, I.M. Pei, designer of the Everson Museum of Art in Syracuse, N.Y., and a host of other notable buildings, says Mrs. Huxtable "can get to the heart of the matter faster than most architects." And Gordon Bunshaft of the New York architecture firm of Skidmore, Owings & Merrill calls Mrs. Huxtable "the greatest architecture critic living and active in the U.S."

True, Mr. Pei and Mr. Bunshaft can be said to be returning Mrs. Huxtable's compliments, or favors, as the case may be. In a recent review of Mr. Pei's extension to the

National Gallery of Art in Washington, Mrs. Huxtable said that the nation's capital "is finally going to have a great 20th-Century building." (She was particularly taken by Mr. Pei's dexterity in working with the "lopsided triangle" of land designated for the building. "I love things that are problem-solving," she admits.) Mr. Bunshaft, on the other hand, was pleased that Mrs. Huxtable agreed to hold off a review of his concave Solow Building skyscraper on Manhattan's West 57th Street; it is known that Mrs. Huxtable's first reaction to the building was one of displeasure, but Mr. Bunshaft hoped that further reflection and exploration would change her mind. (She didn't. She later criticized the building as out-of-proportion and a violator of the "streetscape.")

Mrs. Huxtable isn't prone to rushing out reviews, anyway. A perfectionist, who admits "I'd go crazy if I had to turn out something every day," she does most of her writing in the morning in the den of the Park Avenue apartment (an old, comfortable, but not notably distinguished building) she shares with her husband of 30 years, L. Garth Huxtable. (Mr. Huxtable, an industrial designer, designed all the tableware used by the plush Four Seasons restaurant in New York City—with an assist from his wife. "I've always worked with him, and he's always worked with me," Mrs. Huxtable says. "I show him a copy of everything I write.")

Her appearance in the Times' midtown offices are sporadic, but she goes to the newspapers' headquarters at least twice a week in order to handle the ceaseless flow of letters. Of her mail, she says, "I probably get more than any of the Times' other critics, and almost none of it is crackpot."

Her mail comes from all over—as is only fitting, since the critic herself ranges far and wide on the job, often under the worst possible conditions. For example, she inspected the latest work of Robert and Denise Venturi, a Philadelphia architecture team, on a day that might have intimidated less hardy souls. According to Mr. Venturi,

Mrs. Huxtable visited the Venturis' project, a six-story Philadelphia residence for the elderly, "in one of the worst wind- and rainstorms I can ever remember." He adds: "She also spent a day in our office going over plans for the project and discussing it. It was obvious that she was trying to discover for herself what we were up to."

The Venturis were especially grateful for Mrs. Huxtable's scrupulous attention because, Mr. Venturi says, "we sometimes do what's called second-glance architecture, which means that you don't see everything at once." (They had a subsequent reason for further gratitude: Mrs. Huxtable's review was a rave.)

Among others who have reason to thank Ada Louise Huxtable are some of the architecture critics of the nation's biggest dailies. Only after she was hired by the Times did The Washington Post, the Chicago Sun-Times, the Los Angeles Times and a few other papers hire writers for similar positions. John Pastier, the Los Angeles Times' architecture critic, says he was hired because "the paper was looking over its shoulder at the competition." And Rob Cuscaden, the Chicago Sun-Times' critic, says: "I couldn't have got my job if Ada hadn't won her Pulitzer Prize. She made the whole profession respectable."

Mrs. Huxtable's Pulitzer was granted for her writings. According to some observers, however, her manner while on the job is as important as her critical ability. "She has such a sweet smile and such a way about her," says an architect who has seen her out in the field. "Before you know it, she's got everyone—the builders included—eating out of her hand and telling her everything she wants to know. Then she retreats behind a closed door and out comes this very gutsy critique."

Mr. Robertson of New York's Midtown Planning office has another view. "She's a very charming, feminine, quiet woman who's like a razor blade," he says. "If she were a loud, pushy feminist, she wouldn't be nearly as effective."

Mrs. Huxtable's own opinion of her ability is modest. "I'm only a catalyst for what so many people feel," she says.

She is, however, pleased at the interest generated by her work. "Architecture was once thought of as a little old lady's hobby," she says. "Nowadays, it's a legitimate issue that's of interest to everyone."

—STEPHEN GROVER

The Pianist

His suede coat slung over one shoulder, concert pianist Garrick Ohlsson leans against a wall in the lobby of the Treadway Inn in Utica, N.Y., and gazes forlornly out at the steady afternoon rain. The alternator in his rented car just broke, and he is more than an hour late for a ladies' luncheon being held in his honor prior to an evening concert. As he stands waiting for the manager of the Utica Civil Musical Society to pick him up, several people wander past him, none paying him any mind.

"Yes, this is the glamorous life of the concert pianist," Mr. Ohlsson says with more than a trace of irony. "Terribly exciting, isn't it?"

Perhaps not—but it is terribly typical. For as 24-year-old Garrick Ohlsson hopscotches around the globe playing concerts, he spends a good portion of his time waiting around in places like Utica. And except for the occasional car breakdown, his schedule rarely varies; check-in at a motel, practice at the local theater, a luncheon speech at the local ladies' club, more practice, a nap, a performance with the local orchestra and, finally, a lot of smiling and pumping hands with concertgoers at a post-performance party.

If Garrick Ohlsson's life doesn't sound like a thrill a minute, neither do the lives of most concert pianists. Mr. Ohlsson, in fact, in many respects exemplifies the struggles of the young musician at the crossroads of his career. Having survived the grueling early years of training, the slow ascent to the upper reaches of technical perfection and the sometimes harsh pen of critics, he faces the prospect of seeing his name etched in musical archives beside Liszt, Rachmaninoff and Busoni as one of the great pianists of history—or perhaps of continuing a spate of one-night stands in nonexotic locales, never becoming a household word, to say nothing of a musical phenomenon, and in the end perhaps faltering and withdrawing from the concert circuit altogether.

Waiting in the wings to replace Mr. Ohlsson if he falls are scores of young pianists with equally impressive credentials and the same dreams of playing themselves into keyboard history. For all of them, the road to the top of the profession is a far longer and lonelier one than that for their musical brethren in the world of rock. Whereas rock stars can drink in the glory of overnight success through a gimmick or one smash hit, classical musicians must struggle much of their lives for even the smallest sip of success.

Chiefly responsible for this situation is an apathy—in some cases even a disdain—on the part of the general public toward classical music. An estimated 15 million Americans attended symphony performances in 1972—far less than the 30 million who are estimated to have already seen the movie "The Godfather" and about a third of the number who attended auto races. "As soon as you call something classical, you frighten off a good portion of the population," says Henry Brief, executive director of the Recording Industry Association of America. "It suggests that it requires a foreknowledge and preeducation, rather than just the enjoyment of music for music's sake."

As another example, the recording association reports that classical record sales account for only 4% of total record sales. And of the 1,131 gold records the association had awarded for sales of at least $1 million, only one has gone to a classical musician (Van Cliburn for his 1961 recording of a Tchaikovsky piano concerto). "You're dealing with a rather static unchanging repertoire," Mr. Brief says. "There just aren't any more Beethovens, Tchaikovskys or Bachs."

But there is an Ohlsson. And while it is too soon to tell whether he will ever join the ranks of the musical immortals, he is off to a good start. The Boston Globe reviewed his playing as being "of great intelligence and with an uncommon feeling for architecture" of a work. The St. Louis Post-Dispatch called him "a clean virtuoso, a keyboard tiger who nails down every note." And the Chicago Tribune said he "has a sense of melody and melodic phrasing that brings out sounds you haven't heard before."

At six-foot-four and weighing 240 pounds, the bearded Garrick Ohlsson looks more like a linebacker for the New York Giants than the stereotypically ascetic concert pianist. His massive right hand can span a dozen keys, and his left hand can blanket 11. His personality is almost puckish and belies the solemnity customarily—albeit often erroneously—associated with classical artists.

His stint in Utica provides a good glimpse of Garrick Ohlsson at work. Arriving from New York the evening before his concert with the Utica Symphony Orchestra, Mr. Ohlsson squeezes in a two-hour rehersal and turns in by 11. Rising at 8:30, he gulps down some coffee and scoots over to the theater for more practice. This session is followed by a luncheon of the private Fort Schuyler Club.

During the luncheon, Mr. Ohlsson learns by accident that a second concert he was expecting to give in Utica the following night had been canceled, though no one had thought to tell him. After being fawned over by the club's membership, he then hurries across the street for a final practice session at the antiquated theater where the performance is scheduled. He concludes that the piano "needs a major overhaul," but he is forced to settle for a bit more tuning.

Mr. Ohlssons's next stop is the Civic Musical Society, where he autographs a picture for the secretary and learns, again by accident, that he is scheduled to play during the first half of the concert rather than after intermission, as he had originally been told. Up to that point, he hadn't planned to arrive at the theater until after the concert had begun. But he greets the change with resignation. "It happens all the time," he says.

Driven back to his hotel, Mr. Ohlsson takes a two-hour

nap before the conductor picks him up for dinner at an Italian restaurant with the musical society manager and an officer of the Fort Schuyler Club. Service is slow, and the conductor has to dash off before the end of the meal. The musical society manager drives Mr. Ohlsson to the theater—getting lost along the way and giving him an unplanned tour of some highly unscenic parts of Utica, an industrial city of 95,000.

They arrive at the theater with a half-hour to go until concert-time. Looking over the crowd, Mr. Ohlsson observes: "Mostly old ladies. Typical, typical." Also typical is the fact that the program has his last name misspelled.

Backstage, Mr. Ohlsson is somewhat tense. "I'm usually pretty charged up before a concert," he says. "I'm a little nervous, but it's racehorse nerves, rather than weary nerves. There's always a slight vague doubt whether I can do it this time," When he was 12 years old, he says, he had recurrent nightmares in which he was preparing to open a program before a packed Carnegie Hall with Chopin's "Impromptu" in G-flat major—and found he couldn't remember the piece at all.

No such embarrassments occur in Utica, and Mr. Ohlsson's rendition of Rachmaninoff receives a standing ovation. As he walks off the stage, however, he remarks, "The piano was so out of tune, I couldn't believe it. Right from the very first note." Retiring to his dressing room, he lounges in a chair and sips some soda. Following a concert, he says, "I'm covered with sweat and slightly wrung out. For a half hour, there's a very low ebb and my mind shuts off and I have to sit down and do nothing."

After Mr. Ohlsson rests, the musical society manager-cum-chauffeur takes him back to the motel for a party. All ticket-holders are invited to the affair, and about 100 show up, shake the pianists hand and pose questions that Mr. Ohlsson says he has answered thousands of times in hundreds of other places.

Here's how Mr. Ohlsson describes the typical post-concert party: "Somebody, probably the civic league president, comes up and says, 'Oh, I loved that concert. By the way, where are you going from here? How many hours a day do you practice? Where do you stay? Oh, I mustn't monopolize you.' Then, you are introduced to someone else, who proceeds to say, 'Oh, I loved that concert. By the way, where are you going from here? How many hours a day do you practice? Where do you stay? Oh, I mustn't monopolize you.'"

The Utica affair proceeds along these lines and then breaks up shortly after midnight. All in all, the day has been a success—albeit a restrained one and certainly a far cry from the days when audiences responded to concert pianists much like today's youth respond to their idols in the world of rock. For despite the plethora of concert pianists today—pianists with impeccable technical skills— few have the ability to transport their listeners.

"There isn't the flair with them," says Harold C. Schonberg, senior music critic of The New York Times. "I don't mean dancing on the keyboard. But there is the 'X' factor that leaps out over the footlights and affects audiences."

It wasn't always thus. Contemporaries of Franz Liszt recorded that the showmanship of the flamboyant 19th-Century pianist caused women to fling their jewels at the stage, to shriek in ecstasy and to faint. And only a few decades ago concertgoers listening to the playing of Arthur Schnabel were said to sit spellbound in cathedral silence, nearly hypnotized by the beauty of his playing.

But those days seem gone forever—a fact that music experts attribute to today's more rigid instruction. Old traditions such as improvisation and embellishment, these experts say, have given way to a school emphasizing strength and sobriety rather than charm and brilliance—a school that stresses planning and leaves nothing to chance. By comparison, the performances of today's pop stars— although they, too, may be planned down to the last wiggle or grunt—appear to be spontaneous and correspondingly infect their audiences with a frenzy much like the effect created by the pianists of yesteryear.

Perhaps because of this absence of frenzy, concert pianists today command far less in fees than their rock counterparts. According to a 1971 survey of college concerts carried out under the auspices of the Association of College and University Concert Managers, the average fee for an instrumental recital in 1971 was $2,230, compared with $6,204 for rock concerts. And Harold Shaw, Mr. Ohlsson's manager, says that only two active pianists, Artur Rubinstein and Van Cliburn, consistently earn more than $10,000 a concert.

Mr. Ohlsson receives a standard fee of $2,500 per performance, although he sometimes performs for far less—particularly abroad. "If you're going to compare him to rock and pop stars he's going to look like a crumb," Mr. Shaw says of Mr. Ohlsson. (It isn't uncommon for a rock star to receive upwards of $20,000 a show.) What's more, the $2,500 is a gross. From this figure, Mr. Ohlsson must subtract a 20% commission for his manager and all advertising and travel costs. He also occasionally pays for the rental of a piano; and sometimes, in cases where he wishes to perform on prestigious stages, he must pay the rental of a concert hall. On top of all this, there is a monthly retainer for his press agent—meaning that Mr. Ohlsson's take-home for last season's gross of $175,000 (for 95 concerts) amounted to about $60,000, or $631 per concert (nevertheless, still more than the net taken in by many lesser-known pianists, who often only gross a few hundred dollars a performance).

Garrick Ohlsson concedes that "greed" caused him to enter Poland's prestigious Chopin International Piano Competition in 1970, which he won (becoming the first American to do so). Without such a prize, he explains, "it's very difficult for a young artist to get started. What you have to do is distinguish yourself so when the agents book for Duluth, Minn.; Toledo, Ohio; and Broken Cookie, Neb., they book you."

Mr. Ohlsson's musical interest was spurred by his parents. When he was eight years old and the family was living in White Plains, N.Y., he was placed under the tutelage of a local piano teacher. At 12, he was enrolled in the Westchester Conservatory of Music, and the following year he entered the preparatory division of the Juilliard School in New York. He completed Juilliard's regular division at the age of 22; and since age 18, he has trained under the direction of pianist Olga Barabini, whom he still sees every other week.

The demands of his profession leave Mr. Ohlsson with little time for nonmusical activities. A bachelor, he lives in a tidy, unpretentious four-room apartment on Manhattan's Upper West Side. When he's home, four or five hours a day are reserved for practice on the somewhat battered Bosendorfer piano that dominates his living room. (The room is thickly carpeted, and Mr. Ohlsson claims that neighbors don't complain about his playing—a problem that he had encountered in a previous apartment.) The rest of his waking hours are spent calling on a small circle of friends and taking in an occasional opera, rock performance and concerts by other pianists.

All told, Mr. Ohlsson spent 192 nights in hotel rooms in the 1972-73 season. (The concert season usually begins in September and runs through August.) In the 1973-74 season, to spend more time at home, he shaved his schedule to 65 dates, during which time he drew from an unusually large repertoire of 15 different concertos (most concert pianists play only two or three pieces in public). Throughout it all, along with the applause, there were the staples of the concert circuit: untuned pianos, faulty rental cars, hotel mix-ups, occasional bad notices.

"It is a very grueling life," says Peter Menin, president of the Juilliard School in New Yok. "If you do it out of love and conviction, then you can make it. If it's not done of love, it's better not doing it at all. It's better putting all that energy to work in some other field, and you'll realize more success and be happier."

Garrick Ohlsson agrees. "You've got to almost marry a piano," he says. "At times, it's pretty frustrating. For every time that you really hit it, there are so many times that you'll miss it. But I love music. If I had to stop playing, I'd have to stop living."

—N.R. KLEINFIELD

Part Six

WORKING
FOR THEMSELVES

Some people like to work for a big corporation, others don't care who they work for. But a special breed doesn't feel comfortable working for anyone but themselves. They like being in charge; they like doing things their own way. It is rarely an easy course to take. Just getting started can be a trauma in itself, but keeping going while times keep changing often proves the tougher challenge. There often is a strong element of loneliness—either physical in being separated for long stretches from other people, or emotional and psychological in battling the majority. Only a fundamental belief in oneself can assuage it.

Getting Started

Harry Marcowitz is president of American Hydraulic Paper Cutter Inc., but he doesn't like to use the title. "Does a corporation president dress like this?" he asks, gesturing at his plain shirt and grease-smudged work pants in his rented machine shop in the Chicago suburb of Elk Grove Village. "I'll call myself a president when I can come to work in a suit and tie and spend my time dictating letters to a secretary.

That day might come fairly soon, or not at all. In the fall of 1974, American Hydraulic Paper Cutter Inc. consisted mostly of Mr. Marcowitz, his employe Sigmund "Ziggy" Janiszewski and a 6,000-pound industrial paper-cutting machine he built with his own hands at a personal cost of more than $25,000. The company, incorporated in April of 1974, has yet to make a delivery.

Mr. Marcowitz is negotiating for a $10,000 bank loan that would help enable him to build three machines he would offer for sale. He already had a commitment—and a $4,000 down payment—on one of those three. "When I get the loan and make those other two sales, I'll have the money to go into serious production," he said. "Once people realize how good my machine is, I'll be in good shape."

And what if the loan and the sales aren't forthcoming? "I don't think negatively," declares Mr. Marcowitz, an energetic, strongly built man of 49 years who at various times in his life has been an Army aircraft mechanic, coal-truck driver, baby photographer and life-insurance salesman. "Starting this business has been my dream. If I got discouraged easily, I'd never have come this far."

Going into business for one's self requires more than dreams and an optimistic nature, however. Being a fledging entrepreneur isn't easy in the best of times, and 1974 wasn't the best of times. Besides the usual difficulties that go with turning out a product and beating entrenched competitors to sales, the new businessman, perhaps more than most, must wrestle the twin bullies of tight and expensive money and high and rising costs.

"In more normal times, a guy going into the manufacturing business has about a 60-40 chance of succeeding for, say, at least a half-dozen years," said an official of the federal Small Business Administration in Chicago. "With the economy off the way it is, I'd estimate the odds at no better than 50-50. For other types of new businesses, the risk is even greater.'"

Those who follow the field say that the apparent reasons most new businesses fail are a lack of sales, capital or both, or an inability to control costs. But further search almost always points to the inexperience or ineptitude of management.

"Typically, the person starting the business is a salesman who doesn't know much about production or an engineer who doesn't know much about sales," says Rowena Wyatt, manager of the business economics department of Dun & Bradstreet Inc., the credit reporting firm. She said that the high costs and interest rates prevalent in 1974 have put an added premium on management expertise, noting that her company's statistics showed business failures on the rise in 1974 for the first time since 1970.

Harry Marcowitz knows first-hand about costly money and materials. The bank he was trying to borrow from was asking interest of 11½%, up from about 10% a year earlier, and he says that everything he buys "gets more expensive every time I place an order." As a result, he's had to increase the base price he plans to charge for his machine to about $14,000 from about $13,000 in 1973.

Yet he professes to be fatalistic about such matters. "When's the right time to go into business? I could die waiting for the right time," he says. "My machine is ready and I have to make a living. Now's as good a time as any."

Harry Marcowitz's background of skills and experience would seem to give his endeavor a better chance of succeeding than most. Foremost among these is a mechanical aptitude that amazes those who know him, considering that his formal training in the area consists of a few shop courses in high school and his World War II instruction in fixing aircraft engines. (He dropped out of junior college after a year.)

He has a good knowledge of the printing and bindery industries—his main targets for sales—because he spent four years traveling around the country selling and servicing paper cutters for Schimanek-Universal Co., a now-defunct German firm whose machine his is patterned after. His reputation in those industries is good. "When I need a new cutter, Harry will get the order," asserts Charles Soukup, president of Repro Inc., a Chicago printing firm that has two Schimanek machines. "Getting service is a big thing with our equipment, and Harry never lets us down."

His salesmanship is attested to by his record as an agent and district manager for Equitable Life Assurance Society of the U.S. in Chicago; in two of his eight years with that company his sales of life insurance topped the $1 million mark.

Finally—but not incidentally—people who have done business with Mr. Marcowitz say he is a very nice fellow. "People do things for him because they like him," says David Kayner, his attorney. Mr. Kayner should know. Earlier this year he was approached by Mr. Marcowitz to handle his incorporation; he wound up donating his legal services and investing $1,000 in the business in return for a small ownership share.

All this might not be enough, however, "Harry has an excellent machine and he's selling it at a good price, but the market might not be there," says one large Chicago distributor of printing gear. "Things in the business have been pretty tight lately. They might not loosen up in time to get him off the ground."

Mr. Marcowitz came to his present vocation by a

circuitous route. After leaving college shortly after the war ("It wasn't my bag, as the kids today might say") he spent several years helping out around his father's retail coal business. Then came five years as a baby photographer; he says the business prospered but folded over "partner trouble."

His eight-year stint as an insurance man was remunerative (as he earned as much as $20,000 a year) but unsatisfying. "I've got this thing about machinery—I'm happiest when I'm taking something apart and putting it back together so it runs right," he says. "I can't explain this ability; it must be a gift from God. Gloria, my wife, has perfect musical pitch. She can't explain how she does it either."

He got into paper-cutting machinery by chance. "In 1966, I went to a printing-equipment show with a friend who was in the cutter business," he relates. "When I got there, the thing wouldn't work for them. I'd never seen one before, but I took off my jacket, sat down on the floor and fixed it." The company offered him a job on the spot and he took it, even though it meant less income than he was making selling insurance.

The firm—Schimanek-Universal—"made a marvelous machine, but had problems," Mr. Marcowitz goes on. "It was mostly with the parts—they were slow in coming from Germany. On top of that, some of the owners didn't get along well with each other. They closed down in 1969."

That left Mr. Marcowitz without a job and with a decision to make. "I could have gone back selling insurance, but I really loved that machine," he says. "It was hydraulic, so it didn't have all those gears, clutches and brakes and things that mechanical machines have. I know how it worked and I figured I could make one myself, or even make it better. Gloria, who's a teacher, said she'd support us both until I get going."

So Mr. Marcowitz moved into a friend's vacant storefront and went to work—from memory, without any drawings or specifications. "The German thing was so fouled up I couldn't get their plans, but I asked a patent lawyer about it and he told me I could go ahead," he says. He made a wooden model of the machine's big parts and contracted with a foundry to cast them. Then he went to another friend's machine shop and spent a year making the small parts himself.

In January 1971, the prototype was ready for testing. "The big moment came, and a lot of the guys from the shop gathered around," he says, gesturing for dramatic effect. "I went into the men's room and got a piece of two-ply toilet paper. I separated the layers, put one of them under the blade and pushed the buttons. When the blade came back up, it looked like the paper hadn't been cut and the guys thought I'd blown it. But I wet one finger and peeled back that piece of toilet paper along the cut the blade made. It was as clean a cut as you'll ever see."

A year of more testing and alterations followed, and when 1972 began Mr. Marcowitz was ready to go into production, but problems intervened. One prospective partner—who had a substantial amount of cash to invest—mulled things over for a year before deciding against it. Mr. Marcowitz then took his cutter to a machine shop that had expressed an interest in making many of its parts, but the shop got so busy with other work that it had to decline, too.

Late in 1973, Mr. Marcowitz took a trip to Spain with an eye toward going into manufacture there, but he wound up deciding to set up shop around Chicago. "I might have saved a few dollars by having the machine built in Spain, but it would have meant lots of traveling, a language barrier and all sorts of shipping problems, and I wouldn't have had a good handle on quality control," he says.

"Also, I got to thinking that there are enough Volkswagens and Toyotas on the road. America used to make good, competitive products, and there's no reason we can't again. My parents were immigrants and this country was good to them. Maybe I can pay some of it back by setting up a business that employs people and makes something useful."

The past five years have been expensive ones for Mr. Marcowitz. He has continued to work part-time servicing Schimanek machines, earning about $7,000 a year, and he has put almost all of that into his business. The remainder of the $60,000 or so the company has used has come from investments by a relative, employe Janiszewski, Mr. Kayner and Mr. Marcowitz's accountant.

Expenses were particularly heavy since June 1974, when the company moved into its 3,700-square-foot shop in Elk Grove Village. Mr. Marcowitz purchased—for cash—a lathe, drill press, steel-cutting saw and forklift truck, costing about $8,000 in all. A milling machine, costing another $4,800 had been ordered.

The equipment would have been more expensive if not for Harry's resourcefulness. "I got a terrific bargain on the forklift," he points out. "On the lot, it sounded terrible, but I put in a $25 water pump and now it works great."

And he had some help from his friends. One gave him a welding machine; another sold him the almost-new drill press for $125, one-third its original cost.

The company has kept up with its bills so far, but not without some difficulty; when Mr. Marcowitz's application for a $20,000 bank loan fell through, he had to turn the relative for $10,000 in operating capital. He still needed $10,000 more, but he thought he could get it without too many strings as a result of the $4,000 down payment he collected for his first sale.

He and Mr. Janiszewski, an expert machinist, were making parts for the three machines. There have been enough nibbles to make him confident he will get those sales. He plans to produce 12 machines in 1975, "and after that, who knows?"

Mr. Marcowitz asserts, and people in the business agree, that his paper cutter has some competitive advantages over others. Most paper cutters used in the U.S. are made in Europe, and devaluations of the dollar have pushed up their price so Harry's cutter will sell for about $2,000 less than those models. Its hydraulic operation should cut down on parts and maintenance costs for users, and its safety features are said to be excellent; the cutter's 42-inch blade won't drop unless two widely separated buttons are held down, keeping operators' fingers out of danger.

Automation is the wave of the future and Mr. Marcowitz is providing for that. He's designed a cartridge program that can be attached to his present machine and automatically move the paper to be cut into different positions.

"The main thing will be for Harry to get some machines into commercial operation. That way customers can see how they do," says the printing machinery distributor. "It's kind of a vicious circle—you can't sell many machines unless you've proved they work, and you can't prove they work until you sell some."

—FREDERICK C. KLEIN

The Furniture Makers

Sumner Weinstein stands in a corner of his cluttered Boston workshop, hammering lightly on the handle of a chisel, the blade gently but surely carving a series of abstract, flowing lines into a small piece of dark mahogany.

Mr. Weinstein's pants and shirt are spotted with wood finishes, his once-black shoes are crusted white with lacquer, his hands and fingernails are perpetually discolored by dark finishing stains. These are the marks of his trade—the making of custom furniture.

Today he is working on an armoire, a large cabinet to hold clothing. The job will take weeks, including time off to allow glue and coats of finishing materials to dry, time in which he will work on other pieces. When he is done, his firm, Woodland Furniture Co., will receive about $900 for the armoire.

Obviously, his work doesn't come cheap. Mr. Weinstein and his brother and business partner, Irving, ask—and get—at least $200 for a dining-room chair, $500 for a bed headboard, $2,000 for a set of shelves to hold stereo components, $5,000 and more for a complete dining-room set.

Yet despite these prices, custom furniture making is a craft in decline. For, from the furniture maker's point of view, the prices aren't high enough. Sumner and Irving Weinstein each draw a salary of $200 a week from their business, the same as they have drawn for the past five years. Rarely, after they pay the overhead for their shop and buy the costly woods used for their pieces, is there a profit left to divide between them.

A combination of factors, chiefly greater competition from factory-made furniture, has put a squeeze on custom makers like the Weinsteins. Until the 1950s, Sumner Weinstein says, factory furniture tended to be of markedly inferior quality compared with custom items. But factories are turning out better and more expensive pieces these days. While they may not be unique or as detailed as custom furniture, Mr. Weinstein says, they are of high enough quality to cut into the market of craftsmen like the Weinsteins.

As a result, except for the Weinsteins, "custom makers have all disappeared" around Boston, says Walter Beckhard, an owner of Charak Furniture Co., a Boston retailer of costly furniture that closed its own custom department 15 years ago because of rising costs. The National Association of Furniture Manufacturers doesn't keep a count of custom makers, but John Snow, executive vice president, says, "I wouldn't be able to name one."

Consquently, Sumner and Irving are all but indispensable to the half-dozen interior decorators who regularly rely on the brothers to make furniture for their clients. "If they went, I don't know who else I would go to," says Martin Elinoff, a Brookline, Mass., interior decorator. Sumner and Irving make everything from night tables to dining-room sets for his clients, he says—probably 75 or so pieces a year.

While the Weinsteins' prices sound high, decorators say their work is worth the cost. "They've created some of the most beautiful dining-room sets you've laid eyes on," says Irving Young, another Brookline decorator. He particularly recalls one dining-room set they built for a client of his. The finish required Sumner to lay hundreds of pieces of silver leaf by hand.

Sumner reacts to the praise with confidence and pride. "That's what they're paying me for—to give them something beautiful and unusual," he says, "a work of art."

The skills needed to create a "work of art" have been developed by the Weinsteins during nearly three decades of furniture making.

Sumner and Irving were discharged from the armed services in 1945, and in those days neither knew the first thing about making furniture. Sumner, though, had a long-standing interest in art, and he had studied painting, wood carving and other artistic endeavors at Boston's Museum of Fine Art for about 10 years while growing up in Revere, a town just north of Boston.

In 1945 he decided he would like to get a job as a wood carver. As a way to enter the field, he took a job as an apprentice to a Boston custom furniture builder. Irving joined Sumner on the job soon afterward, and less than two years later the two started their own custom-furniture business, making replicas of early-American lamp tables and end tables for furnitures stores.

"Everybody said we wouldn't last," recalls Sumner, and they almost didn't. During their first few summers, they spent a lot of time outside their shop eating watermelon and waiting for customers to show up.

But in time the customers did come, and as the Weinsteins' reputation grew they took on more and more custom work and made fewer and fewer antique reproductions. By the mid-1950s they had two cabinetmakers and five finishers helping them create the custom pieces—chiefly dining-room sets—they were called upon to make.

By the early 1960s, however, the increased competition from factories began to be felt. As orders became fewer, Sumner and Irving stopped replacing men who retired or quit. For the past several years they have been working alone except for occasional temporary help.

That temporary help during parts of the past three summers has included the two older of Irving's three sons. (Both brothers are married. Sumner has three daughters, who in 1973 ranged in age from 14 to 28; Irving's sons were 15, 20 and 22.) But there seems to be little chance either son will enter the trade permanently. "They'll never wind up in this business," says Sumner. "It doesn't pay well, it's hard work, and there's not a big future."

The hard work and long hours that went into setting up the business are still very much a part of the way of life of Irving and Sumner. They spend all of their time on their feet, hunched over their projects. Their workday starts at 7

a.m. and contintues straight through for nine hours except
for a 15-minute lunch break, which they spend sitting on a
worktable eating sandwiches they've brought from home
and drinking hot tea from glass jars. They take only one
week of vacation annually, and it wasn't until 1970 that
they cut their workweek back to five days from six.

Their shop is on the second floor of a rundown brick
building in a remote warehouse district on Boston's south
end. At first glance, it's difficult to see how anything
resembling beautiful handcrafted furniture could come out
of the clutter that is their workshop. A sign on a huge steel
door outside promises an "office and showroom," but in
fact the 70-foot square shop is filled with odd-sized boards
stacked seemingly at random along the walls up to the
exposed pipes in the ceiling. It is only as you pick your way
around piles of scrap wood and a dozen woodworking
machines that it becomes apparent the place isn't an
abandoned firetrap.

On a table along one wall, amid wood scraps and hand
tools, lie four unfinished chair legs with long hand-carved
lines down each side. Eventually they will be part of two
dining-room chairs Sumner and Irving expect to sell for
$225 each.

"You'd need a shop about twice the size to keep
everything neat," Irving says apologetically as he stands at
a worktable assembling the sides of a cabinet. Irving, a
soft-spoken, husky man of 52 (in 1973), does most of the
machine work—measuring, sawing, sanding and shaping
pieces of wood and then fitting them together.

In a far corner, under the fluorescent lights, his
brother, two years older, works at the finishing of pieces.
Sumner does the final sanding by hand, patches, carves,
antiques and lacquers. From time to time Irving walks over
to ask Sumner's help on a piece; both agree that Sumner
has a better eye for dimensions and proportions.

Sumner is surrounded by pieces in various stages of
completion. Because working on furniture involves endless
waiting for glues and finishes to dry, Sumner says, he and

his brother have "a lot of things started but nothing finished." At any one time they may have a dozen or so pieces under way.

On one side of the finishing area is a five-foot-high bed headboard with abstract flowery designs carved into the top portion. "I carved it all myself," Sumner says proudly. He'll get $500 for the work. Nearby is an elaborately carved vanity sink top that will adorn a bathroom in the home of an interior decorator. The piece will command $200, unfinished. There are also a six-foot-by-two-foot parson's table that will sell for $250 and two four-foot-high knick-knack shelves that will go for about $300 together.

At least the brothers *expect* to get those amounts for the pieces. Sometimes, though, their high prices prove hard to collect. Ten $200 cane-back chairs Sumner started making a year earlier stand piled in the center of the room. He stopped work on them seven months before when the corporate executive who had ordered them suddenly lost his job and said he wouldn't be able to afford them for a while.

"I've got $2,000 tied up right there," says Sumner. And the same executive had ordered a dining-room table and storage cabinet that would have meant another $3,000 sale for the brothers.

Important as money is, the brothers say they get more satisfaction than money could buy from some of their work. "We don't even watch the time," says Irving. "Look at the fun we're having." So much fun is it that he looks forward to pursuing woodworking as a hobby when he retires someday. "Except I don't know what I'd make," he says, remarking that he's already made all the furniture he needs. Indeed, both brothers have filled their homes in Boston suburbs with handmade furniture. Sumner figures he'd probably charge a decorator $10,000 for the articles he has made for his small bungalow-style house in nearby Newton.

Sumner says, though, that perhaps his most satisfying work was carving the 10 Commandments in Hebrew into a thin, six-foot-high piece of wood for a local synagogue. He recalls "holding my breath" while a Hebrew scholar looked it over for errors. There were none, and for Sumner "it was a great moment."

One procedure that would appear to offer considerable satisfaction is the technique known as "distressing." In order to make a piece look older than it is, Sumner hits it with a chain and a steel pipe. Enjoyable as it looks, though, the technique is difficult, Sumner says as he bangs at the $90 armoire. "You've got to bunch the marks artistically so it looks like it was damaged from age," he says. "Most people tend to do it (hit the furniture) too much."

Other easy-looking procedures are also tricky, Sumner says. Spray lacquering is one of them. "This looks easy, but it takes years to learn," he says as he sprays a thin coat of lacquer on two latticed window shutters he has made. "You've got to be careful you don't put on too much or you'll get runs. Runs are the worst thing—customers will never forgive you for runs."

One of the ironies of the brothers' work is that, while they charge seemingly high prices and remain in demand among a small circle of decorators, they seem to be unable to make enough profit to raise their take-home pay. A general mood of economic caution may be part of the problem. During the boom period of 1968 and 1969, the brothers often had an eight-month backlog of work and grossed about $70,000 a year. That left a few thousand dollars in profit on top of their salaries, Sumner says. More recently, the backlog has shrunk to three months, the price of wood has soared, and the profit has disappeared.

Yet the brothers are afraid to raise prices any further lest their potential customers look instead to factory-made items. Actually the customers usually wind up paying considerably more than the Weinsteins receive. That's because interior decorators add their own markup of 20% to 100% so that a dining-room set for which the brothers get $5,000 may cost the customer anywhere from $6,000 to $10,000.

At times, Sumner says, that seems unfair. "We supply

all the labor and materials," he says. "They (the deco-rators) get paid as much for their talk as we do for our labor and materials." Yet he professes a certain admiration for the decorators and acknowledges that they're vital to the brothers' business. "These guys are such great talkers, he says. "They really take some of these old women for a ride."

If the Weinsteins have financial problems, one reason may be that they're neither the most aggressive nor the most efficient businessmen around, skilled though they may be in their craft. Sumner, who runs the business side of the operation, tried to solicit new sales early in 1973 when he phoned an interior decorator he had been told might be interested in custom furniture. The decorator never placed an order, and Sumner hasn't tried soliciting more business elsewhere.

Nor do the brothers keep close track of how much in labor and materials they invest in an individual piece of furniture. Sumner says he and Irving might work six months or more intermittently on a dining-room set or headboard, and it's too complicated to keep track of the hours. "Big companies have cost accountants and all that," he says. "Here we just do it by the feeling."

One feeling the brothers clearly have is that they plan to stick it out in the furniture business as long as they can, low wages, long hours and all. "How can you not like this work?" asks Sumner. "It's always interesting, and it's so varied."

—DAVID GUMPERT

Say Cheese

Rosy-cheeked but somber, a baby squirms on a little wooden stool in Dino Semprini's cluttered studio in New York. Nearby, Mr. Semprini's wife crouches on her hands and knees with a rubber duck on her head, trying to coax the baby to smile. But the baby isn't amused.

Unruffled, Mr. Semprini patiently adjusts his camera and huge lights. "Hey, where's my Woody Woodpecker?" he asks, referring to a toy he can mount on his camera stand. "You say nothing," he explains, "and when you have this real sourpuss, this distinguished man, all of a sudden you tug the string and you hear 'quack, quack, quack.' A guy hears Woody Woodpecker and he breaks up. It'll break up anybody."

By one device or another, Dino Semprini tries to draw a smile or a happy expression from his subjects so he can capture it on film. As a portrait photographer, he makes his living purveying pleasant memories. Whether in his studio or as a practiced interloper at countless weddings, debuts, bar mitzvahs, christenings and other festive events, Mr. Semprini has devoted 27 years of his life to chasing treasured moments. During that time, he has watched people grow up and grow old. He has watched young men and women marry—and marry again. He has seen their families grow and the children themselves wed. Throughout it all, Mr. Semprini has taken pride in depicting man at his best. "My portraits capture a second in a life," he says. "It is likely to be one of the happiest seconds in that life."

In more settled times, the occasional self-conscious trip to a photographer's studio was a mainstay of growing up. Yet in recent years, the portrait photographer has seen the demand for his services gradually wane, partially as a result of changing life styles. According to the Professional Photographers of America, a trade association, portrait photographers now number about 23,000, down 3,000 from 1968. While depressed business can be found throughout the profession, it is the old-fashioned one-man studio such as Dino Semprini operates that is bearing the brunt of the trend, the association reports.

For one thing, portrait photographers are being edged out by the amateur camera bug, who, armed with an Instamatic and a how-to-do-it book, settles for his own snapshots of the kids growing up. For another, portrait photographers are being snubbed by youngsters of the "now" generation who don't share their parents' interest in things that last.

"Today's younger people couldn't care less about portraits," Mr. Semprini says. "It's part of a whole change in society itself. Kids don't care to have keepsakes to remind them of happy days. Kids don't want to buy memories."

What's more, portrait photographers are finding it tougher to compete successfully with the growing number of chain studios that, by consolidating operations, often provide portraits for prices below what the small-time operator is forced to charge. Even the wedding-album business is eroding; more and more catering firms are including this service in their package deals.

The changing character of the business has taken its toll at Mr. Semprini's operation. Over the span of his career, the 60-year-old photographer has shot about 7,000 portraits. Of late, he has been turning out about 200 a year, or about 100 less than his annual production rate a decade ago. Wedding portraits make up about 70% of his business, with baby pictures occupying most of the rest of his time. While he once did more than 100 wedding albums a year, he handles only about 40 now. Because of his advancing age, he began farming out some work outside his studio to local free lancers in 1971, and in 1972 he gave up the practice of doing his own developing and printing at home. He now ships film to a commercial laboratory instead.

Yet, with prices up, his business brought in about $40,000 in 1972—the highest salary ever. Because costs have risen too, however, net income has remained flat for the past few years. Mr. Semprini forgoes promotional tricks practiced by many in the profession, such as buttonholing engaged couples at weddings about their nuptial pictures, or keeping in touch with jewelers and bridal coordinators. He relies solely on word-of-mouth advertising to bring in customers. He charges them $49.50 for an individual 8-by-10 color portrait, which takes six weeks to deliver. A bridal album package containing 36 pictures costs $499 and is delivered in four months (occasionally after the marriage has broken up).

Although he has been forced to make some concessions to changing times, the moustached, bespectacled Mr. Semprini carries on his daily routine in much the same way he always has. He works alone, assisted only by his wife, in a small, sunny studio in Elmhurst, Queens. Behind a wood-paneled reception area hung with finished portraits is the shadowy den where Mr. Semprini spends most of each day hunched behind a $550 Mamiya camera.

If there is one uncompromising law of his profession, it is to never, never deliver an unflattering portrait. At times, Mr. Semprini admits, this rule collides with his artistic instincts. But he is first of all a businessman, and he is well aware his photographs must ultimately suit the whims and vanities of his subjects. With his tools of deception—including oil paints, dyes, pastels, colored pencils, felt-tipped pens, eyebrow pencils and even shoe polish—he manages to obliterate ugly warts, repair crooked smiles and smooth even the most deeply etched wrinkles.

In group portraits, Mr. Semprini can even go so far as to add or subtract people. Once, he shot a family portrait without one brother, who was living in Italy. Supplied with a recent photo of the brother, he snipped the group portrait in half, pasted in the brother's picture, painted over the edges, took a new picture and thus reunited the family.

The photographer is also sometimes called upon to do

the reverse, particularly at weddings and parties. "Lots of families have one relative they don't want in any shot," Mr. Semprini says. "You know, he's sort of the family slob. During the wedding, he'll come over looking to have his picture taken with everyone else. So I'll put him in a group over to one side, snap his picture and get rid of him. When I do up the photograph, I just paint him out."

Mr. Semprini's ultimate deception came about as the result of a near-catastrophe. Once, before a wedding, a child tampered with his camera and threw it out of focus. Unaware of this, Mr. Semprini shot his pictures as usual. When he developed the film, every picture proved worthless. Swallowing hard, he told the bride and groom about the mishap. Then, at his own expense, he restaged the wedding as best he could, renting tuxedos, flowers and other accouterments and returning to the church with minister and guests.

Candid shots taken "on location" often test his skill more than studio work, Mr. Semprini says. Actually the name is misleading, because virtually all candid pictures are posed to reduce the number of unflattering shots. "I could blackmail people with some of the expressions I've got," the photographer says. "You get people snarling and scratching their underarms."

By far the largest chunk of Mr. Semprini's "candid" work is done at weddings. And in recent years, his classic wedding album has undergone a metamorphosis of sorts. In the past, he would try to show a graphic exposition of the day as it progressed. "Now we're trying to put some symbolism into the album," Mr. Semprini says. Instead of the conventional shot of the bride and groom waving goodbye, for example, the last picture might show the couple just looking fondly at each other. He closed one recent album with a closeup of an ash tray holding two lighted cigarets. The final inscripton is always "And they lived happily ever after," although Mr. Semprini says facetiously, "With all the divorces, I'm considering changing it to, 'and they may live happily ever after—and then again they may not.'"

Some occasions demand that the photographer have the instincts of a Perle Mesta to deliver the requisite number of happy shots for a memory album. Mr. Semprini recalls one party where, he says, "Nobody was drinking or smoking. People were going to toast with grape juice in paper cups. They weren't laughing. They weren't talking. They weren't doing anything. So you have to take pictures that don't exist. I told some jokes and put every person I could find together with every other person to get enough photos."

Studio work demands a different bag of tricks—especially if the subject is a child. Mothers are advised to bring babies in after their naps, and always at least a week after a visit to the doctor. If they've been to a doctor recently, Mr. Semprini explains, they identify the photographer with the doctor when their clothes are removed for the portrait—and immediately start howling. If Mr. Semprini has trouble getting a baby to clasp his hands together, he sticks a piece of tape on one finger so the child will try to remove it with the other hand. Although he has a big collection of toys to prod uncooperative subjects to smile, sometimes daubing butter on a child's nose makes him squint and produces a surprisingly pleasant expression, Mr. Semprini says.

Working with adults is far easier. The photographer takes care to arrange groups according to the classic theories of composition, and studies each face to decide which side will photograph best. His wife, Mary, advises customers about what to wear; sleeveless dresses are out, for example, because they make women look fat. In the dressing room, Vaseline is provided to shine up cheeks and lips. Mr. Semprini frowns on heavy makeup because touching up can take care of any necessary highlighting.

Moderating the stuffiness of the studio portrait has helped Mr. Semprini retain some of his teen-age business. Because young people are seldom interested in the traditional grinning-at-the-camera shot, Mr. Semprini now takes more than half his portraits outdoors, usually in a local park. He has also responded to his young customers' demand that a portrait express a mood. "The picture has got to say something," Mr. Semprini says. So he avoids flashbulbs when he can to capture a more natural look. And, he asks his subjects to feel, as much as possible, whatever mood the occasions inspires in them. "If I still did the kind of photography I did 20 years ago," he says, "my business would have gone down the drain a long time ago."

It was a roundabout route to portrait photography for Mr. Semprini, a native New Yorker. Although he was always interested in photography, and even built a camera at the age of 12, his first few jobs were as a button maker, a sign painter and a busboy.

Then, in 1936, he was hired as a waiter at the now-defunct Pete Marden's Riviera in Fort Lee, N.J., then one of the area's hottest night spots. When the management learned of his talent with a camera, they agreed to let him take publicity shots of celebrities when he wasn't waiting on tables. Whenever a star came in—be it Orson Welles, Rita Hayworth, Eddie Cantor or Sophie Tucker— Mr. Semprini would discard his waiter's outfit, slip into a suit and click away. Before the stars had settled down with their drinks, he would return with menus in hand. Late at night after work, he developed the film and sent the best shots to local papers.

When he was drafted into the Army in 1942, Mr. Semprini was stationed in New York City and continued his practice of never going anywhere without his camera. He supplied his battalion magazine with photos, and when he was released from the service in 1946 he decided to open his own portrait studio. His original studio was only two doors away from the one he occupies now.

Although his formal portraits seem somewhat out of place in today's mobile, fast-paced counter-culture, Mr. Semprini still relishes his role as a chronicler of the past. Reflecting on his long career, he flips through some old black-and-white portraits and says, "You know, long after my subjects have grown old and disfigured—perhaps died—my portraits will be as they always were. I'm recording something for tomorrow. In a way, I'm making people immortal."

—N.R. KLEINFIELD

Special Delivery

A dull sun, burning low in a gauzy sky, is about to drop away for the night. On the lifeless plain below, long shadows cast by the scrub trees are starting to go fuzzy and fade. Wayne Sperline, the pilot (aviator sunglasses, Errol Flynn mustache, cigaret dangling from his lip), is crammed in the cockpit of the single-engine airplane, straining to find a landmark. "I don't know where the hell I am," he says.

A sinuous ditch comes into view. The Rio Grande? Wayne rolls eastward and follows the river to the Gulf. But Brownsville, Texas, which is what he is looking for, isn't there. Again, he turns south and happens on a town looking like an oasis on the plain. The water tower calls it Los Fresnos. "I've never seen any of this before," Wayne says, fumbling with the only chart he has—a road map of the whole central United States. Los Fresnos isn't on it. This must be Mexico.

The sun is gone; the land is turning charcoal. Flying nearly blind, Wayne looks for a spot to land and wait for dawn. But then, at last, a lighted road twinkles ahead. "Now that's the road to Brownsville," Wayne says. He follows it in and touches down safely at the airport. A minute later, the sky is pitch-black.

Wayne Sperling is in the process of delivering an airplane 22-feet long from the factory in Cleveland where it was built across 3,100 miles of prairie and jungle and water to a crop-dusting company in Managua, Nicaragua, that plans to use it for making short hops around the banana plantations. The plane is equipped with such useful accessories as armrests, ashtrays and coat hooks, but the crop-dusting company didn't see much use in a lot of buttons and dials, so it ordered only one instrument: a compass, which is what the Wright brothers had.

The company didn't want a gyroscope or a turn-and-bank indicator either, both of which Lindbergh had. And one other thing—the company didn't order any radios.

This doesn't fluster 42-year-old Wayne Sperling, who has been a hard-rock miner, a heavy-equipment operator and a bronco buster and who has "Liberty or Death" tatooed on one arm and a lady in a bikini tatooed on the other. He now is something called a "ferry pilot," and his job is to deliver small airplanes, with or without instruments, to the people who buy them, whether they live in Peoria or Pretoria.

His profession isn't for somebody who wants to make much money or who minds being frequently frustrated, generally bored silly and occasionally scared out of his wits. Nor is it for someone who cherishes longevity. There are only about 300 ferry pilots in the United States, and some knowledgeable people think that around 30 of them get killed every year. Sketchy statistics from the National Transportation Safety Board show 35 major accidents and 15 deaths of ferry pilots in the last five years on flights outside U.S. territory alone. (Two accidents that Wayne himself were in aren't listed.)

But the work is there for the pilots who want it. This country is making a lot of small airplanes—15,000 in 1974—and is supplying 95% of the world market. Exports in the first half of 1974 were up 39%, and business is good on the domestic front as well. Somebody has to deliver the planes, so ferry pilots are doing a heap of flying.

In the month before this flight, Wayne Sperling flew planes from Wichita to New York City, from Elmira, N.Y., to Welsh, La., from Albany, Ga., to Hammond, La. (where he blew an engine), from Albany again to San Salvador, from Wichita to Greenville, Maine, and twice from Wichita to San Antonio.

These are all short hops. To deliver a plane that isn't equipped to fly long ocean stretches from, say, the West Coast to Honolulu, a pilot has to go this way: Wichita, Boston, Gander, the Azores, Malta, Athens, Ankara,

Tehran, Oman, Karachi, Bombay, Calcutta, Rangoon, Bangkok, Kuala Lumpur, Jakarta, Manila, Guam, Tarawa and, finally, Honolulu. It takes three weeks.

The flight to Managua is supposed to take only four days, enough time for a newspaper reporter to get a taste of the life. But the trip ends up taking nine days, and instead of a taste of the life I get a fairly stiff shot.

Wayne hitches a ride with another ferry pilot from Wichita to the small Grumman American Aviation factory at Cuyahoga County Airport outside Cleveland, where we meet at 7:30 on a Monday morning, set to fly out towards Kansas in a little plane called the Traveler. (Grumman American Aviation is a subsidiary of Grumman Corp.) The first person Wayne sees is Gordon Collins, who takes care of shipping planes for Grumman, and the first thing Mr. Collins says is, "For the life of me, Wayne, I thought you were coming tomorrow." The plane isn't ready. "That blows the whole damn schedule," Wayne says. "We're snakebit before we even get off the ground."

We check into a motel, located conveniently between an eight-lane highway and an expanse of flat farmland, to wait around until morning. Wayne breaks out a bottle of Old Charter bourbon and dredges up some memories: a kid hanging around the Butte, Mont., airport; a flight mechanic in the Air Force in the early 1950s; learning to fly and finally becoming a commercial pilot in 1960; chartering out to patrol power lines for Montana utilities; counting antelope from the air for the government. In 1966 he and his first wife split up, and Wayne went to Wichita to become a ferry pilot, living between flights in his old Buick.

Wayne eventually got married again, and three years ago he and his new wife, Arlene, who has a certain amount of business sense, started a little comapny in Wichita that helps ferry pilots hook up with planes that need to be delivered. People who buy planes pay the company a fee. The company finds a ferry pilot to make the delivery, takes a cut and turns over the rest of the fee to them. As the pilot on this trip, Wayne gets $700 of the fee. But he has to use that to buy gasoline for the plane, pay for his own food and lodging, and buy a ticket home on a commercial airline. If he is lucky, he can make the trip in four days and come away with a $200 profit. But he isn't lucky.

The Traveler is ready to go when Wayne, decked out in a blue jump suit, shows up at the airport Tuesday morning. The plane has about two hours of test-flight time on it. Setting off for Managua is somewhat akin to buying a new car, taking it for a spin around the block and then driving it across the Sahara Desert. "The ferry flight is really the test flight," Wayne says. "I shouldn't tell you that, but it is." He does offer the assurance, however, that there is a small radio imbedded in the tail that will give off a signal if the plane hits the ground very hard. I tell Grumman's Gordon Collins how grateful I am for it. "What?" he says. "The emergency locater? This plane doesn't have that."

Wayne, who doesn't seem to be paying attention, climbs into the cockpit, revs the engine, taxis down the runway, slams in the throttle and floats the Traveler off into the Cleveland smog. He has drawn a line on a tattered chart showing the course southwest to Wichita, and as we fly along at a few thousand feet, he peers down for checkpoints: a lake, a drive-in movie, a microwave tower. As we pass one town, Wayne heads for the next, visible in the distance. Thus pass Elyria, Wellington, Willard, Upper Sandusky, Marion . . . .

Lacking instruments, Wayne figures out ground speed by timing the plane's passage across the mile-square section lines that make mid-America look like a vast expanse of green-brown graph paper. He figures the wind's direction by watching the shadows of small clouds creep across the fields. We move along at about 135 miles an hour. Wayne lights the first of many Camels and silently scans the horizon for other aircraft. At one point, he leans back and digs through his beat-up suitcase for a little transistor radio, props it up against the windshield and plays some static interspersed with bits of country music: "Every time I

try to . . . SQUAWK! . . . it turns out . . . SQUAWK! . . ."
Wayne shuts it off. "Naw," he says. "Can't get a thing."

After a stop at a little airport near Terre Haute for some gasoline, the men's room, a Payday candy bar and a call to the weather service, we push on along the Missouri River over the capital dome in Jefferson City, Mo. But the weather suddenly turns foul. The cloud ceiling closes down until we're flying at less than 300 feet above haystacks and backyard basketball hoops. A steady rain falls, turning the highway below into a slick black snake. Visibility is down to a mile. "I think we better head back," Wayne says, turning steeply. "That," he says, "is the safest maneuver in aviation—the 180-degree turn."

Jefferson City airport has a control tower, which means we must request permission to land. But that's hard to do with a crummy transistor radio, so Wayne circles the tower in the rain, wiggling the wings, lowering the flaps, trying to catch the tower's attention. We make a second pass and a third, but we can't seem to elicit the flash of green light that means we can touch down. Finally, Wayne just goes ahead and lands anyway. What happened to the flight controllers? "They can't see, I guess," Wayne says.

It hasn't rained in Jefferson City for six weeks, but it is raining now. It is primary election day; the bars are closed. "Snakebit again," Wayne says. "If I bought a pumpkin farm, they'd do away with Halloween." But things could be worse. Once Wayne was snagged in Elmira, N.Y., for a whole week, and that was nearly as bad as the 10 days another ferry pilot spent in a Baghdad jail and the three months another one spent at an Air Force base in the Aleutian Islands. This time Wayne spends only one night in a Ramada Inn.

In the morning, the rain is still coming down, and a thick fog covers the city. Wayne walks out into the wet parking lot. "Rain!" he yells. "Get out of my sky!" In a few hours it does, and we fly out of Jefferson City into a low haze, covering 240 miles 500 feet off the ground, and glide into an airport near the Cessna factory in Wichita while

F-105 fighters from nearby McConnell Air Force Base rumble above us.

John Howard, a meticulous but not very speedy mechanic, takes the Traveler to his shop near Wichita to squeeze a big metal barrel into the rear of the tiny cockpit so we can carry an extra 35 gallons of fuel. The additional gasoline will allow us to fly from Mexico to Nicaragua without landing in several Central American countries, each of which charges several different fees for doing so. John doesn't finish the job on Wednesday, so we stay in Wichita Wednesday night. John doesn't finish the job on Thursday, so we stay in Wichita Thursday night. On Friday, he finishes, but there are tornadoes tearing through the Midwest, so we stay in Wichita Friday night.

Saturday the weather is "passable," and we take off. A curl of smoke rising from a barnyard indicates a tailwind. "Hope it stays that way," Wayne says. "We deserve some kind of good luck." Then he breaks out some Saltines and Spam, and we sail across Oklahoma into Texas—and into a long, dark line of thunderstorms.

Wayne aims the plane at the one light spot on the horizon, and we slide between storms, lightning cracking the sky on both sides. The Traveler is bouncing like a peanut in a boxcar when suddenly the engine coughs and dies. Wayne's eyes widen as he quickly snaps several switches and, after a few terrifying seconds, the engine kicks in again. He had allowed one of the gas tanks to go dry. "That put the hair on the back of your neck up," he says, lighting a Camel.

Soon we enter territory covered by the next aeronautical chart, but Wayne doesn't seem to have the next chart. We know we're heading south toward Brownsville, but that's all. It looks like we have to land someplace and buy a chart. Wayne spots a weedy little airstrip, and we put down. Nobody home. We fly out to another tiny airport. Deserted. Then we land at a place that has some friendly people—but no charts. They sort of point us to Brownsville, and we eventually arrive, after a half-hour of terror at dusk.

Exhausted, we check into a motel. Just as Wayne steps into a welcome shower, the motel generator goes on the blink, and every light and air conditioner in the place conks out. Snakebit again.

Next morning we're all set to cross the border into Mexico when Wayne finds out that Mexican customs officers don't work on the Sabbath unless you pay them about $60 in overtime. Wayne isn't in that much of a hurry, so he puts in another day poaching in 103-degree heat at the pool. At night Wayne escorts me across the bridge over the Rio Grande in a tour of the tawdry *zona roja* of Matamores, and we spend several hours drinking beer and watching a lewd floorshow in a dilapidated hall that is called a bar but is in fact a bordello.

Late Monday morning, with two hours of bureaucratic fussing behind us, we finally fly into Mexico. It has taken a week to get out of the U.S.

Wayne flies low along the Mexican coast, waving at fishermen casting their nets into the surf and passing over a desolate swamp where he landed two years ago when the engine on a crop duster he was delivering blew up in midair. A cylinder had cracked on that plane, throwing off balls of fire and splashing hot oil over the windshield. "I thought for sure I'd burn up in that damn thing," Wayne says. But somehow he landed and walked five hours through swamp water two feet deep until he found help in a little fishing village called Lo Pesca. In a stroke of luck, our engine doesn't blow up today, and we breeze into Vera Cruz for another inebriated evening watching the mariachi bands in the city square.

From Vera Cruz we must cross the Isthmus of Tehuantepec to the west coast of Mexico, flying over thick, hilly jungle with 10,000-foot peaks of the Sierra Madres on either side. The weather in Vera Cruz is fine. So is the weather in Ixtepec on the other side. But there isn't any weather report—ever—for the interior, nor are there any airstrips or many open fields flat enough to land on.

As we fly over the jungle, the clouds are building and

mists are gathering between the mountain peaks. "This is always a problem, getting through here," Wayne says. "Once you get through here, you've got it made." Past the last ridge, the Pacific comes into view. We have it made. Wayne turns and follows the coast into Guatemala, past smoking volcanoes and over the thatched huts of Indians living at the edge of the sea.

Our last hurdle is the Gulf of Fonseca, 60 miles wide. Without landmarks below, Wayne sets a compass heading and sticks to it until land comes into view on the far shore. Many of the ferry pilots who don't come back get lost during longer overwater stretches. They simply miss their objective, usually an island layover, and fly on until their fuel is gone. If something goes wrong with an engine, precautionary landings aren't much use. "The biggest sharks in the world are there, they tell me," Wayne says, looking down at the blue water.

Thankfully we regain the land and go on to Managua. Wayne nearly lands at the wrong airport, then finds the right one and buzzes the control tower for 15 minutes before he gets a green light for landing. After seven straight hours in the air (30 in all from Cleveland), we put down with a thunderstorm raging behind and the needle on our last tank of gas on the empty mark. "Survived another one," Wayne says.

He leaves the Traveler in an airport lot for the owner to retrieve and immediately buys a ticket on a jetliner leaving for Miami in just one hour. From there, Wayne will head for Albany, Ga., where a crop duster is waiting for another ferry flight, right back to Managua.

Before boarding the jet, Wayne pulls out his beat-up wallet to count what's left of the $700 he got for the job. For nine days' work he counts up a clear profit of $80, plus a few assorted Central American coins.

—BARRY NEWMAN

Part Seven

NOT WORKING

In a land where people often think of themselves and are described by others in terms of what they do for a living, people who do nothing are a perplexing exception. "Oh, he's retired," or "He's laid off," identifies them in terms of their past work, but what it is to be a dropout from society or a skid-row alcoholic is beyond everyday experience. Yet, the large dimension that work has in most people's lives is made more comprehensible by looking in on those lives where it is absent, by choice or by chance.

Laid Off

When William L. Marsh got the word, his first reaction was relief. For weeks, rumors had been flying that more layoffs were in the offing. So, when his turn came, at least it ended the uncertainty. That particular uncertainty, anyway.

"The first couple of weeks I was off, it was sort of like a vacation," says 33-year-old Mr. Marsh. "I felt pretty sure I'd be recalled. I kept thinking it was just a matter of time." But days turned into weeks. Weeks stretched into months. "Finally, after about two months, I realized that I was out of a job for good, and then the scary part began."

On layoff from his job as a welder for National Cash Register Co. in Dayton, Ohio, unable to find a job that pays what he believes he's worth, uncertain about his own future and the welfare of his family, Bill Marsh is but one soldier of a legion of workers on layoff at plants and factories around the country.

Some are on layoff because their plants are outmoded and the work load is being switched to other facilities; others are out of work because technology has made their labor too expensive. Still others have the misfortune to be working in industries in which business is slack.

Says Dr. Sidney Cobb, a physician and research scientist at the Institute for Social Research at the University of Michigan, who has studied the psychological effects of layoffs on blue-collar workers: "When a man is laid off and then can't find work that measures up to what he was doing before, there's a natural loss of self-esteem and self-confidence."

All too often, Dr. Cobb adds, such men give up. They don't try very hard to find new worlds because they're "sick of being disappointed, or being told time and time again that they're not worth what they think they are." Some

294   *Laid Off*

men, he adds, reach a point where they're afraid of further exposure, of again and again looking like a failure in the eyes of their families and friends. One tendency in such cases, Dr. Cobb says, "is to withdraw," mope around the house and just hope that something good comes along.

A vague hope that something good will happen along is about all Bill Marsh, the father of two young sons, had going for him in the late winter of 1973 after being laid off for eight months. Dressed in his customary brown denim pants and dark-green work shirt, wearing white socks but no shoes, Bill spends a lot of time in front of the Zenith color-TV in the living room of his comfortable, three-bedroom brick house on a three-acre lot on the outskirts of Vandalia, a village about 12 miles north of downtown Dayton.

With the TV sound turned low, Bill reflects on his inability to find work and declares: "Welders have gotten a bad name. Everybody that comes out of the mountains" of neighboring Kentucky and other nearby Appalachian states "calls himself a welder. What that means is that they can burn a rod." But being able to burn a rod doesn't make a man a good welder, Bill snaps, and the "quality of a lot of their work is terrible—it just falls apart."

Because of a glut of men calling themselves welders and the shoddy kind of work they do, Bill says, most employers in the Dayton area refuse to pay their welders much more than $3 an hour. And to Bill, who earned about $5.25 an hour before his layoff and who considers himself a highly skilled welder, working for $3 an hour would be demeaning. Drawing a deep breath and glancing at his 31-year-old wife, Harriet, Bill adds: "I'll just hold out until I can get at least $4 an hour—either that or I'll go and do something else."

(Although Bill considers himself a highly skilled welder, he was classified by his employer as a semiskilled production-line welder. Indeed, Class A welders, as the most highly skilled type of welder is classified in the trade, usually have little difficulty in finding jobs.)

In some ways, Bill still can hardly believe what has happened to him. After all, it was barely a year earlier that it seemed that his job and his future were secure. "Look at it this way. I had better than six years seniority," says Bill, a tall and muscular man who sports a jaunty handlebar mustache. "You would think that that much time on the job would mean something, but it didn't. Not for me, anyway."

What Bill and countless other workers at National Cash Register, which is usually called NCR, didn't foresee was a dramatic shift in NCR's basic manufacturing methods. The maker of cash registers, computers and a variety of other business machines for years had made mechanical and then electro-mechanical devices in its sprawling factory just south of downtown Dayton. But in 1972, due to changing technology and other factors, the company began a rapid switch to electronic business machines. They require far less labor than mechanical devices. Moreover, a multitude of parts for electronic machines are purchased from suppliers rather than being built in-house.

In June of 1972, NCR announced that it expected to lay off up to 2,00 Dayton production workers by the end of that year, reducing its local work force to about 13,000. Early in 1973, the company disclosed further layoff plans, this time involving about 1,800 white collar workers.

Bill Marsh, who got the ax in late June 1972, was among the first to go. "The funny part of it all is that two weeks before the layoffs started, we were working overtime in my department," Bill recalls. "They even brought in three extra men" to beef up the welding crew.

That brief spurt of overtime and those three extra men were critical considerations in Bill's early layoff. The three extra men, like all the other welders in his department, had more time in service with NCR than Bill did. Thus, when the layoffs started, Bill was the man with the least seniority. About six weeks before his actual layoff, Bill says, he knew it was coming. By then, he had been bumped downward to what's called general service—"that means pushing a broom and picking up trash, the lowest thing they've got," Bill said.

Both Bill and Harriet can remember the day of his layoff as if it were yesterday. "They called here at the house and told Bill to come in half an hour early," says Harriet. "Well, we knew what that meant." Adds Bill: "I went to the employment office, and they told me about my rights to unemployment benefits. Then they said that when my shift was over that day, I was on layoff. Zap. That was it."

Bill and Harriett were more than slightly familiar with layoffs. Both of their fathers, now retired, had worked in factories and had been laid off at one time or another. In fact, Bill was laid off from the first full-time job he held—in 1960 at a Chrysler Corp. unit in Dayton—after he had been graduated from high school and had learned to weld in the Army. Moreover, after going to work for NCR in early 1966, Bill had had a two-month layoff early in 1971. And he had been out of work at NCR for almost five months in late 1971 and early 1972 as a result of a strike by the United Auto Workers, of which Bill is a member.

When the latest layoff came, Bill wasn't particularly worried, he says. He was confident he would sooner or later be recalled, and he and Harriet, who once worked at NCR herself, had built up their savings to about $7,000. Moreover, the Marsh family lived frugally. Both their cars—a 1970 Plymouth sedan and a 1966 Falcon station wagon—were paid for. Their only debt was about $8,000 they owed on their house, which Bill values at about $35,000.

In a way, Bill says, at first he welcomed the layoff. For one thing, it gave him more time to devote to his hobby—building and racing dragsters. Since 1962, he says, he has built or owned seven dragsters, and at the time of his layoff, he was anxious to finish and race a car he had been working on. "Every weekend during the summer, Saturday and Sunday, the only thing we would ever do is go racing," says Bill.

In addition to tinkering with his race car, Bill erected a chain-link backyard fence and started pouring a concrete driveway from the street to his house. Bill also spent considerable time looking for a job. Shortly after he was laid off, Bill admits, his efforts were somewhat perfunctory. One reason was that he was receiving $76 a week in unemployment benefits. That was quite a comedown from his before-tax pay of $210 to $225 a week at NCR, but still, says Bill, "It was grocery money."

To qualify for his unemployment benefits, Bill had to have at least two job interviews per week. And at about the same time that it began to become clear he wasn't likely to be recalled, Bill also realized that he was going to have a hard time finding a job that paid anywhere near what he had been earning at NCR. "Most of the places I went to weren't hiring, and those that were weren't paying anything," Bill says. "The best I could find paid $3.49 an hour, and then I would have had to pay half of my own insurance and supply my own hood."

When it became apparent that he was going to have a hard time finding a job that paid well, Bill got serious. For one thing, recalls Harriet, "He had had a full beard. It was all black and bushy, and it looked pretty bad." Says Bill of his beard and his job hunting: "I thought I might make a better impression if I looked better, so I shaved it off."

But a clean-shaven Bill fared no better than a bushy Bill. Soon he began to think of ways to cut expenses. Since his family lived so frugally to begin with, there was only one thing to do. He sold his race car for $2,000, taking a loss of about $1,000, but eliminating the cost of racing every weekend. For her part, Harriet stopped having her hair done every Saturday.

As time went on, Bill became increasingly discouraged with the job market. Thumbing through a tattered appointment book that lists perhaps 100 companies where he applied for work, Bill says: "It was the same thing everywhere I went. They weren't hiring or they weren't paying. I got pretty discouraged."

Just before Christmas 1972, Bill got the last of his unemployment checks. That meant he and Harriet had only their savings to live on, and that nest egg was going fast. Since Bill was laid off, the couple's savings account has dwindled to less than $3,000 from the original $7,000. "It just makes me sick to go to the bank. I'm always withdrawing, never depositing," says Harriet. Adds Bill: "That money is all that's keeping us going. If I didn't have the money to meet my bills, I would really be low. I wouldn't be able to sleep at night."

If Bill has become so disheartened that he has given up in his search for a job, the Marsh family is also displaying some of the other symptoms common to laid-off workers that Dr. Cobb of the Institute for Social Research outlines. Among other things, Bill and Harriet have stopped going out entirely.

Until about August 1972, the couple had periodically dined out with their sons, nine-year-old Tom and five-year-old David. In addition, they had taken in an occasional movie. Now, says Harriet, "We just stay home all the time and play cards or watch TV. It's been so long since we've been out, I wouldn't know how to act in public."

Indeed, Bill hardly ever got away from house in March 1973. He says he spent most of his time "out in the garage piddling around with stuff—nothing important—just piddling" with a small welding rig he owns. On occasion, he adds, one of his friends stopped by with a little welding job. "I never get paid for it. I just do it for the fun," Bill says.

What the future holds for the Marsh family is difficult to foresee. However, Bill says has about had his fill of living around Dayton and being unable to find a job that pays as much as he things he's worth. "Why should I stay here and fight it?" Bill asks. "I'm not going to get anywhere." Discouraged and despairing, nowadays Bill merely whiles away his time, waiting for summer.

"As soon as the warm weather gets here, I'm going to finish paving the driveway and get some grass up and the place looking nice," he says. "Then we're going to sell the house and move to Florida," where Harriet's retired parents live. 'If we can get $35,000, we'll pay off this house and pay cash for one in Florida. Then, with a house that paid for, I can pump gas or do anything else just to get grocery money, just enough to live on. That's all I want now."

—EVERETT GROSECLOSE

Drop-Out

Once there were two sawmills in Wellington, Maine. There were three stores, a hotel and a dance hall. But a few decades ago, the sawmills finished cutting down all the trees worth selling. So the sawmills closed, and so did everything else.

Wellington today is a scattering of weathered frame houses, trailers and tar-paper shacks sunk in the deep snow of Piscataquis County, at the edge of Maine's "big woods." On the road into the town of 231 people, there's a little tumbledown house with windbeaten shingles and a few old cars hibernating in the yard. This is where Milton Christianson came to live in August 1972.

As a curl of smoke rises from the chimney, Milton stands inside at a wood stove, stir-frying onions and peppers in a wok. The paint on the floor is worn through to bare wood. A picnic table is pushed up against one wall, and an old cot leans against another. Towels hang drying over the stove, and an herb garden grows on the windowsill. A hole cut in the ceiling lets heat into Milton's bedroom upstairs.

"I've lived a lot of places, and this is the best so far," Milton says in his soft voice. "I've wanted to leave every-place else."

In May 1973, Milton Christianson was 26 years old. During his high-school years in suburban Minneapolis, he was vice president of his class, captain of the swimming team, feature editor of his school newspaper, editor of the literary magazine and a public-speaking champion. He was graduated cum laude from Wesleyan Universtiy in 1969, an anthropology major.

Ten years ago, a young man leaving college with those credentials almost surely would have gone on to graduate school and become a professor or perhaps taken a job in a social-service agency. But with his long, wispy blond hair and full beard, Milton is a child of the youth culture of the late 1960s. Like many of his contemporaries, a few of whom have also journeyed to Wellington, it was his intention from the day he lef school to live on the "outside." "I never learned anything in college that I've used since," he says.

The only full-time steady job Milton has ever had was during a college summer when he drove a station wagon through the mountains of Ohio and West Virginia for a seed company, picking up unsold seed packets from little stores in little towns. Since then, he has subsisted through a bagful of devices that include painting signs for storekeepers, watching over property, doing odd chores, growing some of his own food and scrounging through dumps. (A torn tendon in his hand exampted him from the draft.)

He has also benefited from an enterprising spirit worthy of a budding capitalist. A case in point: Early in December 1972, Milton had exactly $3. By the end of the month he had $1,500, enough to last all this year. His stroke of genius was to design, print and market 300 pretty silk-screened calendars as Christmas presents. The scheme worked so well that he intends to do it again, boasting, with a nod toward Detroit, that his calendars are endowed with "planned obsolescence."

"I guess I'm poor by most standards," Milton says. "But I have all the space I need and good food. So I have everything I want. I can always get money if I need it."

Milton says he is happy now. But his path to Wellington and to this measure of psychic (if not financial) security has been a difficult one. "I didn't know what I wanted when I got out of college," he says. "I needed time to figure myself out." So, after a dose of Jack Kerouac's books about traveling, Milton was on the road. For a year after graduation he "just bummed around, living off the fat of other people."

"I made a special effort to get to know people who were bad," Milton says, "because I had always been good, and I didn't want to be good any more."

In Santa Fe, he tried some psychedelic drugs "with an Apache Indian I met in a bar." The pair stumbled into a cafe owned by "a guy who was busted out of the Marines for being a speed freak." They formed a "tight bond," and Milton hung out at the cafe for close to two months. "Nobody knew how to make the place run," he says. "So all we'd do is close it down every night at about 8 o'clock, buy some wine and have a party."

Eventually, the ex-Marine gave up the cafe. He and Milton and another friend who owned a van set off on a lazy ride to San Francisco. "Every place we stopped," Milton remembers, "I said, maybe I'll stay and work here. But I kept on going."

In San Francisco, he holed up with an old friend from college and was briefly inspired to look for a "straight job." Clutching his anthropology degree, he made the rounds of agencies doing work with Indians. No luck. "There weren't any jobs like the one I wanted," Milton says. Then he saw an ad in the Stanford student newspaper asking for help in decorating a chain of bars for $1.75 an hour. Milton showed up, was handed a paint brush and spent the next few weeks painting scenes from his travels all over an old barn that was being converted into a singles bar.

"You got a free lunch and all the beer you could drink after 5 p.m.," he says. But it wasn't enough, Milton was getting tired of the road: "Here I was, dropping in on everybody's life and never having anything going for myself. I wanted some roots. I wanted to be around people of different ages. I wanted a home."

Like others his age, though, Milton felt the home he wanted wasn't the one his parents were offering. His father, an administrator for a Minneapolis prison, and his mother, a legal secretary, were "very strict" and too "uptight"' to suit him. So instead of going back to Minneapolis, Milton hitchiked to Boston and moved in with some more college buddies. He flirted with a few jobs (including one in a mental institution where "you couldn't tell who was crazy and who wasn't"). And then Milton formed a commune.

With two girls and a male friend, he moved to Maine in May 1970. One of the girls had some money, and with it she bought an old farm near Waterville without electricity or running water. "We were all going to share it as equals," Milton says. "We were going to live there forever. We were very dumb." To supply the commune with tools, Milton contributed his share painting signs. And he spent a great deal of time forming a community arts center for Waterville. But relationships within the commune became badly strained.

"It's incredible that we stayed together for the entire winter," Milton says. "It's mostly because once you get settled in Maine and the snow comes, it's impossible to budge." The commune fell apart with the spring thaw. "Then I just camped out. I didn't have any belongings."

As a last resort, Milton borrowed $100 from his parents and rented a room in Waterville. The first night, three trains roared past under his window. The next day, he moved out. Finally, putting his debater's skill to work, he persuaded the owners of an empty 12-room mansion to let him live there as a caretaker.

"If you're a landlord," Milton says, "you're much better off having someone staying in an empty house. And I'm one of those someones."

The place had 11-foot ceilings and seven marble fireplaces. The previous tenant was an eccentric inventor who left enough equipment for Milton to set up his own silk-screen studio. Without much formal training, he perfected the ability to make silk-screened prints. (Silk screening is a color-printing process that can sometimes become quite complex.) While working on his craft, Milton made do by designing brochures part-time at nearby Colby College, doing some house painting and fixing up around the mansion.

But, as before, it wasn't enough. "There were days in that big house," he says, "when I would just sit and look at that wood stove in the kitchen. I just couldn't get anything done." So when some friends decided to travel farther into the wilds, Milton went along and ended up in the little house outside Wellington.

Surviving in Wellington has been tough. Unlike some of the other hippies in the area, Milton doesn't collect welfare. He doesn't borrow money, and he doesn't buy on credit. But with a good deal of ingenuity, he has made $400 last from summer into the dead of winter. And thanks to his calendar sales, 1973 started off good.

The owners of the house he lives in are Clair and Marjorie Cross, a middle-aged couple who have never traveled south of Augusta, Maine. Clair is first selectman of Wellington, a taciturn Mainer who wears baggy overalls and lets Milton live on his land in return for some help caring for his "creatures."

At dawn each day, Milton walks across the road to Clair's barn and shovels manure into a pit below the cow stalls. The body heat from the dozen calves and cows fogs the barn windows. The animals squirm and moo and grunt as Milton does his work. Then Clair ambles into the barn.

"Mornin'," Milton says. "Up a little late this morning." Clair gazes through a clear spot in a window at the sun coming up over the snow-covered fields. "Ayup," he says in his Maine drawl. "Days are getting longer."

In January 1973, after a heavy snow, the roof of the barn nearly caved in. Milton and others in the town spent several dangerous days shoring it up. "It's not like working for Clair," Milton says. "It's just being neighbors. Besides getting a pretty nice house, I get manure for my garden, and I can borrow tools and use their phone. Clair and Marjorie come over for ice cream after dinner. They have lots of stories."

When he came to Wellington last summer, Milton and some close friends, Richard and Sheila Garrett, put in a garden near the house and lived almost exclusively on the vegetables they raised. They canned tomatoes and applesauce, and Milton has carrots and turnips buried in sand in his basement. But in the winter he buys most of his food—largely grains and vegetables, although Clair bagged a deer in the fall and Milton has shared in the venison.

His clothes aren't high-fashion: a scruffy assortment of

faded shirts and rumpled pants, all with holes. Once, he brought all his old clothes into a Waterville thrift store and traded them for a whole wardrobe of new old clothes. "I rely on rummage sales a lot," he says. And he has also discovered that college dormitories at the end of a school year are a prime source of discards.

In fact, Milton has found that many things society casually consigns to the junk heap can be valuable. Much of the wood he uses, for instance, comes from edgings tossed out by sawmills. His woodshed is loaded with rusty old tools, bits of rope, tin cans, and piles of unwanted nuts and bolts. The cars in his yard are his chief supply of spare parts. Some of his furniture was salvaged from old buildings before they were torn down.

"Having a lot of junk around is pretty handy," Milton says. "Lots of things that aren't useful for other people are useful for me. I never pay for anything if I can help it."

If he does pay, it isn't much. Take his car. A few years ago, he bought an ancient Volkswagen for $75. When the body rotted away, he removed the engine and put it into a relatively recent 1964 VW body that he bought for $35. The bumper droops and the muffler sputters. Remarkably, the car runs. "You always have to fool around with it. It doesn't start all the time. But it's cheap," Milton says. Insurance? He doesn't have any.

There are a few amenities around Milton's house: a blender in the kitchen and, surprisingly, a modern freezer in the woodshed, a few steps from the outhouse. These are on loan from a "benefactor" who is temporarily away from the area. Milton doesn't go to movies or buy books and magazines. He doesn't have a television set or a telephone of his own. When a reporter took him to Shirley's Restaurant in nearby Skowhegan, it was the first time he had been out to dinner in two years. But he does support a dog named Visions and a cat named Bruno. (Bruno was weaned by Visions, incidentally, and is convinced she is a dog.)

Milton's greatest pleasure in the winter is skiing—not

the kind that requires fancy togs, expensive equipment and the purchase of lift tickets. He avoids all that by going cross-country skiing. For well under $75 he outfitted himself, and he spends at least an hour every day gliding quietly across the fields and through the frozen woods on his skis. And every morning after cleaning the barn and eating a big breakfast, he skis to the center of town to a one-room former schoolhouse where he has set up a silk-screen studio.

The studio is spacious and well-lighted by a wall of windows. Milton spends much of his time there. But he doesn't own the schoolhouse, and he doesn't pay rent either. He uses it in return for the work he did last summer renovating it with the owner, a 27-year-old woodworker.

Besides the money he made from his calendar, Milton picks up a few dollars printing posters for local events, selling T-shirts he silk-screens (one has the word "Artichoke" in big, green letters over a picture of an artichoke) and making the rounds of craft fairs. For the most part, he trades his work for materials or for help from other people. "We help each other out, so there's hardly any money exchanged," Milton says. The practice, by the way, cuts down on income taxes.

Milton has been so successful at silk screening that he talks about the possibility of getting some of the townspeople interested in taking up similar crafts as a source of much-needed income. "The old people really like having young people around," he says, because most of their own children tend to leave the town instead of staying and trying to create work there.

Some of the young people who have moved in to replace them have already gotten together to help reactivate the Grange. Some plan to run for town office someday. However, it may be a long time before any of them are accepted as natives in the closely knit community. (Milton tells of asking a woman in another tiny hamlet on an island off the coast if she was born there. "Oh, no," was the reply. "I come from the other side of the island.")

Still, Milton is planning to spend at least a few decades in Wellington, possibly with a wife if he can find the right girl. "I'm coming to the point where I can choose the work I want to do," he says. "Maybe I really won't be home until I have some land of my own. But I don't have any now, and I'm not suffering on account of it. I'm willing to wait."

—BARRY NEWMAN

Skid-Row Alcoholic

Here is his world: a hotel cubicle, barely big enough for a cot; no windows; green walls lit by a bare overhead bulb; an overpowering stench of stale urine and alcohol.

These are his friends: down the hall, a man hunched over a toilet, retching and gagging; sitting next to him on another toilet, another man, shaking uncontrollably and crying.

This is his life: at night he sleeps with the light on. Otherwise, he would see things—imaginary, nameless things; crawly things. What he wants is to see is his pint of muscatel wine. Besides the grimy clothes on his back and the 28 cents in his pocket, that jug of "musky" is his only possession. He needs its warm sweetness before the night is out to escape his fears, his guilt, his remorse. That's where he'll find the peace to quiet his nerves, the strength to keep from screaming.

This is the world of Tommy Dunn on Chicago's ski row. It's not pretty—Tommy Dunn can tell you. He has wandered in and out of its flophouses, bars and hockshops, stumbling over the broken bottles and bodies, for almost 20 years. He knows it well—he knows the guilt and remorse, too. "When I look in the mirror I cuss at myself," he says. That's because he sees a man, 50 years old, who once was a university student, a promising baseball pitcher, a combat Marine and a fairly prosperous young self-employed businessman. Once.

Today, Thomas Francis Dunn is a Chicago skid-row alcoholic, divorced from his wife, out of touch with his three children and penniless. He is unemployed, and it has been years—so many that Tom can't remember—since he has held a job regularly. He's supported mainly by the charity of the Catholic church, which runs a skid-row mission, and by the largesse of his bottle buddies. Sometimes, when he's sober, he works at odd jobs—most skid row habitues do—but never for long. Whenever he accumulates a little cash, he drinks it up and slides back into the gutter.

Sociologists say skid row is a phenomenon peculiar to the U.S. that originated about the time of the Civil War, when thousands of persons were left homeless and destitute. The term itself originated in Seattle as Ski Road, a local trail down which logs were skidded to the sawmill and along which rough-and tumble, hard-drinking lumberjacks lived in squalor. The country adopted the name and corrupted it to skid row.

After the Civil War, such areas grew rapidly. Thousands of young men were needed for lumbering, seafaring, laying railroad track and harvesting; in between jobs, that's where they lived. Skid rows became huge pools of unskilled labor. In 1917, World War I virtually drained them. The Great Depression refilled them, and World War II again emptied them.

Today, for one reason or another, the number of faceless bums in those skid row gutters is again declining. Chicago today has only about 10,000 skid rowers, compared with around 50,000 in 1915. New York's Bowery is down to about 6,000 bums from 75,000 in the early 1900s. Sociologists estimate that the U.S. total now is around 500,000, a third less than a decade ago. And the young have disappeared almost entirely as the character of skid row has changed—from a rough labor market to a pathetic last home for drunks and other outcasts of society.

If skid rows are declining in population, so, too, are they declining in area, giving way to the bulldozers or urban renewal. "The property is worth more for parking lots than flophouses," says Ronald VanderKooi, a sociologist at Calvin College in Grand Rapids, Mich., who has studied skid rows extensively.

But most cities still have at least a shadow of their old skid rows—dilapidated collections of saloons, greasy restaurants, cheap hotels, pawnshops and missions. Chicago still has three, the largest being the one not far from the

Loop on West Madison Street, where Tom and 7,000 others hang out.

Dr. Jekyll and Mr. Hyde is one way Tom likes to describe himself and to anyone who has seen him sober and then drunk that's how he seems. Sober, he has a certain charm and good looks—boyish blue eyes, an engaging smile and straight, white teeth that one wouldn't guess were false. When he is sober, he stays closely shaven, he keeps his graying, wavy hair neatly combed, and he dresses in clean and neat clothes—he was wearing dark slacks, a blue plaid shirt and a lightweight red jacket on one of his sober days. "Tom's got a thing about cleanliness. He'll sober up and be taking a shower at 10, two, four and six," says a friend who used to drink with him on "the street."

But Tom is a different man when he's drunk. "Then he won't wash his face for three months," says the friend. His clothes are torn, soiled and infested with lice. His face is bloated with drink and covered with an inch-long growth of beard. Usually, he's toothless: he has lost five sets of false teeth in 15 years. "I don't know where—heave them out when I'm sick, I guess," says Tom. The friend recalls coming upon a group of men on day, "down on their hands and knees in the gutter, looking for Tommy Dunn's false teeth." In vain, as it turned out.

Tom believes his journey to skid row started at age 17 when he took his first drink. He was a freshman at the University of Illinois, and two friends asked him to have a beer with them. "I got drunk that night. I liked it, and from then on it was straight down hill. I kept missing class—one day, two days, three, four," Tom recalls. The university suggested he not return the next year, that he wait two years until he had more "emotional maturity."

That suited Tom fine. He hadn't wanted to go in the first place, but as he puts it: "My people are sticklers on education. It was just kind of understood from the beginning that everybody went to school." Then, at college, he wanted to study dramatics, something he had enjoyed in high school. His father, however, insisted on accounting.

"He thought all actors were immoral," says Tom. "If I'd taken up dramatics, it would have hurt his feelings." He pauses, laughs, and then adds: "I hurt his feelings worse by . . .," and his voice trails off.

For the next two years, Tom worked at an ordnance plant in Joliet, Ill., and played semi-professional baseball. A left-hander, he had a good enough fastball to get a tryout with the St. Louis Cardinals and Cleveland Indians, plus an offer to sign with a Cardinals farm team. "My dad frowned on that. They were only paying $75 a month, and I was making $55 a week at the ordnance plant," says Tom. So he didn't sign.

The drinking continued. Once, late at night, he stalled his car on a railroad crossing near his home in Kinsman, Ill., about 85 miles southwest of Chicago—and then passed out at the wheel in a stupor. The lights of an approaching train were visible when a neighbor happened along and pushed him off the tracks.

In July 1942, he enlisted in the Marines, hoping the service might help him control his drinking. Apparently, it did; he landed in a Marine guard house once for drinking, but never again. Eventually, Tom saw combat on Guadalcanal, Bougainville and Guam, where he was wounded in the left shoulder by an exploding shell—"and no more speed for pitching," he says.

After the war, he and his father opened a bulk-fuel oil business, selling to farmers. He married a girl whom he'd known slightly in high school, and he stayed sober for 18 months. Then he fell off the wagon. He recalls a bartender telling him that one night he drank 40 shots of whisky and then went out and drove home just as if he were cold sober. "I didn't remember a thing," says Tom.

The business suffered, and after two years, the Dunns sold out. Tom went to work as an oil compounder for a company that showed remarkable patience with his drinking. In two years the company fired him five times, and five times it rehired him. More than once he was promised whisky to drink on the job, if he would just come to work and tell others what amounts of additives to mix with the motor oils.

As he sank deeper into drink, his home life disintegrated. On New Year's Eve, 1953, Tom told his wife he was going to the drugstore for cigarets. Two months later—or was it four? Tom isn't sure—he wired her from Seattle for money to come home, "and do you know, that girl took me back," says Tom. But their life together was all over.

Where did he go and what did he do? The weeks were mostly an alcoholic haze, but he remembers some things. He left with $300 and the family car and headed for Las Vegas. He won $1,500 at the dice tables, got drunk, lost the money gambling and was jailed overnight. He drove to Portland, Ore., sold the car for $100 to buy liquor, went on to Seattle, and, to raise money for more liquor, pawned his proudest possessions—the last things he had with him—his Purple Heart and Marine discharge papers. They brought $5.

By this time, in the mid-50s, Tom's drinking was legendary around his home town, so to find work he came to Chicago. He was attracted to West Madison Street, he says, because "you can let your hair down here—the neighbors are very understanding." He found a comfortable acceptance. At home everybody always expected "me to look like I had on a Brooks Brothers suit and a million dollars in my pocket. Here, if a guy is a friend and has a fault, to hell with the fault; he's still a friend. There's a loyalty—not so much emphasis on how he looks or smells," he explains.

Much of Tom's nearly 20 years on skid row is a mystery to him. Part of the reason is simply that when he's drunk, he can't remember what's happening. "Believe me, you lose track of time—you lose track of everything. You don't even know what month or year it is. You walk around blacked out," he says.

Part of it is the grinding boredom of the street itself, where one day blends perfectly with a thousand others. And part of it is something that worries Tom more and more, the alcohol's gradual but steady destruction of his mind—Korsakoff Syndrome is the medical term. "In high school memorizing lines used to be a snap. Now my memory isn't worth a damn," he says. "Of course, sometimes that comes with age, but I'm not that old."

When Tom isn't drinking, and that's perhaps a third of the time, he passes the days in a variety of ways. For a while, he was rising at 5 a.m. and going to the Catholic Charities mission to help clean the basement where skid-row men read, watch television and are fed from a soup line. Often, he hung around part of the day washing dishes, moving boxes, shoveling snow or running errands. He got no money for all this, but did get fed—coffee, eggs and toast for breakfast; meat and a potato for supper—and Catholic Charities buys him a bed ticket ($1.50 a night) at the Starr Hotel, a West Madison Street flophouse.

His room there measures six by 10 feet. It has a cot, steel wall-locker and wooden stool. The green, paper-thin partitions don't reach all the way to the ceiling, so chicken wire is nailed across the top, as it is in all the rooms, to keep next-door occupants from reaching over and helping themselves to Tom's valuables.

Not that Tom has what many would consider valuables. His total possessions one day were 26 cents, a razor, soap, hair oil, deodorant (he mentions this item with a chuckle), three shirts, a pair of pants and an extra pair of shoes. The clothing comes form castoffs donated to the mission.

When Tom is sober, and when he isn't at "home" in his cubicle at the Starr or else helping out at the mission, he spends his time walking around, watching television at the Starr, standing around talking—mainly about sports, women and drinking—and occasionally having a Pepsi or shooting a game of pool in one of the skid row taverns. He also likes to read newspapers, True magazine and, sometimes, historical novels. (Books are available free at a nearby reading room maintained by the city.)

Occasionally, through one of the street's day-labor

agencies—skid rowers call them slave-labor markets—Tom finds a paying job: "pearl diving" (dish washing), gandying (railroad track repair), unloading trucks and boxcars, cleaning up after conventions or distributing handbills.

Sometimes he raises cash by pawning his false teeth (if he hasn't lost them) for a dollar or two or by selling his blood at $10 a pint. He used to receive a $30-a-month veteran's disability allowance paid in connection with his war wound, but four or five years ago, Tom says, his two sisters somehow arranged—he doesn't understand how—to have the money paid to them. "I guess you can't blame them," he says resignedly. "Everytime I'd get the money, I'd get drunk." Tom's sisters refuse to discuss the matter or to talk about their brother at all.

At times, Tom has no desire for drink, but when the urge strikes, it's terrible and virtually uncontrollable. Usually, he can tell about a week ahead when it's coming. "I get shaky and irritable," he says. Sometimes candy or milkshakes help fight off the craving. When he starts drinking, though, a bender can last for weeks or months. The longest (so far as Tom remembers) was three months, and he lost 45 pounds.

If he has the money and a "good front" (clean clothes), he sometimes starts a bout of drinking at the Conrad Hilton Hotel or the Palmer House. "I like a change. Live high—drink champagne on a beer income," he says. When he's broke and desperate for a drink, he'll try almost anything. Once it was gasoline and milk. "It was another guy's idea. I don't know how he got it, but it doesn't work. I got so sick I thought I was going to die," he says.

Usually, he falls back on his cronies on the street who will pool their nickels and dimes from their welfare or Social Security checks to buy 65-cent pints of wine that they all share. "I can go out right now without a penny in my pocket and get drunk," he declares. "The guys down here are pretty generous, if you want something to drink. They don't like drinking alone." By the same token, when Tom has money, he's expected to share, and he does. "I went through $30 in 20 minutes one day buying drinks and flops for everyone." Ironically, he forgot to buy himself a flop and ended up spending the night outside.

That is not unusual. He has slept under viaducts, covered with newspapers and cardboard to keep warm. In warm weather he will sleep by the Chicago River, which runs a few blocks from skid row. One night, sleeping on the bank, he rolled the wrong way and fell in. The police fished him out, and the judge, thinking Tom might have tried suicide, ordered a psychiatric hearing for him. "I wasn't trying to commit suicide," says Tom with disgust. "I was just drunk." He was sentenced to five days in jail.

He estimates that he has been jailed around 100 times, mostly for loitering or vagrancy and sometimes simply for his own safety. One night when he wasn't locked up for safekeeping he stumbled and fell headlong on the street, his face and mouth smashing into the curb. The fall loosened all his teeth and eventually he had to have them pulled. The work was done free by dental students at Loyola University.

When Tom needs medical care (or a new set of teeth), he heads for one of the area's Veterans Administration hospitals. In the summer of 1972, he couldn't get into a nearby facility because it was full, so he walked nearly 50 miles to one near Waukegan, Ill. The trip took three days; he took along three pints of wine and spent the nights in parks along Lake Michigan.

At night alone in his tiny cubicle, Tom sometimes thinks about all the worry and aggravation he has caused others, all the years he has wasted drinking. He shows no bitterness over the way his life has turned out. He says he doesn't know why he drinks except that he's "a born alcoholic." He does resent, however, not being able to drink normally, and he seems particularly hurt that he never could emulate his father's drinking habits. "Dad drank quite a bit, but just on weekends, never during the week when he was working," he says. A social worker on the street observes: "Tom was always impressed with the idea that a good man could hold his liquor."

Tom says his biggest regret is losing his wife. "That was definitely my fault. She gave me every break in the world. Most women would have got rid of me long before she did," he says. She is remarried now, and Tom rarely sees her.

Tom still might kick his habit and go on to a useful life, but his time to do this is getting short. He has been on the street for about 20 years now, and though his health seems remarkably good—all things considered—the odds are that he'll die an early death. The life expectancy on skid row is cut about 10 years, medical experts say. Studies show that the death rate from pneumonia is 14 times higher for men on skid rows than among men in general, and the tuberculosis death rate is 37 times higher.

Indeed, Tom is often called on to act as a pallbearer as the years roll by and as more and more of his friends from the early days pass on. Few mourners gather at these funerals, for these men had no life outside the little world of West Madison Street. Some had no families, and others had long ago lost touch with their people. These funerals make Tom pause, because he himself is out of touch with life beyond skid row.

Tom's father died five or six years ago, and he says his senile mother is in a nursing home. He hasn't seen his children—two boys and a girl—for at least four years. Two of them are married, he says, but he doesn't know where they live. The third, a son, lives at home with his mother, Tom thinks.

"I always sent them birthday cards, but I never got an answer, so I quit," he says. "I know all their birthdays." He pauses. "I used to feel sad that I don't see them, but not any more. This street makes you kind of callous."

—RICHARD D. JAMES

Retired

Roy L. Atkins remembers his retirement party very well. Co-workers from his 20 years on the job have turned out to give him two huge cakes, a camera and a scale-model Lincoln Continental, his dream car. Supervisors thanked him, younger employes shook his hand and wished him luck. And then, for the first time in 45 years, he could do as he pleased.

Today, the cake is eaten, his youngest granddaughter has broken the bumper on the toy car, and eight color snapshots help preserve the memory of the party. And Roy Atkins has discovered the difference between not having to do anything and not having anything to do.

"I'd still be working if I could," he says. "It was a routine I've had since I was 22 years old. I don't believe there's one out of a hundred persons happy doing what he damn pleases."

Mr. Atkins, or "Okie," as his fellow workers call the Shawnee, Okla., native, worked in the shop at Texas Instruments in nearby Dallas. As a methods and tooling engineer, he helped shape bits of metal into parts for computers and ballistic missiles and also taught in the firm's trainee program. Under company policy, he retired at age 65 in September 1971.

Okie's retirement—although by no means harsh—passes slowly and, for the most part, uneventfully. To some degree, he shares problems common to many of the more than 14.5 million retirees nationwide. But some of his restiveness is unique to him, a machinist with a degree in English literature, a gentle, portly man who spent the prime of life working with his hands.

Financially, he isn't as troubled as many retired persons, and he can still get by without working. When Okie retired, he was making about $12,000 a year, and he and his slim, attractive wife, Carmen, had expected to live rather comfortably on a budget of around $450 a month from Social Security and a lump-sum pension from Texas Instruments. However, Carmen, also 66, recently suffered a series of injuries and illnesses that cut substantially into their savings, but so far they have been able to meet the expenses.

Naturally enough, Okie also feels somewhat left out of the mainstream. None of his closest friends is retired— most, in fact, are in their 30s and 40s. Carmen and Okie feel they enjoy a special camaraderie with younger people. To neighborhood children, they're "Paw-Paw" and "Mammy," often called on to pump up a bicycle tire or taste a new cake. More than once, Okie has reached in his baggy trousers for "a fiver till payday" for a young neighbor up the street.

Yet, despite his rapport and daily contact with neighbors, Okie's most persistent problem is finding something to do with his time.

On one fairly typical day, he rose about 7:30 (the time he gets up depends on when he fell asleep the night before), fixed toast and coffee for Carmen and read the morning newspaper thoroughly. When the milkman knocked on his midmorning rounds, Okie chatted with him about fishing for catfish as he placed quart carton in the refrigerator. "What kind of lies have you got today?" Okie asked with a grin. The milkman left, and as Carmen began to watch one of her favorite television soap operas, "Search for Tomorrow," Okie muttered, "I'll run the errands now."

He drove to a nearby dry cleaning shop to drop off a skirt and stopped by a bank, where he and the teller greeted each other by name. Afterward, Okie drove to a grocery store to buy dog food for Bee-Gee, their Pekingese. While counting out eight cans he said, "Can't buy too many— won't have anywhere to go in four more days."

On the way home, he peered through the windshield and squinted. "The sun's beyond the yardarm," he said. "Might as well get a beer." When he saw Okie enter, the manager of a package liquor store reached for a six-pack of malt liquor, and Okie counted out exact change.

Then it was home again for a lunch of pinto beans, fried potatoes and cornbread. Okie helped Carmen clear the table before ambling out to the backyard, where he examined the first spring flowerings of a willow and a peach tree. Stooping to pet the Pekingese, he remarked, "When it rains and you can't get outside, you get very bored just sitting around in the house."

During the afternoon, two neighbors dropped by to chat, and another borrowed an aerosol can of cleanser. About 4 p.m., Okie and Carmen drove to their daughter's apartment in Arlington 20 miles away. There they picked up Shawna, their youngest granddaughter (they have five grandchildren), to spend the night with them. Once back home, Carmen realized the 17-month-old girl didn't have enough diapers, so Okie was dispatched to buy some. In a drugstore, he rummaged through several shelves before finally asking a female clerk about the best brand for the occasion.

When he returned, Okie snapped open a can of malt liquor (he also dips snuff) and leaned back in his reclining chair to watch "Young Dr. Kildare." It's not unusual for Okie and Carmen to go to bed at 8 o'clock since they each have a small television in their bedrooms. Okie's is equipped with a two-hour timer that switches off the set if he falls asleep. But with mowing the lawn his only exercise, the sleep is often fitful, and Okie sometimes wakes up at 1 or 2 a.m. and reads for an hour until he can fall back asleep.

"The days go by faster, but the nights have gotten longer," he says.

Some of his restlessness can be traced to his past, some to his personality. He learned early about working from his parents, who were tenant farmers in Indian territory before Oklahoma became a state. After he was graduated in 1926 from the University of Oklahoma with a degree in English, he taught school in Valley View, Texas, and Elk City,

Okla., where he met Carmen. Following a courtship that included moonlit dates in a Whippet Overland convertible, they were married in 1928.

During the Depression, Okie left teaching and worked variously as a mail sorter on an automobile assembly line, as a potter, at a dairy, at a bakery and as a cotton-gin operator. When World War II began, he went to work in the machine shop at Tinker Airfield in Oklahoma City, though he had never had any machine training. He eventually became a shift foreman there, but after the war he began looking South. In 1951 he went to work for Texas Instruments in Dallas as a machinist in the grinding section. Later, he again stepped behind a podium to instruct new employes in the company's training program.

"He was the first one to help out with our classroom work," remembers Ed Hendrick, a supervisor at Texas Instruments. "He taught people who came off the street— hard-core, disadvantaged people—how to run these machines, how to read a blueprint or measuring tool. He even taught them motivation."

Of his stint in the training programs, Okie flatly states: "It was the most satisfying thing I've done in all my life."

Because of his extensive vocabulary, avuncular manner and teaching background, the gravelly-voiced Okie was tagged with several other nicknames at Texas Instruments. He was known as The Professor (on one of the retirement cakes, there was a frosting sketch of him in a mortar board), 'Fess, Dr. Atkins, Father Time, Santa Claus and Burl Ives—these last three because of his hoary beard.

Then he retired. "For two weeks it was like a vacation," he says. "Then I started climbing the walls. It became a whole new world." He paid off several small debts, bought a car (an Oldsmobile, not a Continental) and with Carmen planned a trip to Norfolk, Va., to visit their son, Richard, who was in the Navy.

At first, he frequently stopped by Texas Instruments to talk with friends and otherwise "just keep in touch." (He proudly displays a laminated lifetime identification badge for "Okie Atkins.") When he was still working, he would go in as much as an hour and a half before his shift began "because I liked to visit and see what was going on and what I should do." Carmen recalls that he didn't like to wait around the house when he worked the 4 p.m. to 12:30 a.m. shift. "He'd stay down there all day if they let him," she says with a smile. "For awhile he didn't think Texas Instruments was going to run without him after he left." Okie hasn't been back to the shop for a long time now, but he still likes the people—"and they like me. I think. I hope."

In January, 1972, Okie was asked to be on the Dallas County grand jury, and for the next three months spent half a day five days a week listening to cases and petitions. "I didn't have anything else to do," he says. When his tour of duty was over in March, he and Carmen left for Norfolk.

It was there that Carmen fell and broke her knee, the first of several problems that were to introduce her husband to his first and only full-time occupation in retirement. He became, in his words, "a housekeeper, cook, nurse, launderer and gardener," jobs he still performs while his wife has recovered from a blood clot on her lung, a cerebral hemorrhage and another broken knee.

Like many retired couples who spend their savings and free time traveling, Okie and Carmen had made plans to visit Mexico with three other couples. However, her second fall postponed the trip. Before his wife's illness, Okie considered going back to work part-time in a hardware store, but that possibility hinges on her full recovery. He used to bowl weekly with cronies from Texas Instruments, but he now insists he's getting too old. Occasionally, he goes fishing with one of his old friends or drives alone to a local lake "just to walk around."

Okie has found that retirement provided few of the spare-time rewards described in counseling programs. For several months before he retired, he faithfully attended sessions sponsored by the American Association of Retired Persons. The sessions were designed to teach senior citizens fine points of diet, wills, health, insurance, investment and generally how to use eight more hours in a day. But Okie refused several opportunities to enter volunteer programs in local hopsitals, the Small Business Administration and other agencies. "They offered me very little," he explains gruffly. "It's hard for me to sit there and listen to someone making $20,000 a year tell me how much he needs me to work—for nothing."

Consequently, Carmen's recuperation absorbed most of his time and energy for nearly a year. She's now able to walk unaided and is resuming some of the household chores. As his wife recovers, Okie grows even more restive.

For several years before he retired, Okie wrote poetry, keeping what he calls a few "fair" poems in a vinyl binder and closeting the "rotten" ones in a cardboard box. Stroking his beard, he recalls many nights sitting in a small office in the shop at Texas Instruments, feeling the hum and throb of big and small engines, letting their rhythm flow into his verse, seeking the cadance of his favorite poet, Poe. A minister at his church once read one of Okie's poems during a sermon, but Okie has never tried seriously to publish. And he hasn't written anything since he retired. "I don't know why I haven't written anymore," he shrugs. "I'd like to, but I just haven't felt like it."

He wrote his last poem shortly before the retirement party. It was called "A Bitter Old Man Retires," and one of the stanzas reads:

Pass time? Oh God, is that all
That I have in store as I go?
My arts are as precious to me now
As they were in the short, short ago.

—MIKE THARP

2913 1